EAST ANGLIAN ARCHAEOLOGY

# Life and Death on a Norwich Backstreet, AD 900–1600: Excavations in St Faith's Lane

by Iain Soden

with contributions by
Trevor Anderson, J. Andrews, Philip L. Armitage,
Paul Blinkhorn, Wendy J. Carruthers, Andy Chapman,
I. Hodgins, Tora Hylton, I. Mack, G. McDonnell
and E. McMullen Willis

illustrations by
Jacqueline Harding, Chris Jones, Mark Roughley and
Alex Thorne

East Anglian Archaeology
Report No. 133, 2010

Northamptonshire Archaeology

EAST ANGLIAN ARCHAEOLOGY
REPORT NO. 133

Published by
Northamptonshire Archaeology
2 Bolton House
Wootton Hall Park
Northampton NN4 8BE

in conjunction with
ALGAO East
http://www.algao.org.uk/cttees/Regions


Editor: Brian Ayers
EAA Managing Editor: Jenny Glazebrook

Editorial Sub-Committee:
Brian Ayers, Director, The Butrint Foundation
Owen Bedwin, Head of Historic Environment, Essex County Council
Stewart Bryant, Head of Historic Environment, Hertfordshire County Council
Kasia Gdaniec, Historic Environment, Cambridgeshire County Council
David Gurney, County Archaeologist, Norfolk Museums and Archaeology Service
Adrian Tindall, Archaeological Consultant
Keith Wade, Archaeological Service Manager, Suffolk County Council
Peter Wade-Martins, Director, Norfolk Archaeological Trust


Set in Times Roman by World Tree using Adobe InDesign™
Printed by Henry Ling Limited, The Dorset Press


© NORTHAMPTONSHIRE ARCHAEOLOGY

ISBN 978 0 9555062 1 5


This volume was published with the aid of funding from Norwich School


*East Anglian Archaeology* was established in 1975 by the Scole Committee for Archaeology in East Anglia. The scope of the series expanded to include all six eastern counties and responsibility for publication passed in 2002 to the Association of Local Government Archaeological Officers, East of England (ALGAO East).

For details of *East Anglian Archaeology*, see last page

**Cover illustration**:
One of the burials in the Greyfriars cemetery: the mouth is packed with ash
*(Northamptonshire Archaeology)*

# Contents

| | | |
|---|---|---|
| List of Plates | | vi |
| List of Figures | | vi |
| List of Tables | | vi |
| List of Contributors | | vi |
| Acknowledgements | | vii |
| Summary/Résumé/Zusammenfassung | | vii |

## Chapter 1. Introduction
| | | |
|---|---|---|
| I. | Planning background and the circumstances of excavation | 1 |
| II. | Geology and topography | 1 |
| III. | Historical and documentary background | 3 |
| IV. | Excavation methodology | 6 |
| V. | Post-excavation methodology | 6 |
| VI. | Research priorities | 7 |

## Chapter 2. The Excavated Evidence
| | | |
|---|---|---|
| I. | Phase 1: Late Saxon industrial and domestic occupation (10th–11th centuries) | 8 |
| | Summary | 8 |
| | The excavated evidence | 8 |
| II. | Phase 2: Early medieval domestic occupation (11th–13th centuries) | 10 |
| | Summary | 10 |
| | The excavated evidence | 10 |
| III. | Phase 3: The medieval cemetery (late 13th–16th centuries) | 13 |
| | Summary | 13 |
| | The excavated evidence | 13 |
| | Character of the burials | 20 |
| IV. | Phase 4: Post-medieval garden soils | 22 |
| | Summary | 22 |
| | The excavated evidence | 22 |
| V. | Summary of dating evidence for key contexts | 22 |

## Chapter 3. The Human Skeletal Material, by the late Trevor Anderson, with E. McMullen Willis, J. Andrews and I. Hodgins
| | | |
|---|---|---|
| I. | Overview | 23 |
| II. | Demography | 23 |
| III. | Pathology | 24 |
| IV. | Conclusion | 24 |

## Chapter 4. The Finds, by Paul Blinkhorn, Andy Chapman and Tora Hylton
| | | |
|---|---|---|
| I. | Post-Roman pottery, by Paul Blinkhorn | 26 |
| | Analytical methodology | 26 |
| | Fabrics | 26 |
| | Discussion | 30 |
| | Chronology | 32 |
| | Pottery occurrence | 32 |
| | Fragmentation analysis | 33 |
| | Vessel use | 33 |
| II. | The small finds, by Tora Hylton | 34 |
| | Introduction | 34 |
| | Phase 1 (Late Saxon industrial and domestic occupation: 10th–11th century) | 34 |
| | Phase 2 (early medieval domestic occupation: 11th–13th century) | 34 |
| | Phase 3 (medieval cemetery: late 13th–16th centuries) | 35 |
| | Phase 4 (post-medieval garden soils) | 35 |
| | Discussion | 35 |
| III. | The ironworking waste, by Andy Chapman with I. Mack and G. McDonnell | 40 |
| | Introduction | 40 |
| | Tuyere plates | 40 |
| | Hammerscale | 40 |

## Chapter 5. Economic and Environmental Evidence, by Philip J. Armitage and Wendy J. Carruthers
| | | |
|---|---|---|
| I. | Faunal remains, by Philip L. Armitage | 41 |
| | Introduction | 41 |
| | Descriptions of the main livestock species | 41 |
| | Descriptions of the fish species | 42 |
| | Interpretation and discussion | 43 |
| II. | The charred and mineralised plant remains, by Wendy J. Carruthers | 45 |
| | Introduction | 45 |
| | Methods and results | 47 |
| | Discussion | 47 |
| | Comparisons with other sites and conclusions | 48 |

## Chapter 6. Discussion
| | | |
|---|---|---|
| I. | Pre-Friary | 50 |
| | Street origins and street/plot layout | 50 |
| | Cultural exchange and trade | 50 |
| | Industry and craft | 51 |
| | Domestic arrangements: change and decay | 52 |
| II. | The Franciscan Friary | 52 |
| | Church-planting and expansion | 52 |
| | Burial rights and rites: the dead of the cemetery | 53 |
| | Enclosure of the precinct and the use of space | 55 |
| | The Dissolution and beyond | 55 |
| III. | Envoi: site context and future research objectives | 56 |
| | Limitations of the evidence | 56 |
| | Moderating factors and benefits | 56 |

| | |
|---|---|
| Bibliography | 58 |
| Index, by Sue Vaughan | 63 |

# List of Plates

| | | | | | |
|---|---|---|---|---|---|
| Plate I | The site during excavation of the Phase 1–2 Saxo-Norman street frontage | 11 | Plate IV | The trackway | 14 |
| | | | Plate V | A section of the precinct wall including foundations | 14 |
| Plate II | Pit *644*, half-sectioned | 11 | Plate VI | A typical skeleton in the cemetery | 20 |
| Plate III | The site during excavation of the Phase 3 cemetery | 14 | Plate VII | Skeleton detail: the mouth is packed with ash | 20 |

# List of Figures

| | | | | | |
|---|---|---|---|---|---|
| Fig. 1 | General site location | 2 | Fig. 9 | Plan of graves | 16 |
| Fig. 2 | Trench location | 3 | Fig. 10 | Plan of graves; age of skeletons | 17 |
| Fig. 3 | Site plan, all features Phases 1 and 2 | 8 | Fig. 11 | Plan of graves; sex of skeletons | 18 |
| | | | Fig. 12 | Plan of graves; burial details | 19 |
| Fig. 4 | Site plan, 10th–11th century | 9 | Fig. 13 | Section 6, graveyard and later deposits (south–north) | 21 |
| Fig. 5 | Site plan 11th/12th and 13th centuries | 10 | | | |
| Fig. 6 | Section drawing conventions | 11 | Fig. 14 | Medieval pottery, nos 1–24 | 28 |
| Fig. 7 | Section 1, pit *644* | 12 | Fig. 15 | Medieval pottery, nos 25–35 | 29 |
| Fig. 8 | Section 2, pit *592*; Section 3, Pit *613*; Section 4, cart ruts; Section 5, Cart ruts | 15 | Fig. 16 | Small finds, nos 1–15 | 38 |
| | | | Fig. 17 | Small finds, nos 16–22 | 39 |

# List of Tables

| | | | | | |
|---|---|---|---|---|---|
| Table 1 | Ceramic phases, including the amount of pottery per phase, all fabrics | 32 | Table 5 | Small finds quantified by material type | 34 |
| | | | Table 6 | Finds ordered by functional category | 35 |
| Table 2 | Pottery occurrence per ceramic phase, expressed as a percentage of the weight of pottery per phase | 32 | Table 7 | Coins | 36 |
| | | | Table 8 | Faunal species | 41 |
| | | | Table 9 | Pig remains | 42 |
| Table 3 | Mean sherd weight per fabric type per ceramic phase | 33 | Table 10 | Details of cod remains | 42 |
| | | | Table 11 | Percentage of 'backyard farmed' animals present | 44 |
| Table 4 | Vessel occurrence per ceramic phase, all fabrics, expressed as a percentage of each phase assemblage, MNV | 33 | Table 12 | Charred and mineralised plant remains | 46 |

# List of Contributors

**the late Trevor Anderson MA**
formerly freelance osteologist, Canterbury

**J. Andrews BDS BSc FRSM**
sometime associate of the late Trevor Anderson

**Philip L. Armitage PhD**
Freelance archaeozoologist

**Paul Blinkhorn BTec**
Freelance ceramicist

**Wendy J. Carruthers BSc MSc MIFA**
Freelance palaeobotanist

**Andy Chapman BSc MIFA**
Senior Archaeologist, Northamptonshire Archaeology

**I. Hodgins PhD MB BS**
14 Lyndrick Road, Hartley, Plymouth PL3 5TA

**Tora Hylton**
Finds Officer, Nothamptonshire Archaeology

**I. Mack**
former research student, Ancient Metallurgy Research Group, University of Bradford

**G. McDonnell PhD**
former Senior Lecturer in Archaeological Sciences, University of Bradford

**E. McMullen Willis**
formerly PhD research student, University of Bradford

# Acknowledgements

This report is the product of many people's efforts, from excavation to the page. The list above names only a few but thanks are due to all who have contributed to the project to any degree, particularly Steve Morris, the site supervisor. Gratitude is extended to the staff and students of Norwich School for their enthusiasm in visiting the site during the excavation, including those who took part during appalling weather in April 1998. Thanks also go to the following for their help and encouragement: Nick Cooper (Norwich School) and Henry Rolph (Purcell Miller Tritton); Keith Fuller and Paul Knowles (formerly of Bidwells); Brian Ayers, Phil Emery, Andy Hutcheson and Andrew Rogerson (Norfolk County Council). The academic analysis and reporting has elicited the help of Dr Sarah Hamilton (University of Exeter), Dr Frances Andrews and Dr Angela Montford (University of St Andrews), Dr Victoria Thompson (New York University in London) and Dr Margot Tillyard (University of East Anglia). A debt of gratitude is owed to Fr Ninian Arbuckle, archivist at the Franciscan International Study Centre (Canterbury) and Fr Austin McCormack, Provincial Minister for the Order of Friars Minor. Thanks to Norfolk Archaeology Unit for sight of Phil Emery's draft report on the wider excavations at the Mann Egerton site 1990–5 and to Andy Hutcheson of Norfolk Landscape Archaeology for his comments on the first draft of the present report in April 2002.

# Summary

Excavations and a watching brief at St Faith's Lane over nine months in 1998 uncovered a portion of a 10th–12th century street frontage containing both domestic and industrial material and comprising incomplete remains of timber structures, pits and ditches. Finds relate to domestic occupation and a metalworking presence that may denote the proximity of a forge. In the 13th century, after a period of decline and possible abandonment, the site was incorporated into the precinct of the Franciscan Friary. The Greyfriars soon began burying their dead in a cemetery laid out here, halting only to dig for minerals in a nearby building programme, probably in the 14th century. The burials have an unusual demographic profile which it is felt may relate, at least in part, to a Franciscan school of international renown. The site was fully enclosed by the present precinct wall in the early 16th century. After the Dissolution the site was predominantly garden until increasing encroachment and redevelopment from the 19th century onward. Fittingly, the site is now once more part of a school.

# Résumé

L'équipe du Northamptonshire Archaeology a effectué des fouilles à St Faith's Lane et les a complétées par un compte-rendu d'observations, ce qui a permis de mettre à jour des bâtiments donnant sur la rue qui dataient d'une période comprise entre le dixième et le douzième siècle. Ces bâtiments comprenaient les restes incomplets de fosses, de fossés et de structures en bois de construction. Les objets découverts se rapportent à une occupation domestique et révèlent la présence d'un travail du métal qui indique peut-être l'existence d'une forge à proximité. Au treizième siècle, après une période de déclin, voire d'abandon, le site fut intégré à l'enceinte de l'ordre franciscain.

Probablement au quatorzième siècle, les Greyfriars ne tardèrent pas à enterrer leurs morts dans un cimetière installé à cet endroit, alors qu'ils s'arrêtaient uniquement pour creuser le sol à la recherche de minéraux dans la perspective d'établir des constructions à proximité.

Les tombes ont un profil démographique inhabituel qui s'explique peut-être, du moins en partie, par la présence d'une école franciscaine de renommée internationale. Le site fut complètement entouré par un mur d'enceinte au début du seizième siècle et après la Dissolution, il fut principalement transformé en jardins jusqu'à ce qu'il se développe à nouveau au dix-neuvième siècle. A l'heure actuelle, le site fait à nouveau partie d'une école, ce qui est dans l'ordre des choses.

(Traduction: Didier Don)

# Zusammenfassung

Bei Ausgrabungen und einer Baustellenbeobachtung durch Northamptonshire Archaeology wurden in der St Faith's Lane Teile einer Straßenfront aus dem 10. bis 12. Jahrhundert mit unvollständigen Resten von Holzkonstruktionen sowie Gruben und Gräben entdeckt. Die Funde deuten auf Siedlungstätigkeiten und Metallverarbeitung hin, die auf eine nahe gelegene Schmiede schließen lässt. Im 13. Jahrhundert ging die Stätte nach einer Phase des Niedergangs und vermutlichen Aufgabe in das Gelände des Franziskanerklosters ein. Die Greyfriars (Graubrüder) begannen kurz danach, ihre Toten in einem an der Stätte angelegten Gräberfeld zu bestatten, eine Praxis, die vermutlich im 14. Jahrhundert nur durch die Gewinnung von Mineralien für Bautätigkeiten im Umkreis unterbrochen wurde. Das ungewöhnliche demografische Profil der Grabstätten könnte zumindest teilweise auf eine Franziskanerschule von internationalem Rang hindeuten. Die Stätte wurde zu Beginn des 16. Jahrhunderts vollständig ummauert und fungierte nach Auflösung der Klöster bis zu ihrer erneuten Nutzung im 19. Jahrhundert überwiegend als Garten. Heute gehört das Gelände erneut zu einer Schule.

(Übersetzung: Gerlinde Krug)

# 1. Introduction

## I. Planning background and the circumstances of excavation
(Figs 1 and 2)

Archaeological excavations took place during Norwich School's redevelopment of the former Wallace King warehouse premises in St Faith's Lane, Norwich, between 1997 and 1998 (Site 373N, TG 2347 0870: Fig. 1). This involved evaluation in three trenches by the Norfolk Archaeological Unit (Emery 1997) and the subsequent controlled excavation of *c.* 600 sq m of the site supported by a periodic watching brief, both carried out by Northamptonshire Archaeology (Fig. 2). The site is now occupied by a purpose-built gymnasium constructed for Norwich School. This stands upon an augered-pile foundation, the design of which has been largely sympathetic to the deeply buried archaeology still remaining over much of the plot.

The site had been cleared of buildings and most post-medieval foundations and drains before the present excavation works began. It was clear that these former foundations had been extensive and widespread (Fig. 2), and previous disturbance was observed over a wide area as the remaining post-medieval material was removed. In places the deepest foundations — particularly concrete stanchion pads, still with cut-off steels affixed — had been missed during demolition. These were removed where possible, but one was left *in situ* while work proceeded around it. Disturbance by such foundations was not unexpected, as human remains had been reported previously during construction work close by in 1950 (Site 394N) and on this site in 1991.

The excavation scheme was intended to mitigate the loss of archaeological deposits from a specific part of the new gymnasium building's footprint. As such the precise location of the site was not driven by any specific archaeological research agenda, and excavation effort was focussed upon areas where significant archaeological deposits appeared to be under greatest threat of destruction. Evaluation trenching provided an overview of the significance of the buried archaeology, and led to excavation work being concentrated in the western part of the site of the proposed development. However, the design of the 1998 excavation area was ultimately determined in detail by the perceived threat to deposits posed by the development, at the expense of exploring some of the archaeological potential determined by the evaluation. Thus there was no metalworking focus within the trench where one had been hoped for. Nor was any evidence recorded for the site's Middle to Late Saxon context, which would have been of value given the significant finds of these periods that came from evaluation (Emery 1997). Wider-scale excavation might have elucidated the former, but Saxon-period evidence may have been destroyed by the greater intensity of medieval pitting in the eastern part of the development area.

The excavated area is known to have contained part — but only a part — of the cemetery associated with Norwich's Franciscan Friary, founded in 1226. Consequently any demographic conclusions to be drawn from the research must be tempered by the limited size of the sample, although the sample of 136 burials that was eventually recorded must be regarded as a significant one. It is not known how many more graves lie undisturbed to the south, and possibly also to the west (although relatively poor survival may be envisaged in the latter area on account of disturbance by post-medieval buildings).

The earlier phases of archaeological activity in the excavated area were constrained by the need to ensure safety when working at depth, as well as to prevent disruption of ongoing activities on adjoining plots. To the north lay St Faith's Lane — at that time still open to vehicular traffic, with all the stresses that this imposed upon the medieval Friary precinct wall which still marked the northern site limit (Fig. 2). Building work was ongoing within standing structures immediately to the west, and a driveway to the south of the excavation area had to be maintained, both during this construction work and subsequently to provide access to these premises when they reopened for business. The upcast from excavation was deposited to the east of the excavation area, filling the whole of the remainder of the plot except for the space required to accommodate three vehicles and on-site offices and mess facilities. There was therefore no physical room to extend excavation eastward to clarify any outstanding archaeological issues.

The size and location of the site present a number of problems in archaeological and historical terms. It does not constitute the whole cemetery and the pre-Friary levels do not comprise an entire medieval plot in any sense: all that may be said about this historic land division is that it fronted St Faith's Lane. Any suggestions as to Anglo-Saxon or medieval plot size or shape are therefore matters of archaeological conjecture. A fuller discussion of the pre-Friary townscape in this part of Norwich may be found in Emery 2007, 36–40.

## II. Geology and topography

The site lies in the centre of the City of Norwich on the 25-foot contour (7.6m above OD). Today St Faith's Lane is a gently sloping, narrow, pedestrianised thoroughfare which is aligned roughly east to west, with a sudden and pronounced dog-leg at its mid-point, which follows the northern limit of the precinct of the Franciscan Friary (Figs 1 and 2). The excavated area lay in the western angle of this dog-leg on the south side of the lane. The natural geology comprises a *c.* 1.5m thickness of Norwich or Red Crag (sands with gravel pockets), overlying chalk. The surface of the natural sand lies 6.0m above OD at the north-west corner of the excavated area, dipping to 5.18m at the east, 4.79m at the south and 4.64m at the extreme south-east. Overlying archaeological deposits comprised sandy soils which had built up from the 10th–11th centuries to the present.

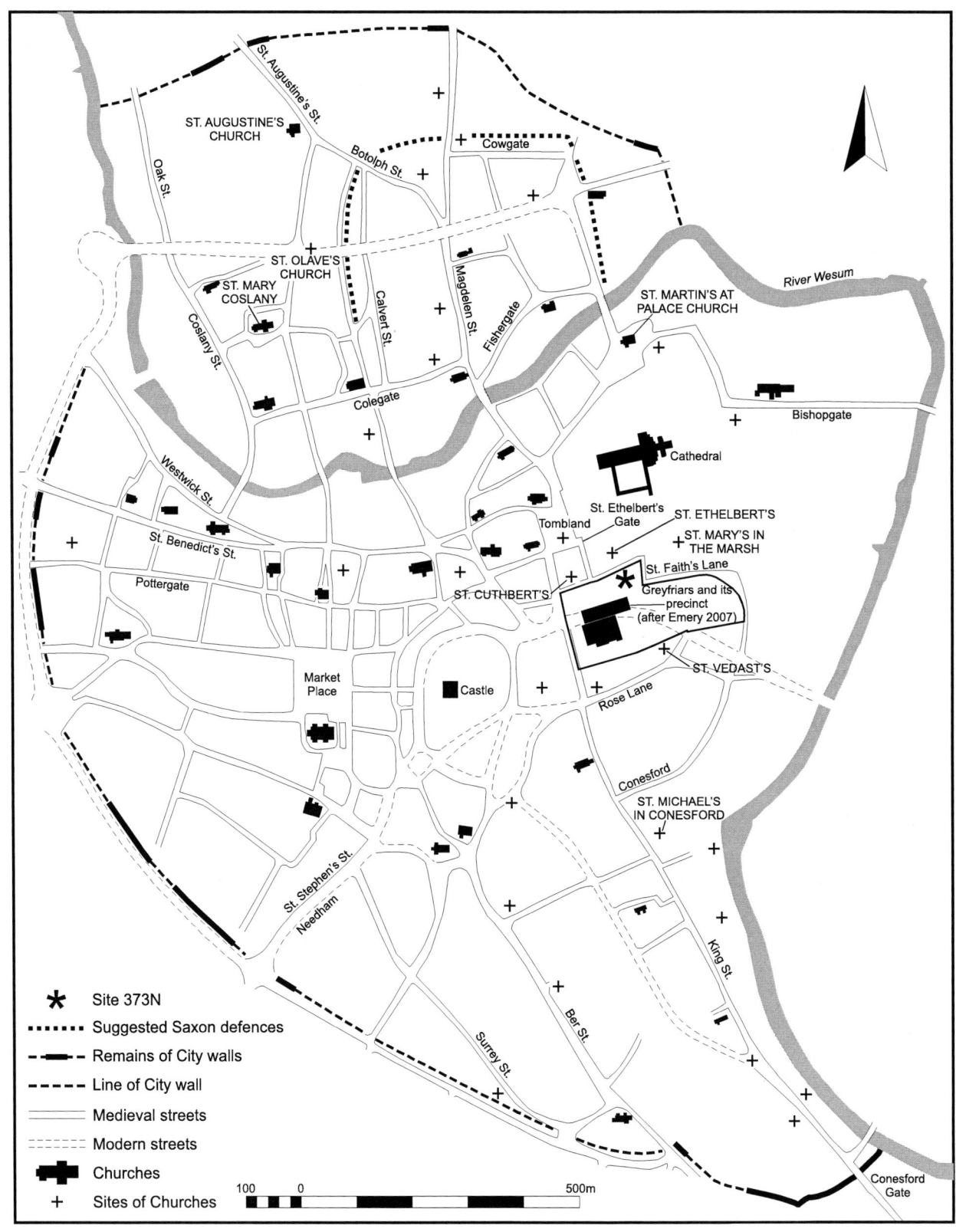

Figure 1  General site location

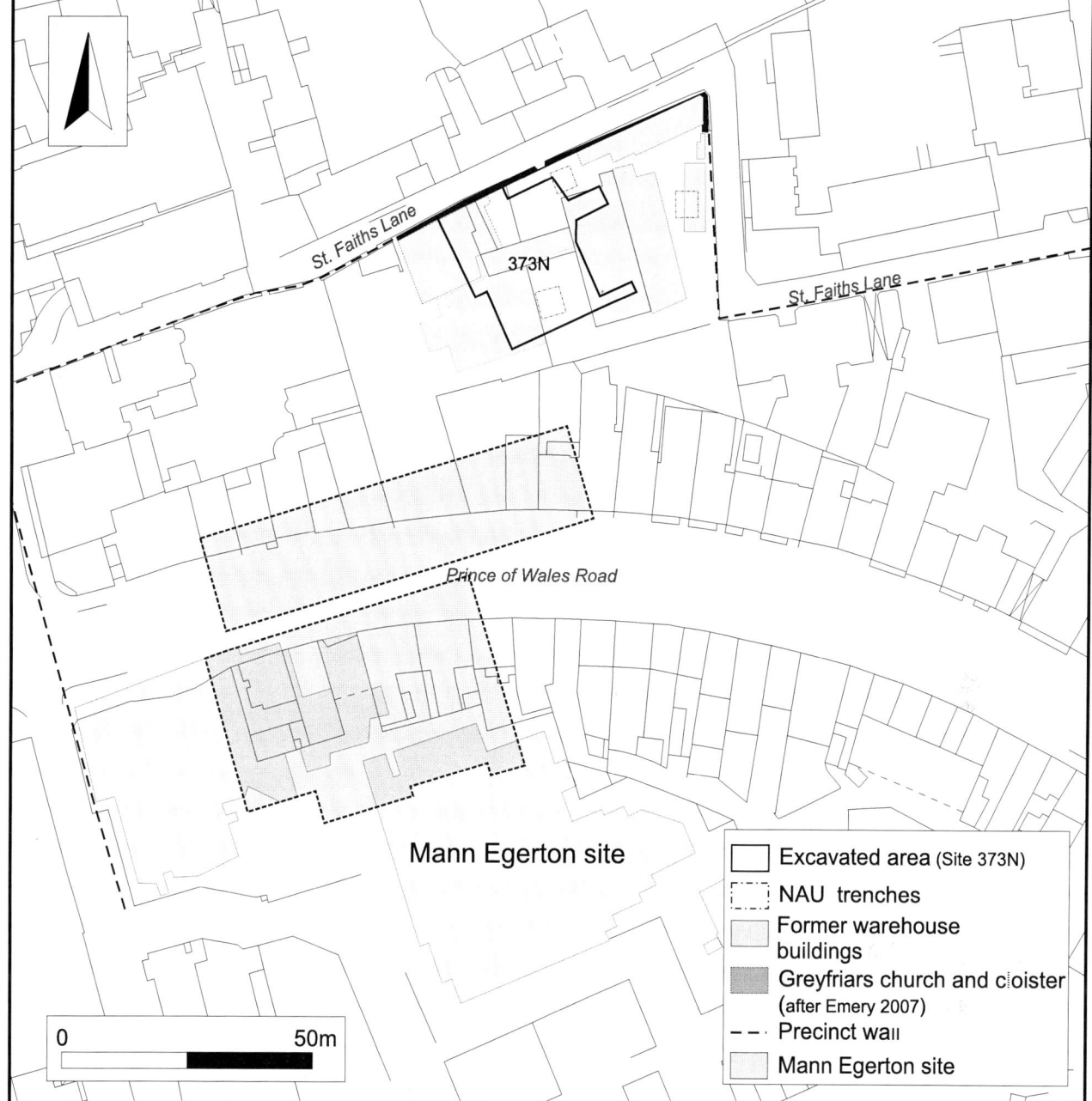

© Crown Copyright. All rights reserved, Northamptonshire County Council; License no. 100019331. Published 2009

Figure 2 Trench location

## III. Historical and documentary background

The historical and archaeological evidence for the origins of Norwich have been discussed at length in numerous major reports (Atkin *et al.* 1985; Ayers 1988, 2003). The consensus of interpretation suggests that the city began as a number of distinct settlements which coalesced into one urban mass for mutual economic benefit or to rationalise defence, or possibly for both these reasons. This is thought to have taken place in the 10th century, possibly being marked with the creation of a *burh* under Edward the Elder in *c.* 917. The survival of the early settlement name of Norwich suggests that it may have subsumed its (perhaps no less substantial) neighbours of Needham, Conesford, Coslany and Westwick, and their names thereafter remain only as districts within the whole.

From the 10th century onward the site would have lain within an area of the early core of Norwich. This tract of land saw a variety of industrial activities and domestic occupation, and may have featured a highly developed road system which is now mostly obscured (Emery 2007, 36–40). Such industrial zones or groupings based around specific craft activities are not uncommon in early Norwich, and local specialisation of this kind persisted into the medieval period (*e.g.* the ironworking focus around Alms Lane: Atkin *et al.* 1985, 3). A variety of industries might have existed cheek-by-jowl, sharing key resources such as fuel or water. The association between an area and a specific industry could be a persistent one — for example, Pottergate has retained its name from the production of Thetford-type ware in the 10th–12th centuries, even though the pottery itself was no longer produced here after this period (Atkin *et al.* 1983).

Some elements of the pre-Conquest street layout survive in parts of Norwich, and recent work has enabled the reconstruction of the former alignments of further streets lost beneath later topographic changes. A series of north–south and east–west streets or lanes has been postulated and in some cases been confirmed by excavation (Ayers 2003; Emery 2007, 26, 36–40). St Faith's Lane may be a remnant of this early topographic landscape and its curious dog-leg form may be due to later partial lane closures to the north and south, those to the north probably resulting from the imposition of the Cathedral Close onto the Late Saxon townscape (Ayers 1996).

Thus by the 11th century Norwich was already established as East Anglia's principal urban centre, and it was the base for many administrative functions relating to Suffolk as well as Norfolk. This pre-eminence continued into the Norman era, Norwich hosting not only a cathedral but also, for a century, the only royal castle in the region. The Castle supplanted earlier occupation wholesale and it would appear that even the church authorities were powerless to resist, as witnessed by the discovery of a Late Saxon church and at least one cemetery beneath the north-east bailey (Ayers 1985, 63–5).

While the Castle to the west would have influenced both growth and stagnation in the area of St Faith's Lane, the Cathedral, too, would have had an impact. With the Norman establishment of the new marketplace in its current position to the west of the Castle, at the expense of the previous Late Saxon focus at Tombland, St Faith's Lane became further removed from the urban commercial centre. Furthermore, with the Normans came many of their own artisans and craftsmen. The demise of a specialist ironworking industry on the excavation site in the 11th century may have had something to do with the new physical presence of the Castle but equally might relate to commercial pressures if these smiths' wares were no longer required in large quantities. From 1093 Tombland was dominated by the Cathedral and Bishop de Losinga's new Close spread in all directions, subsuming former plots and frontages. It is not known to which church the inhabitants of St Faith's Lane paid their tithes, since the later medieval parish boundaries may have borne little resemblance to those of the later Saxon period, which for the most part leave no trace (Ayers 1985, 64). The cloistered existence of the Cathedral's Benedictine community also meant that wherever the new precinct wall supplanted former buildings, a physical screen was erected which cut off one side of a street from its neighbours on the other. Such a drastic transformation could make an entire street 'non-viable' in a commercial or social sense, especially if the 'wrong' side contained (for instance) the communal water source or the common oven.

Thus the location of St Faith's Lane, or at least in its western course, may have been at the mercy of a whole series of developments during the Norman transformation of Norwich which may have had significant impacts on this locality. There were opportunities for industry and commerce within a wider local network of activities, but there were real risks that this could be disrupted or curtailed and the site eventually lay on a thoroughfare with reduced prospects for future development. As a result, from the 12th century onward it became run down and provided an ideal space on which a Friary might be founded and grow.

The site came within the purview of the Order of Friars Minor — the Franciscans or Greyfriars — from 1226, when the Friars were settled very close by (Luard 1859, 113; Emery 2007, 45–7). It had, however, been dominated from the late 11th century onward by the precinct of the Benedictine Cathedral Priory on the north side of the lane. Indeed, the western end of St Faith's Lane connected with the south-western corner of the Cathedral Precinct and the Priory's almonry and granary close to St Ethelbert's Gate. In general terms the arrival of the friars, in Norwich as elsewhere, was a cause of some ecclesiastical disapproval. Although ostensibly because of the friars' then-unconventional approach to evangelism, this was as often as not due to bitter wrangling over contested burial fees, the rights to which were perceived to have been wrested by friaries from local parishes. Many of the Norwich parishes owed their allegiance to the Cathedral Priory (Page 1906, 236–7). So serious was the bad feeling that in some places the new orders drew impassioned statements and pleas from the established Black Monks and Nuns: 'O sorrow, O worse than sorrow, a tiresome plague! The Franciscans have arrived in England' (Thorpe, 1848, quoting Florence of Worcester). In Norwich, the situation was worsened by the Franciscans obtaining papal indulgences to offer burial in a purpose-built 'pardon cloister' adjacent to the nearby St Vedast's Church, giving them an advantage in attracting mortuary business (Page 1906, 236). Their need for revenue may have been acute at this time since at least part of their new house burnt down either before 1238 or 1242, at which time Henry III, probably taking a lead, granted twenty pounds for reconstruction of fire-damaged buildings (see Doucet 1953, 86 for discussion of the two dates, which are at odds in different texts). The quarrelsome Benedictines at the Cathedral Priory may not have helped their own cause. They and the Prior and Bishop were often also in dispute with the city, culminating during the tenure of Bishop Roger de Skerning and Prior William de Brunham in rioting by citizens in 1272 (Campbell 1975, 13, *inter alia*). Suffice to say their cause was lost, as by then the Franciscans were popular amongst the citizenry and remained so right up to the Dissolution.

To the south of the lane lay the former course of the Dallingflete, one of the many small watercourses in the city, which flowed into the River Wensum to the east as it exited the city. As late as the 19th century a substantial medieval stone bridge spanned what still remained open of the Dallingflete, which Kirkpatrick (1845, 4) called the Greyfriars Creek. It is now culverted, although it has been suggested that culverting of the headwaters may have begun in the medieval period. It was formerly thought that the Creek was to some extent navigable and thus of special value to the Franciscans, since it gave direct private access to the River Wensum (Kirkpatrick 1845, 118; Blomefield 1806, 108; Hudson 1910, 118). Most of the monastic orders in the city had private access to the river and its commercial traffic and even houses with only a nominal presence in the city fought hard to obtain and retain similar access (Hudson 1892, 21).

St Faith's Lane is a relatively modern name, derived from the nearby former church of St Vedast (*cf.* Hudson 1892, note 9). The lane was variously known as Sevencote Rowe at about 1300 (later Seven Coal Row) and, further round, Little/Nether Conesford or, in part, Rose Lane

(Hudson 1892, 2 and note 4; Campbell 1975, 25, maps 3 and 6).

The friars' purposeful acquisition of the area adjoining St Faith's Lane was part of a series of land transactions, constrained by the Franciscan Rule that only land adjoining that relating to their initial grant could be acquired subsequently. On the basis of the survival of monastic documents, the Norwich Franciscans appear to have been at their most acquisitive in the late 13th century. However, this may reflect biases in the creation and survival of documents resulting from the introduction in 1279 of the Statute of Alienation in Mortmain, which required Crown ratification of all property gifts to monastic institutions where no reversion was envisaged. Quite simply, from that date more copies of documents had to be made as the Crown was involved in transactions of this kind.

Between 1285 and 1299 the Franciscans enlarged their site by enclosing adjoining lanes and acquiring adjacent tenements by gift (Hale and Rogers 1991, 13). These transactions, fully explored by Emery (2007, 49–53), may be summarised as follows:

*1285:* Leave to close a lane 211 feet x 12 feet on the south to enlarge their close (Page 1906, 430).
*1292:* Eighteen properties granted from nineteen benefactors (Kirkpatrick 1845, 110; Page 1906, 430).
*1297:* Leave to enclose a lane 100 feet 6 inches x 10 feet for the enlargement of their dwelling (*ibid.*).
*1299:* Bestowal of three messuages in gift (*op. cit.*)

This expansion process was not entirely trouble-free, however. In 1289/90 the friary was arraigned before the Leet: 'Iurati presentant per sacramentum quod ... fratres minores appropriaverunt sibi plura tenementa que solebant dare Domino Regi langabulum.' [The jurors witnessed under oath that ... the Friars Minor had appropriated to themselves several tenements for which they had been accustomed to paying landgable to the Lord King] (Hudson 1892, 36). It is clear that such complaints were not without substance as these inclosures had far-reaching effects. Hudson records that in the Leet Rolls of 1364, 1375 and 1391 two Conesford parishes were amalgamated, partly due to the Friars' inclosures, which greatly reduced the number of persons tithing (Hudson 1892, xix).

Of the properties given in 1292, fifteen were said to be void. Although Kirkpatrick stated that they lay in the order in which he presented them, the work of Margot Tillyard shows them to have been sited in disparate places. She was unable to place them with accuracy and suggested that the whole area may already have been run-down (Tillyard, *pers. comm.*). Documentary studies connected with the Mann Egerton excavations show that the area was indeed in serious decline, with abandonment attested in several locations: these included the site of the current excavations, which lay within a larger plot (Emery 2007, 49–53). In such circumstances it might be argued that the gift of such lands to the new friary was less a matter of pious devotion than a fortuitous transfer of parcels of low-quality urban wasteland which had previously stood idle, earning little for their owners.

No documentary evidence relating directly to the excavated area itself pre-dates the later 13th century. The Franciscans' occupation has left little documentary trace after they obtained the area, with no deeds being enrolled by the city. There is no documentary evidence for the site in the period *c.* 1300–1539 other than the record of wills or abstracts of wills in various sources, which indicate eight requests for burial in the Franciscan cemetery (Emery 1997, appendix 5). To these can be added a ninth from the will of Robert Wymbergh in 1509 (Smith 1895, 592). Unfortunately none of these specifies burial in the excavated cemetery or at the Pardon Cloister. Likewise, some make no distinction between intra- or extramural burial. It would be unwise to speculate further on such a small group of requests.

At the Dissolution, the Norwich friaries were assessed as relatively poor: in salvage terms they had 'no substance of lead', and only some had 'small gutters' (Hale and Rogers 1991, 32). Such observations probably reflect the local use of ceramic roofing materials. On 12 March 1539 the entire site, including the cemetery (specifically mentioned), was granted by the Crown to the Duke of Norfolk who sold it to the city in 1559 (*ibid.*, 37). Demolition of the main buildings took place in 1565–6 (*ibid.*, 40–1) and the Norwich City Lease Book records that in 1566 the site was leased as a garden to Lawrence Wood amongst others (*ibid.*, 42). The terms of the lease required lessees to repair the (perimeter) walls. In addition the three main lessees of large orchard or garden plots abutting the main stone walls to north and south were to leave seventy-six existing ten-year-old apple trees intact and replant a number of walnut trees if they were lost (*ibid.*, 45). The leases were renewed in 1607/8, when the City Chamberlain's accounts record that the Greyfriars site remained undeveloped (*ibid.*, 47). This situation appears unchanged in Cleer's map of Norwich of 1696 which shows the whole site as gardens with no buildings along St Faith's Lane. Hochstetter's map of 1789 (transcribed in Campbell 1975) continues to show a site given over to horticulture amidst a city which was beginning to infill large areas of its former gardens and backyard plots.

During the 19th century the fortunes of the excavated plot began to change markedly, with increasing encroachment onto the former gardens by new building. The creation of Prince of Wales Road in the mid-19th century introduced a new frontage to the south of the site, which was now abutted by the rear frontages of nos 22–40 Prince of Wales Road. While the gardens still dominated the site on the first large-scale Ordnance Survey map of 1885, there were also numerous buildings — some already hinted at in Hochstetter's map, but now augmented by greenhouses between carefully surveyed paths and steps. These indicate changes in the levels of the garden, with some hard landscaping implied. There is no indication as to the use of any of the buildings. By about 1900 private deeds show the site further built upon, including the entire eastern quarter, with the greenhouses swept away. New steps show repeated changes to the landscaping (*ex inf.* Purcell Miller Tritton and Partners). Along the St Faith's Lane frontage a house was constructed over extensive cellars, and this became the first cellared building on the plot.

During the 20th century was constructed a series of buildings which became the premises of Wallace King's furniture warehouse. Some of these were very substantial two- and three-storey structures which covered parts of the site that had not previously been built upon. They had considerable foundations comprising brick and concrete strips (generally externally) and concrete stanchion bases for interior steel supports. A new arrangement of rainwater pipes, soakaways and sewers accompanied them (*ex inf.* Chaplin Farrant drawing in archive). The complex reached its greatest extent by about 1978, when the 1:2500 Ordnance Survey revision of that year shows widespread warehouse footprints joined to the precinct wall at the north along most of its length. This had contracted considerably by 1997 just before total demolition began; Purcell Miller Tritton and Partners surveyed its remains in a photomontage (June 1998, in archive). The wall has been preserved and repaired as befits its Grade II listed status, especially since the excavations have established its antiquity and significance.

## IV. Excavation methodology

The layout of the warehouse buildings dictated the configuration of a series of three evaluation trenches dug by the Norfolk Archaeological Unit in 1997 in yards and car parking areas, in the context of the planning application to develop the plot (Emery 1997). Following demolition of the buildings and removal of the foundations and services, Northamptonshire Archaeology was commissioned to excavate and record a predetermined area of the footprint of the new Norwich School Sports Hall as part of a Section 106 planning agreement. Fieldwork took place during 1998–9. The brief for archaeological excavation, which was prepared by Norfolk Landscape Archaeology on behalf of Norwich City Council, required that an area with an east–west width of *c.* 20m should be excavated, with two trenches extending eastwards to establish the extent of the cemetery. One of the previous evaluation trenches was subsumed into this more extensively excavated area, while the other two remained beyond its edges (Fig. 2). The excavation was complemented by a watching brief on service installation and other groundwork during development, as required by the archaeological brief.

Contingencies were in place to ensure a quick response to unanticipated needs for excavation and recording which emerged during the course of the project. In the event, these became necessary beyond the new building footprint in two specific instances. The first was to enable the recording of the surface of exposed remains (before their re-covering, undisturbed) of a further 13m of the north precinct wall, since maintenance of a soil baulk against the wall during construction had proved impossible for engineering reasons. The second was to excavate and record a strip of ground in the south-west part of the area where a terrace had to be created to allow close access by a piling rig to the western side of the building at a depth which would affect upper layers, principally further cemetery remains.

A 12-ton 360° mechanical excavator was used under archaeological control to remove post-medieval garden soils beneath a residue of hardcore and backfill left by previous demolition and levelling of the site. The area had been cleared of recent building foundations and drains prior to the archaeological programme being commissioned. The overburden was removed in spits which were metal-detected to retrieve ferrous and non-ferrous metal artefacts. The mechanical excavator returned to remove up to 700mm thickness of grave-earth later in the programme.

Hand-excavation in an area of over 600 sq m recovered evidence of a monastic cemetery and its bounds, together with underlying industrial and domestic remains. This sequence was tied in stratigraphically with a 13m length of the boundary wall of the plot to the north, which confirmed that this latter feature was indeed a vestige of the former Franciscan Friary Precinct Wall. While large areas of deeply intercutting pits were sampled at their unexcavated upper surface to obtain dating evidence, closer attention was given to discrete pits since these presented fewer problems of residuality. Sampling for environmental remains was concentrated upon pits showing visible potential for preservation of macroscopic plant and faunal remains. In addition, a widespread sampling programme covered the abdominal cavities of skeletons in order to retrieve gall, kidney or bladder stones or any preserved stomach contents.

In summary, the site embodied archaeological deposits of *c.* 2m thickness, with Late Saxon and early medieval features cut into natural geological layers at the base of the excavation (Fig. 3; Pl. I). The different horizons can be summarised chronologically as follows:

*Phase 1:* Late Saxon industrial/domestic occupation features cut into natural deposits;
*Phase 2:* early medieval domestic occupation features cut into natural deposits;
*Phase 3:* medieval cemetery with building-site type features;
*Phase 4:* post-medieval garden soils.

After the pre-emptive archaeological excavation, the new building was constructed on piles which were drilled using a flight-auger working from an imported piling mat. The formation level of the new build makes it likely that the unexcavated portions of the pre-cemetery horizons (comprising those features cut into the natural sand) remain relatively undamaged between piles. Pile caps, ground beams and some of the accompanying new services lie at a higher level. Beyond the excavated area to the east, it is likely that most archaeological deposits remain unaffected.

## V. Post-excavation methodology

Following the completion of fieldwork, individual finds were washed, dried and labelled with the appropriate Norfolk SMR site code (373N), as well as their context number, before being prepared for specialist assessment. Apart from human bones, which were sent immediately for full reporting since it was agreed they would warrant detailed analysis, the site data and assemblages were assessed for their archaeological potential in accordance with the English Heritage procedural document *Management of Archaeological Projects 2* (1991). An Assessment and Updated Project Design resulted (Soden 2000b). The archive has been deposited with Norfolk Museums Service. The skeletal material was re-buried by the Roman Catholic Order of Friars Minor, the heirs to the medieval Franciscan tradition, in their cemetery at East Bergholt, Suffolk. Samples of teeth and ribs from each skeleton have been retained in the archive.

## VI. Research priorities

This report has been compiled in the light of the two-part regional archaeological research framework *Research and Archaeology: a framework for the Eastern Counties* (Glazebrook 1997; Brown and Glazebrook 2000). While the excavation results have in some ways not realised the potential that evaluation and preliminary research had indicated, their value has exceeded expectations in other areas. Thus it will be seen that the project has addressed a number of identified research priorities in a way which is limited only by the fact that the results derive from a single site. It is hoped nevertheless that the work usefully complements the results gained from the investigation of the Greyfriars precinct that took place at the nearby Mann Egerton site (845N; Emery 2007).

# 2. The excavated evidence

## I. Phase 1: Late Saxon industrial and domestic occupation (10th–11th centuries)

### Summary

Late Saxon remains comprised post-holes and pits of 10th–11th century date. The structural elements relate to buildings fronting St Faith's Lane, one entirely domestic and others which may have had a partly industrial purpose, specifically for ironworking. An area of ironworking debris was recorded in the north-eastern corner of the site but assessment of the slag indicates that the forge which produced it lay beyond the excavated area. The building footprints at the frontage were fragmentary as large portions had been cut away by a later sand quarry, and by the construction trench of the later monastic precinct wall on the same alignment.

### The excavated evidence
(Figs 3 and 4; Pl. I)

In the southern part of the site, furthest from the lane, features of the earliest phase were relatively few. What there was comprised a scatter of post-/stake-holes (such as *484, 850–1* and *862*) and disparate pits (*472, 583, 788, 810, 815–6, 838–9, 843*). One narrow timber slot (*485*) indicated the former presence of a structure in the south-western corner. However, although apparently associated with at least one of the post-holes, it lacked further association and was surrounded by later intrusions.

Closer to the St Faith's Lane frontage, at about the midpoint of the excavated area, there were even fewer features of this date. Four discrete pits (including *269, 792* and *618*) were accompanied by a much larger one (*613*) which, at 1.65m depth, was substantial enough to reach the underlying chalk bedrock and contained a series of distinct fills (*593, 614–7*: Fig. 8 and Section 3).

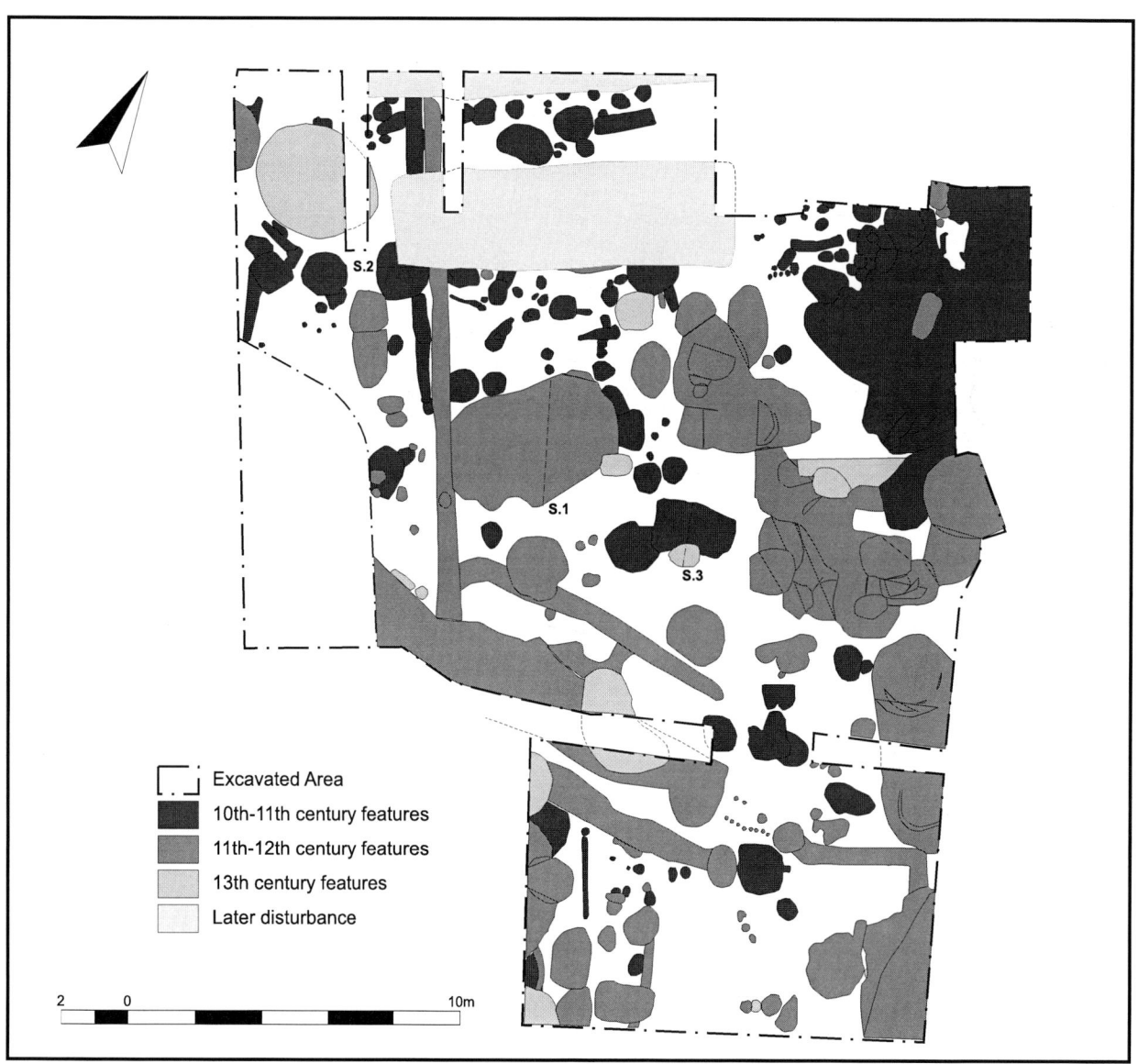

Figure 3  Site plan, all features Phases 1 and 2

**Building A**

Adjacent to the street frontage a widespread complex of post-holes, small pits and slots interspersed with a few larger pits appeared at first sight to represent a somewhat haphazard array of features. They may, however, largely derive from a single rectangular building or sequence of buildings on the same spot. The whole layout has been confused by the massive intrusion of a late medieval sand quarry (*529/893*) and the loss of the postulated frontage itself to the construction trench for the later Friary precinct wall at the north (*885*).

It is not possible to reconstruct the layout of the building. However, some sections of probable beam-slots (*1018, 883, 530, 1065, 700, 386*) were aligned approximately with the street frontage and the group of small pits and post-holes lay within the area that these features enclosed, which measured *c.* 14m by 10m.

None of these features is individually noteworthy but as a group they probably represent part of a building. No hearth or any specific internal focus was present; it is likely, however, that if any such feature had existed that it would have been removed by the later sand quarry.

There were few visible post-pipes to help the process of differentiating pottery finds associated with the date of the building's construction from those dating to the time of its removal. Consequently the building may only be assigned broadly to the 10th–11th centuries. It is possible that some of the recorded structural elements belong with Phase 2 since it is noticeable how the features positively dated to this later phase tended to avoid the street frontage.

**Building B: part of a nearby forge?**

A dense concentration of features filled with ash, charcoal and ironworking slag lay to the east of Building A. They comprised numerous intercutting pits, post-holes and stake-holes, and a curving slot 1.6m long which resembled a beam-slot but had not necessarily held a timber. While all were cut into natural sand, the constant churning of the top of the pits by intercutting produced an irregular and extensive spread of burnt material, which masked many features. The basic colour of every fill was dark grey to black, with little variation. This material, variously identified as deposits *435, 442, 444* and *445*, thickened considerably to form a massive lens of material towards the east.

The post-holes, stake-holes and slot probably derive from a single structure or a sequence of structures in the same location. The rest of this putative structure probably lay beyond the area of excavation. The Norfolk Archaeological Unit's evaluation Trench 2 uncovered features of a similar date nearby (*84* and *85*) but they too lacked associated structural elements. Both complexes of features point to the existence of a forge close by, probably somewhere near the existing frontage. The excavation area did not extend to the precinct wall in this part of the site, leaving the frontage here unexcavated over a distance of some 7m. The forge structure probably extended into this unexplored area.

The majority of slag recovered is somewhat unusual, comprising the actual hearth or furnace lining (Chapman *et al.*, Chapter 4, p.40). Typically material of this kind is deposited within metres of ironworking activity but is readily destroyed by later disturbance. There was little more evidence of any related structure. Phase 1 (and Phase 2) material at such a depth (4.5m above OD) was largely undamaged by

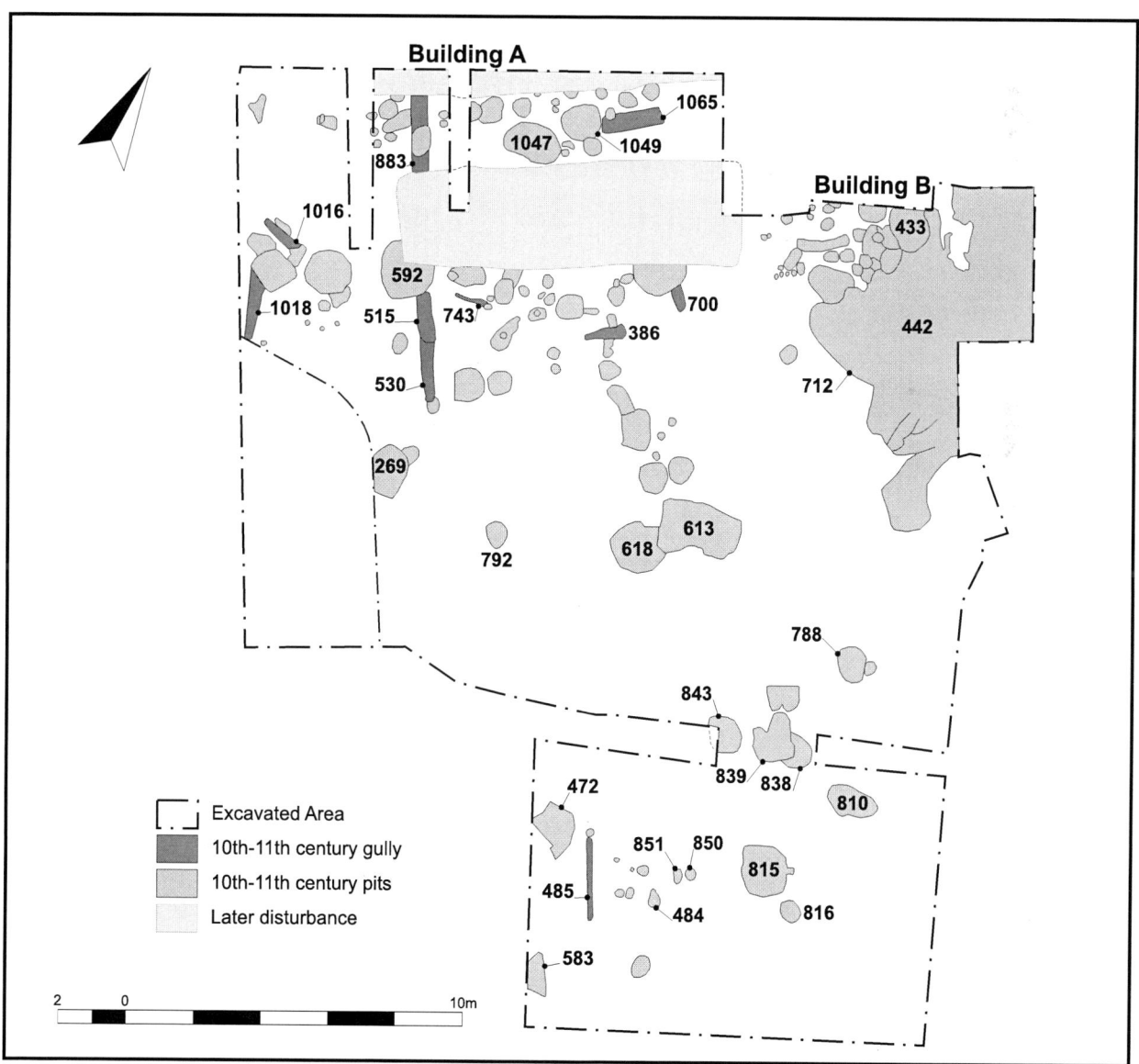

Figure 4 Site plan, 10th–11th century

pile caps and ground beams in the development, so further remains are preserved *in situ*.

## II. Phase 2: Early medieval domestic occupation (11th–13th centuries)

### Summary
Early medieval occupation dated from the mid-11th century into the 13th century. The zone fronting onto the lane was probably occupied by buildings, but few post-holes can be positively dated to later than the 11th century. Elsewhere there was very intensive pit-digging. None of the new pits impinged upon the footprints of the frontage buildings; in fact, pitting seems to have spread progressively southwards over time.

Small enclosures or plots were laid out during this period, perhaps to formalise the existing layout at the frontage which previously may not have been fully demarcated. Such a need to subdivide the frontage might imply either increased pressure for space or an administrative rationale connected with clarifying ownership or rental calculation.

The number and density of features of this phase tailed off sharply in the 13th century and it might be concluded that the focus of occupation had shifted dramatically by this time, with occupation along the frontage ceasing altogether. These changes were almost certainly the result of the foundation of the Franciscan Friary in 1226. A large circular pit close to the frontage at the north-western corner of the excavation may have been the first of a number of sand quarries to be dug, perhaps in connection with the construction of the Friary.

### The excavated evidence
(Figs 5–7; Pls I and II)

The excavated area seems to have been divided into two plots by a discontinuous gully aligned east to west (*541* and *846*), broken by an entrance flanked by large post-pits *555* and *813*. The entranceway may have been blocked, or at least narrowed at some stage, since a line of nine stakes was driven across it, possibly to support wattle hurdles. There were other post- and stake-holes in this area. Another possible boundary gully (*598*) to

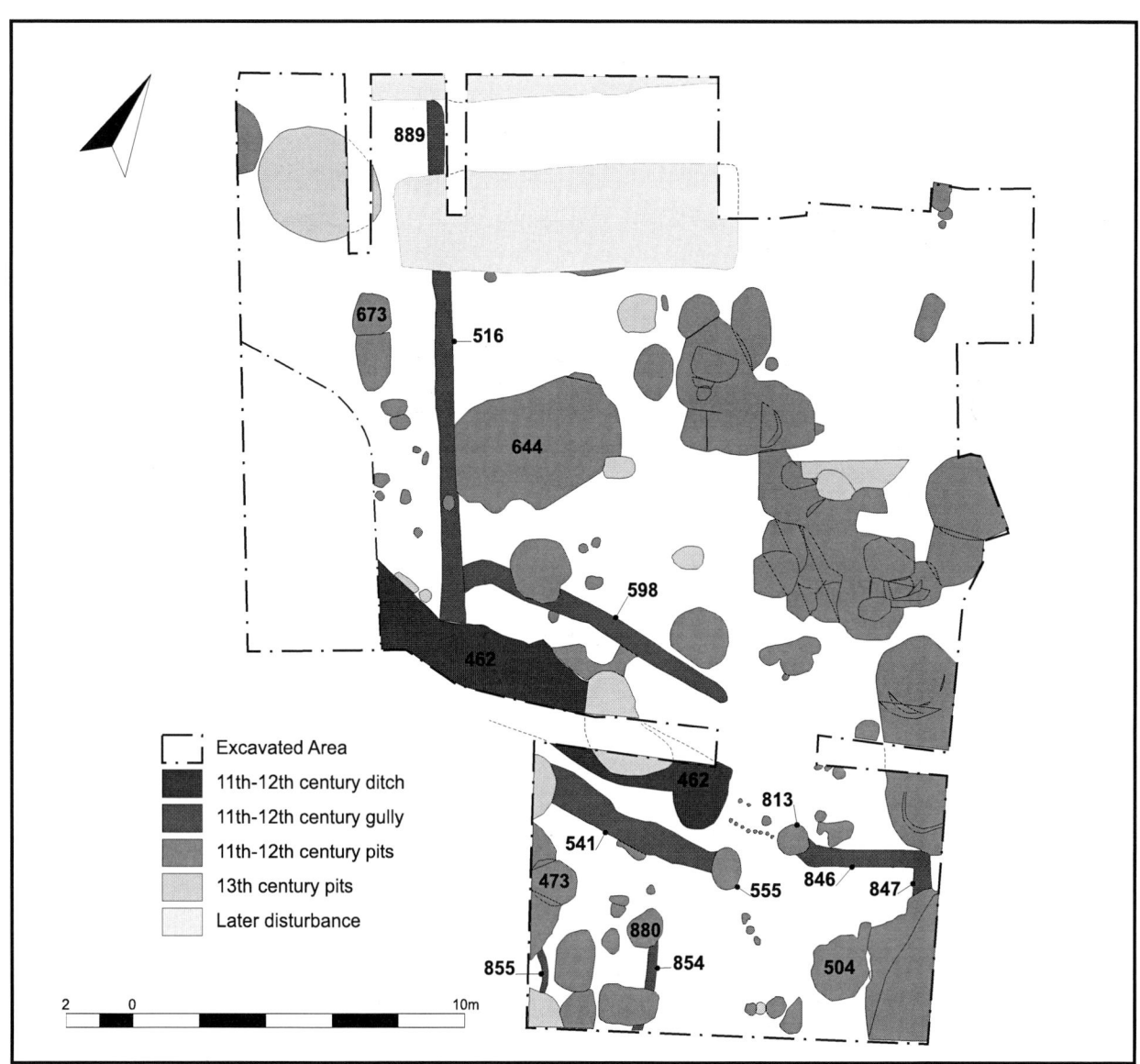

Figure 5  Site plan 11th/12th and 13th centuries

Plate I The site during excavation of the Phase 1–2 Saxo-Norman street frontage

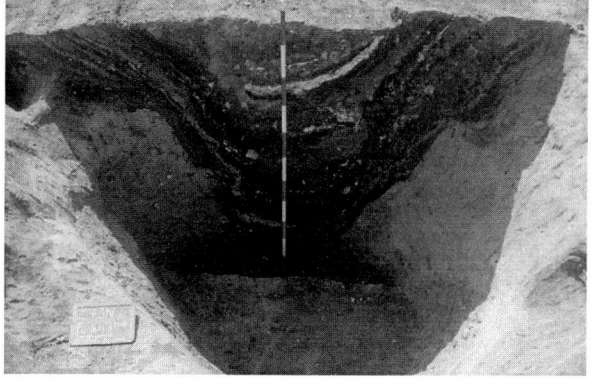

Plate II Pit *644*, half-sectioned

the north lay roughly parallel to *541*. This was probably related to the others, the position of its eastern terminal (mirroring that of *541*) suggesting a corresponding entrance opening. A gap of 4m between gullies *541* and *598* suggested there may have been a pathway between them, perhaps providing access to the southern plot.

The southern plot contained some structural evidence, denoted by slots (*854* and *855*) and a collection of small pits. There were also a few larger pits, including two (*473* and *504*), which were sampled for environmental remains (see Carruthers, Chapter 5, pp.45–9). Of these (*473*) produced primarily evidence for crop processing, while (*504*) produced evidence of the burning of fuel, including heathers.

In the northern plot a zone of densely intercutting pits lay on the eastern side of the site. These were partly examined and found to contain mainly domestic, rather than industrial, waste. However, on account of their location they contained a large proportion of residual material, including ironworking slag. The complicated stratigraphy of this area indicated that further investigations would have been of limited value due to problems of residuality.

Features were sparser towards the western side of the plot, comprising scattered pits and discrete post-holes that were not arranged in any recognisable pattern. One of the pits (*644*) was enormous, measuring 5.0m by 3.3m at the surface and at least 2.4m deep (Fig. 7; Plate II). It differed from almost all others in this phase not simply because of its size but by surviving as a discrete feature. It was therefore half-sectioned and recorded as extensively as safety considerations would allow. Numerous distinct infill layers (*286, 284, 283, 280, 278, 690, 645, 738* and *691*) were recorded along with a mass of 40 discernible lenses, some wafer-thin, dipping at such steep angles from both sides as to suggest that many were liquid when deposited, perhaps as night soil. The contents of the pit were of outstanding significance. It yielded the best faunal assemblages and archaeobotanical specimens from anywhere on the site, together with good dating evidence. Analysis of the resulting information provides a useful guide to the status of the site, and its environment, at this period. It may have been at least filled partly with midden waste.

After it had been infilled, the pit had been cut on its south-western periphery by a long beam-slot (*516*) running back from the frontage. This was over 14m long

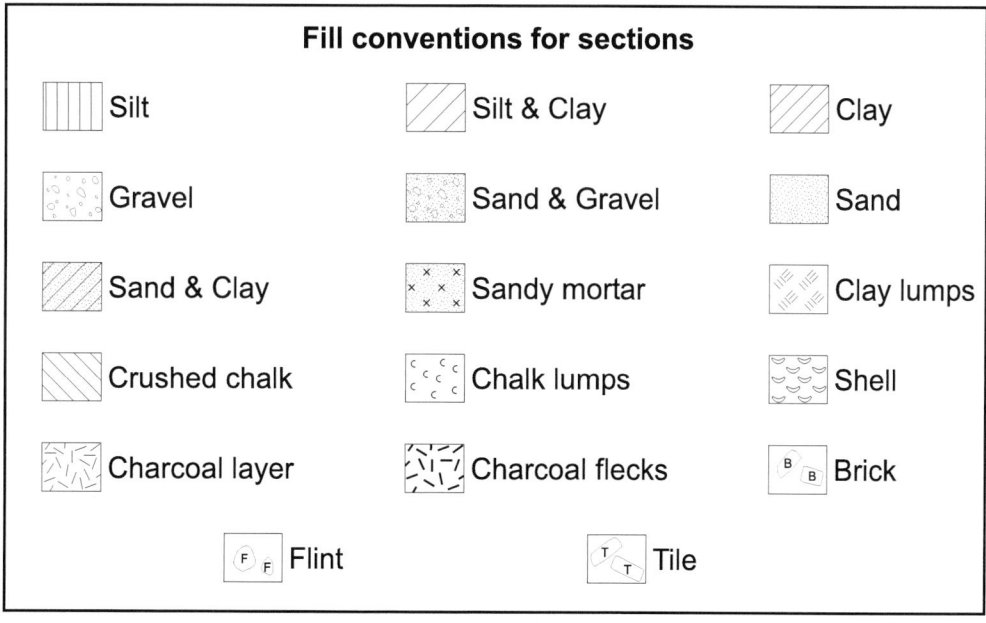

Figure 6 Section drawing conventions

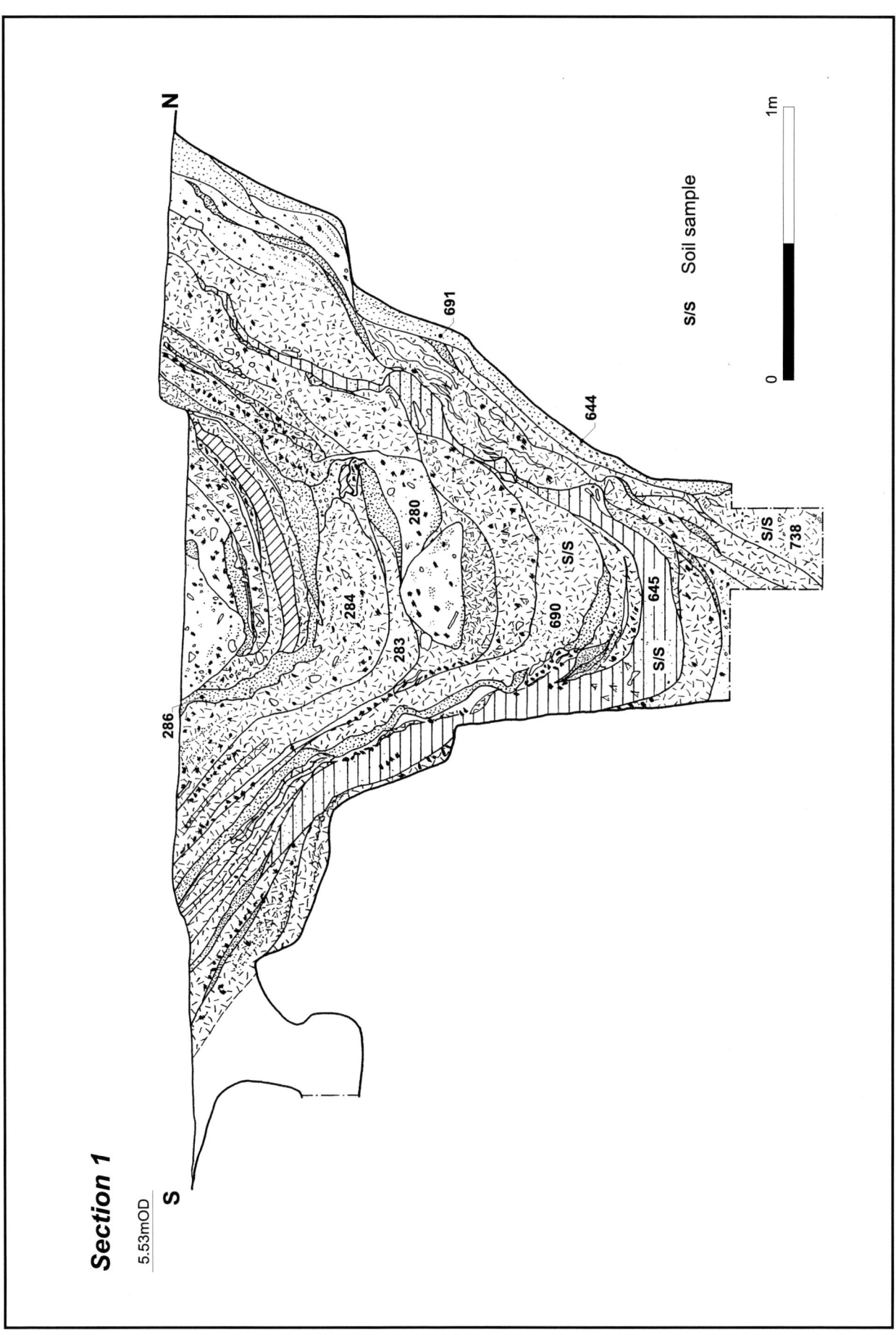

Figure 7 Section 1, pit 644

and may have formally demarcated separate eastern and western plots. It seems likely that Building A had gone out of use by this time and that the pathway between gullies *598* and *541* was blocked.

Towards the end of the period a massive trench (*462*) cutting a swathe between the two parallel boundary gullies almost certainly reinforced the division marked by these earlier features. It was 1.3m deep and 3m wide, with a flat base, and was at least 10m long, extending westward beyond the excavation limit. It is one of the latest features to be dated to the 12th century.

A small scatter of pits and a few post-holes are the only features which can be positively dated to the 13th century. While it is possible that some features of this date contained exclusively residual material, analysis of the pottery indicates a marked decline in deposition in the 13th century, strongly suggestive of a change in land use (Blinkhorn, Chapter 4, p.32). It is possible that pits were concentrated to the east of the site in the area, where several intercutting pits of this date were found in evaluation Trench 3 (Emery 1997).

## III. Phase 3: The medieval cemetery (late 13th–16th centuries)

### Summary
Evidence of 14th–16th century activity relates entirely to the Franciscan Friary, chiefly comprising burials within a cemetery. Of these, 136 were excavated, including six previously located but left *in situ* during evaluation by the Norfolk Archaeological Unit. The graves had been dug into a soil horizon which had probably constituted the former occupation soil. This contained finds of all dates, from the Late Saxon period to the late medieval periods, and its upper horizon also represented the ground surface at the time of the cemetery's use. None of the earlier features could be seen to cut this soil horizon, suggesting that the intercutting of numerous pits and other negative features had probably 'churned' it on many occasions. Almost all of the graves were then cut into this layer, with the result that residual finds within the soil became redeposited once more. The layer, which lay up to 700mm thick over almost all of the area, was intensively surveyed by metal-detector before its removal, partly by mechanical excavator under archaeological supervision and partly in hand-excavated control areas.

A large spread of stone hardcore in the middle of the excavated area suggests that building work may have been going on nearby from the late 13th century. Sand quarrying was once again important during this period: a massive quarry-pit was dug hard by the frontage of St Faith's Lane and served by a haphazardly metalled track. Three early burials lay in its path but the track simply ran over them. Interments in this period initiated a burial pattern which in places was regularly spaced but in others without any apparent order. Some clusters of burials may have been deliberate.

The cemetery continued to be used for interments in the 15th century. However, in the south-western part of the site there was evidence of considerable building work nearby, denoted by numerous dumps of builders' waste and mixed soils laid down in a spread, which was thicker to the south and thinned out to east and north. Such dumping built up the ground to the extent of forming a terrace, which was revetted in stone along the eastern edge but later robbed out. The only grave to contain 15th-century pottery had been cut into these terraced dumps. The burials hereabouts were laid out in a seemingly orderly fashion, unlike those elsewhere on the site.

Towards the end of the Friary phase 16th-century remains were also dominated by construction work to the north. It was probably early in the 16th century that this part of the Friary precinct was finally enclosed by the northern boundary wall that survives in part today (Plate V). The wall was tied archaeologically into the stratification over a distance of 14m (Fig. 13). A ditch (Fig. 9, F307) lay parallel to the wall and separated the latest graves from the sand quarry, which by then had been backfilled and sealed. This ditch probably denoted the northern edge of the area that had been designated for burials. Its exact coincidence with the edge of the sand quarry might imply that some continuing subsidence had been noted — or was still anticipated — long after the pit had been infilled. An area of crushed stone and mortar between the ditch and the wall may relate to construction work on the new perimeter wall. It was cut by a slot which may indicate the former presence of a pentice around the northern edge of the precinct. The last interments within the excavated area appear to have been laid right up against the enclosing ditch, implying that the graveyard at this point was regarded as 'full'. A jetton from the boundary ditch shows that it was backfilled in the period *c.* 1550–74 or soon after. Late medieval burials may have existed in further lines to the west, but post-medieval terracing and redevelopment suggest that archaeological remains have been increasingly denuded in this direction, and beyond the excavation site along St Faith's Lane, by the foundations and floors of 19th-century buildings.

### The excavated evidence
(Figs 8–13; Pls III–V)

#### Sequence
The former occupation surface (*109/190*), a sandy loam heavily stained and contaminated by the detritus of the preceding phases of occupation, covered the entire site and formed the surface upon which the Phase 3 re-use of the land as a cemetery took place. Extensive dumps of sand and pebbles were laid down across the southern part of the site, and in one area a considerable dump of mixed chalk, stone chips and mortar was spread liberally around. The earliest of these layers (*195*) produced pottery of the 14th century. Nearby lay a spread of roof tile fragments (*183*, *212*). Four graves (graves *21*, *22*, *23* and *24)* had been cut into layer *301*; while they may not be the earliest, they are the only ones that appear demonstrably 'early' graves, due to their stratigraphic link with the dumped materials.

Crossing over the former occupation surface, dumped materials and three of the four 'early' graves were the deep, near-parallel, gravel-filled ruts of a former cart track (*183–6*, *196*). They ran continuously on a north–south alignment over a length of 12m, and further discontinuous patches of rutting were suggested further north (Pl. IV). The evidence suggests numerous heavily laden cart journeys, causing wheels to sink into both the soft sandy material and the compacted chalk and stone layer. The three graves had been heavily disturbed by these ruts, although the bodies within them were not affected. Elsewhere the ruts penetrated the make-up layer *196* and deformed the spread of tile beneath (*212*), pressing it into dumped layer *195* and displacing it into the rut sides. Although the ruts themselves were not dated they cut through the layers of dumped material, the earliest of which (*195*) was dated to the 14th century: thus they are clearly of this date, or slightly later (Fig. 8, Sections 4 and 5).

Eventually the wheel ruts had been filled with gravel to restore the ground surface and give wheels more purchase on subsequent journeys. They led towards a massive rectangular pit in the northern part of the site (*529/893*) which measured 10m (east–west) by 3m (north–south)

Plate III  The site during excavation of the Phase 3 cemetery

and had been cut through earlier features. It had vertical sides and was at least 1.5m deep; three separate localised sondages suggested a depth of over 1.8m. It seems to have been used to extract sand and gravel (and possibly chalk and flint) for building purposes. The quarry would have produced 45 cubic metres of builders' sand, weighing about 90 tons. The backfill of the quarry pit contained 14th-century pottery. An outlying pit (*254*), roughly square and measuring 3m x 3m x 0.7mm deep, lay beside the cart ruts and seems to have represented a more modest quarry. It barely reached the level of undisturbed natural sand and may have been a trial hole or the beginnings of an aborted quarry; it does not appear to have been used for rubbish disposal. It was cut by later graves. The quarrying observed here seems to form part of a pattern observed elsewhere in the Friary precinct (*e.g.* Emery 2007, 61).

The cart ruts were covered with sandy loam following backfilling of the two quarries. Grave-digging resumed, although the soft material in the backfilled quarry may have precluded extending the existing alignment of three graves across its fill for some time. Long continuous lines of burials were dug across the area, probably forming part of a wider burial pattern which extended beyond the excavation area to both west and south. It is likely that the eastern edge of the cemetery was identified within the excavation area, while the northern edge was delineated by a precinct wall or boundary ditch. The majority of graves in the excavated cemetery had no stratigraphic relationship to any features other than the ubiquitous former occupation surface *109/190*. Some stratigraphic relationships were noted within small clusters of adjacent graves, but virtually none produced pottery or other datable material which might have been of value in producing any relative seriation.

- The following graves were cut directly into the former occupation soil and no other context: graves *2, 3, 26, 30, 34, 36, 37, 39, 47, 49, 53, 55, 56, 58, 63–9, 71, 73, 75, 78–82, 84, 85, 87, 89, 94, 95, 98, 100, 103–5, 113, 117–24, 127, 128* and *132–4*.
- The following may be regarded as 'secondary' interments on account of their cutting other graves (bracketed numbers denote the earlier interments that were affected): graves *1 (2), 27 (75), 28 (65), 29 (65), 31 (84), 33 (119), 38 (63), 43 (79), 48 (94, 104), 51 (118), 57 (80, 81), 62 (84), 72 (82), 76 (131), 93 (103), 96 (123), 97 (49, 98), 105 (134), 109 (103)* and *116 (121)*. Graves *100* and *132* were also probably secondary as they seem to closely respect another secondary interment (*109*) although there is no firm stratigraphic relationship that demonstrates this.
- A third phase of interment, indicated by the cutting of 'secondary' interments, was represented by graves *32 (62), 52 (51), 70 (76), 86 (96), 42 (132), 91 (109), 92 (93), 101 (97)* and *115 (116)*.
- Three graves (*73, 112, 135*) contained sufficient disarticulated bone to suggest that an initial burial had been entirely displaced by a secondary, deliberately placed burial, occasioning the wholesale (and seemingly casual) redeposition of a skeleton.

Although these burials, representing the majority of the excavated cemetery, had no physical links with datable layers, a few others did. In the southern part of the site a half-line of burials cut through the gravel-filled cart ruts and the dumps put down to form the base of the track. They comprised 'primary' graves *12, 13, 14, 15, 17, 19, 64, 66, 67* and *83*, which were partly succeeded by 'secondary' graves *18 (17), 59 (11, 83), 60 (14, 15)*. A third phase of burials was represented by graves *61 (60)* and *16 (18)*. Two graves (*102* and later *99*) cut the smaller of the two quarry pits (*254*). Some of the graves in this area may have had markers, possibly denoted by an irregular configuration of shallow post-holes or planting holes, although the dating of these features is uncertain. With so much building material spread around the cemetery area there may have been an urgent need to mark, at least temporarily, the positions of graves that might otherwise have been rapidly obscured.

At the south-western corner of the site lay an area in which widespread dumps of building materials were laid down, probably connected with the creation of the track and the need to extract sand. The dumps comprised sands, loams, chalk, stone chips and gravels (Fig. 13, Section 6: *943, 940, 942, 941, 939* and *937 inter alia*). Only context *937* produced datable material, in this case 14th-century pottery. Interments began again with graves *138–41, 145* and *146*. The fill of grave *138* (*944*) contained 15th-century pottery. Thereafter further dump layers were spread around (up to the latest layer *976*) before further graves (*142, 135, 136* and *137*) were dug. This suggests that the graves which constituted the westernmost excavated row may have been of 15th century or later date.

Plate IV  The trackway

Plate V  A section of the precinct wall including foundations

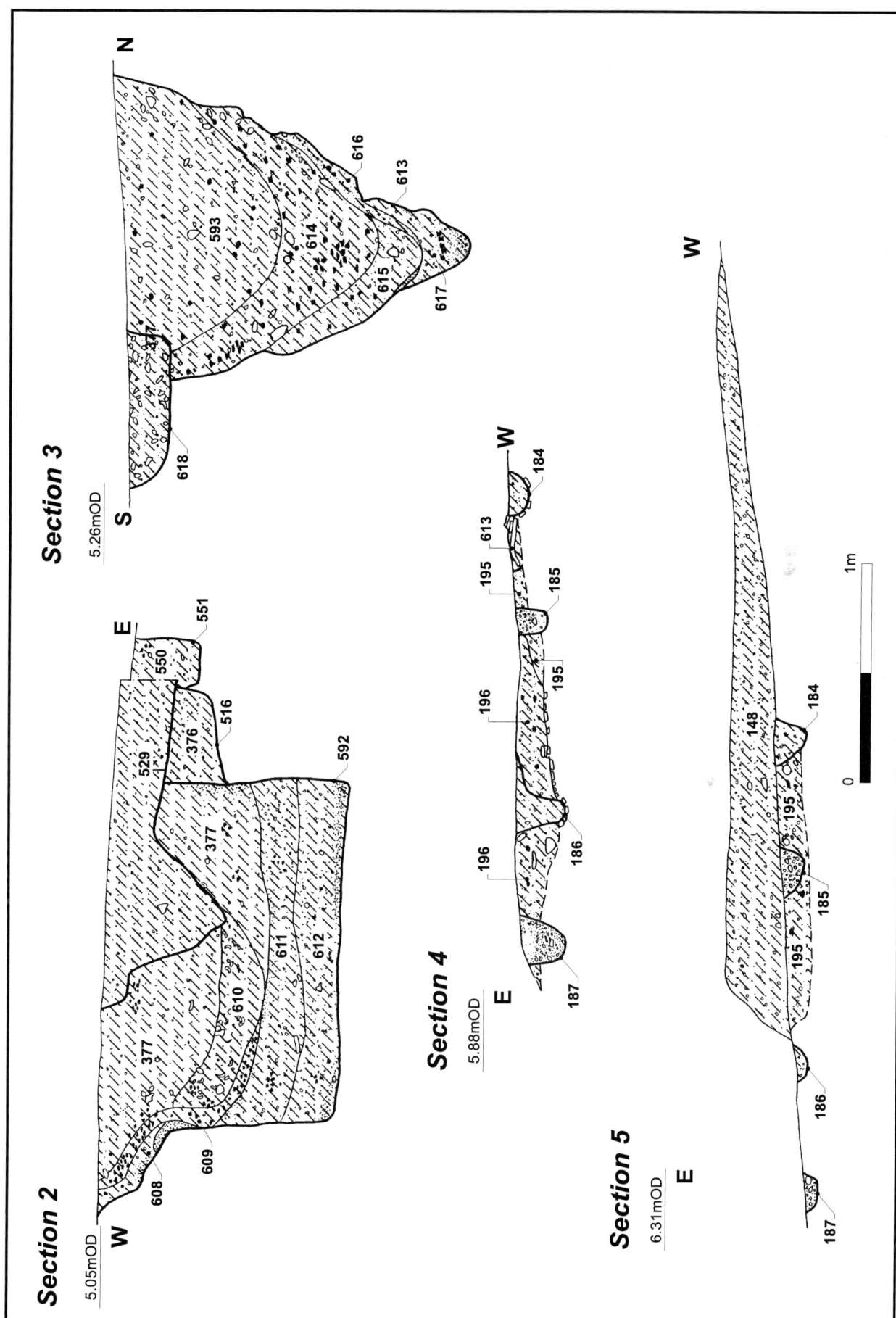

Figure 8 Section 2, pit 592; Section 3, Pit 613; Section 4, cart ruts; Section 5, Cart ruts

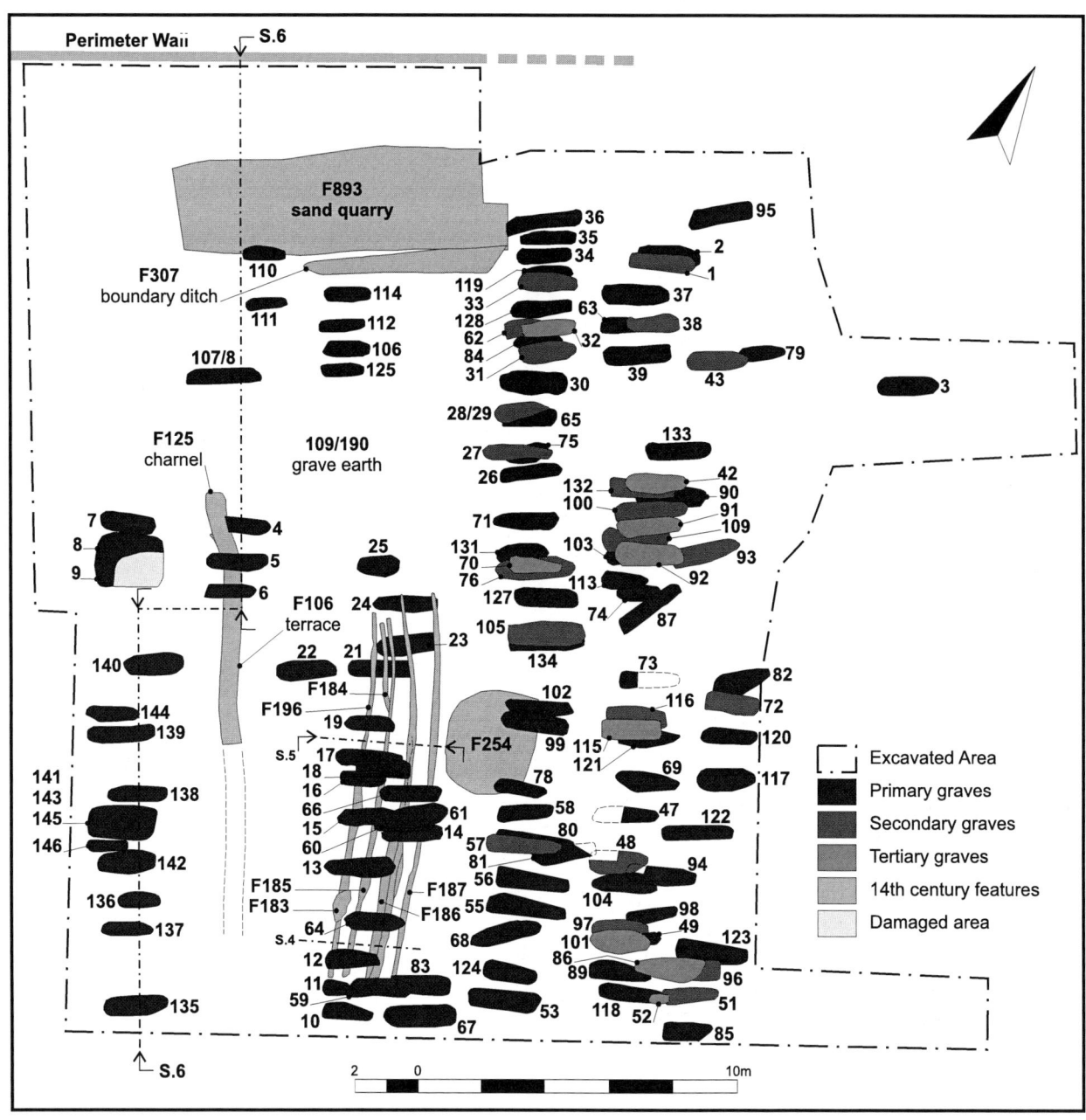

Figure 9  Plan of graves

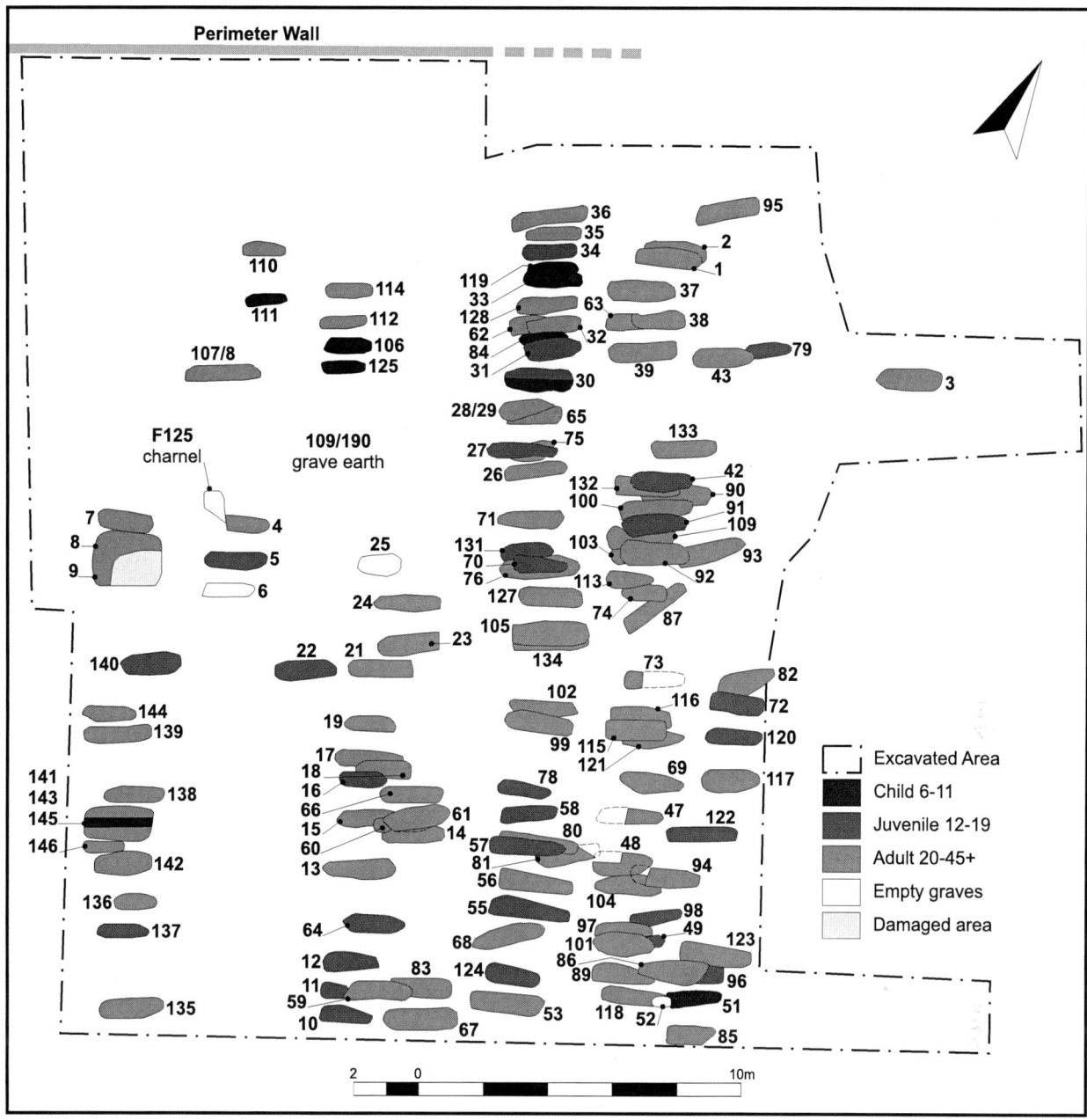

Figure 10  Plan of graves; age of skeletons

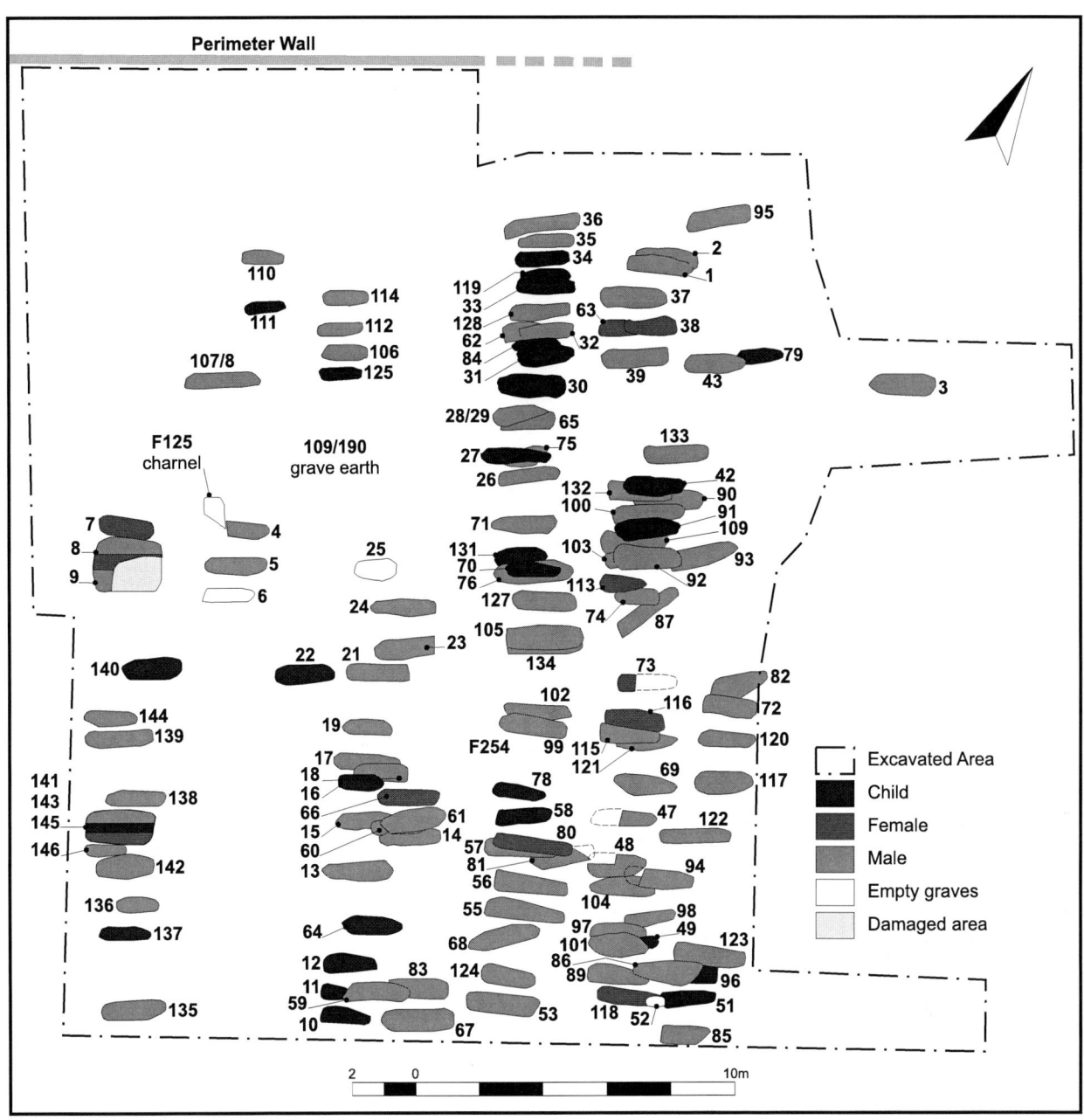

Figure 11 Plan of graves; sex of skeletons

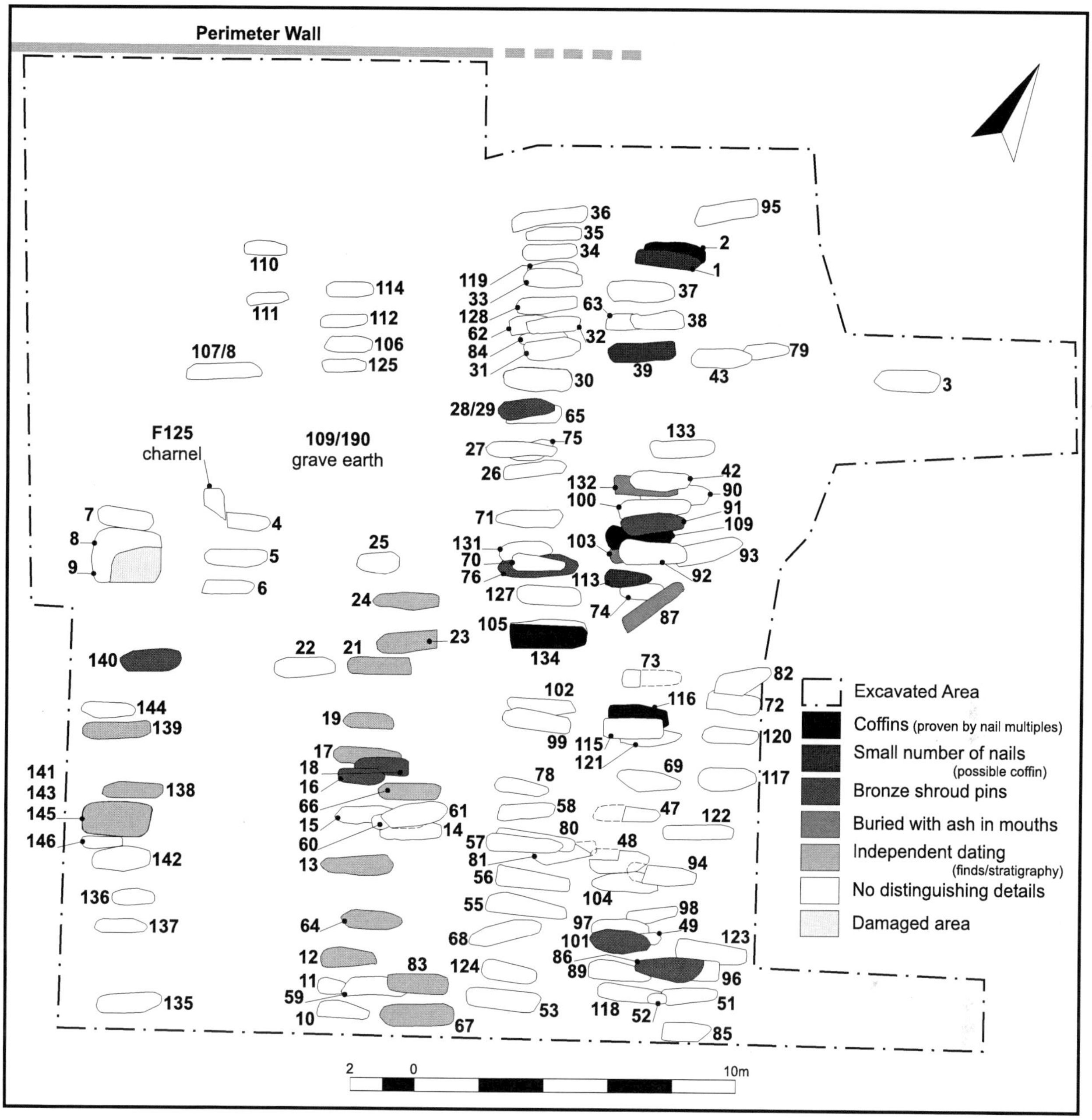

Figure 12  Plan of graves; burial details

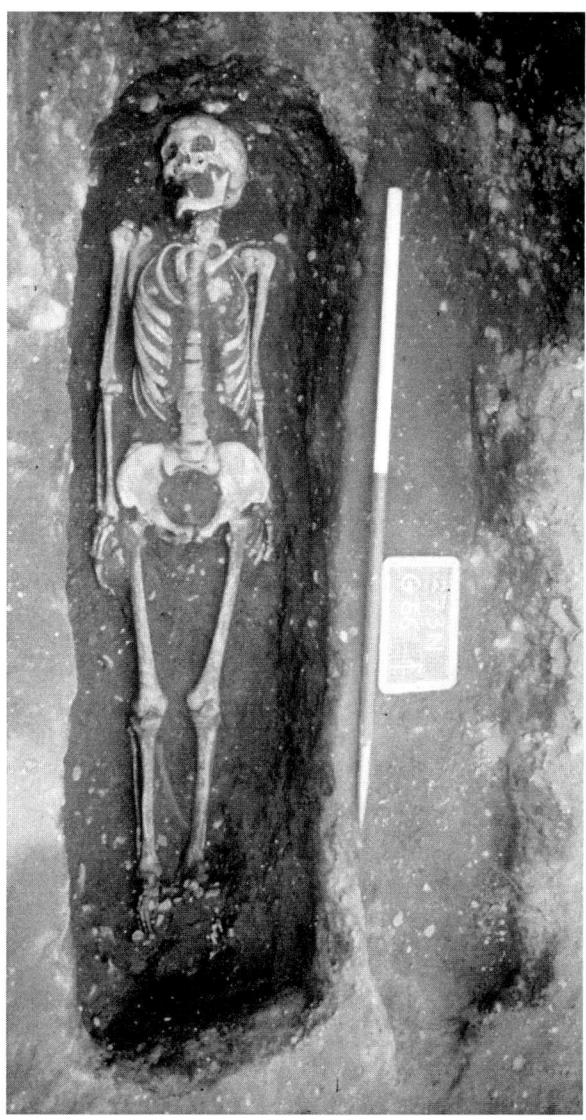

Plate VI   A typical skeleton in the cemetery

Plate VII   Skeleton detail: the mouth is packed with ash

At the northern extremity of the dump layers at the west end of the site, a group of burials had been cut into the dumped material where it thinned out to only 0.20m thickness (layers *108*, *110* and *107/921*: Fig. 13 and Section 6). They comprised graves *4*, *5*, *7*, *8* and *9*. Grave *8* was a triple grave which had been truncated by a concrete stanchion of the former Wallace King warehouse. At this point a robbed-out foundation (*106*) appears to have delineated the dump layers over a distance of at least 5.5m from north to south, showing that the material had been shaped into a hard terrace edge rather than left as a steep bank. During construction the builders had disturbed graves *4* and *5*, setting the disarticulated bones aside in a charnel pit (*125*) adjacent to grave *4*.

A group of graves to the north may have been among the latest on the site. Few of them were intercutting, but they related stratigraphically to deposits that had been laid down during construction of the precinct wall (Fig. 13, Section 6; Pl. V). A total of eight graves (graves *106–8, 110–12, 114, 125*) together with the construction trench for the precinct wall (*882*) cut a substantial dump of loose, clean chalk (*308/921*) which had been introduced above the backfilled sand quarry (*529/893*). The construction trench contained alternate layers of loamy sand (*886, 961*) and gravels (*960, 962*) — the type of fill seen everywhere within the precinct within the foundation of monastic walls of any size (Emery 2007, fig. 3.13). A large pit (*966*) cutting the same layer contained 16th-century pottery in its fill *967*. Ditch *307*, over 10m long and sharing an alignment with the northernmost graves, appears to mark the limit of burials in the region of the former sand quarry, perhaps because the ground was soft and liable to sink, or else was frequently wet due to drainage from the adjacent precinct wall. A Hans Schultes jetton of *c.* 1550–74 came from the backfill of the ditch. A series of post-hole bases just inside the wall (*315, 915, 917* and *919*: not illustrated) probably relate to later scaffolding used in its repair, but a slot (*964*: Fig. 13) dug through *308/921* and parallel with the wall may have contained the sole plate of a pentice which had allowed perambulation of the cemetery in all weathers. It lay parallel to ditch *307*: 17th-century pottery in its fill *965* suggested that any beam that it had housed was not removed until post-medieval times.

## Character of the burials
(Figs 10–12; Pls VI and VII)

Throughout the cemetery's existence the majority of burials seem to have been made in winding sheets, leaving no discernible remains. However, the discovery of multiple nails confirms the use of wooden coffins in five burials: graves *2* (31 nails), *109* (21 nails), *116* (18 nails), *132* (29 nails) and *134* (21 nails). Similarly, eight shrouded burials can be inferred from the presence of pins: graves *16*, *18*, *29*, *76*, *86*, *91*, *101* and *140*. Neither coffins nor shrouds were restricted to specific gender or particular age.

The position of the arms in each burial was recorded. Only where both arms lay in identical alignment could the intended burial posture be gleaned: in ninety-six instances overall. Among consistent female burials (eight out of eleven), all but one (grave *80*) had both arms lying directly by their sides. Otherwise the burials of both genders and all ages displayed a mixture as follows: arms by sides, including the eight females (38/96); arms by side with hands on thighs (2/96); arms crossed with hands on pelvis (15/96); arms crossed with hands on midriff, including the one anomalous female (30/96); arms crossed with hands on chest (11/96). The remainder displayed inconsistent arm positions or lacked one or both arms due to disturbance by other graves. These included three females.

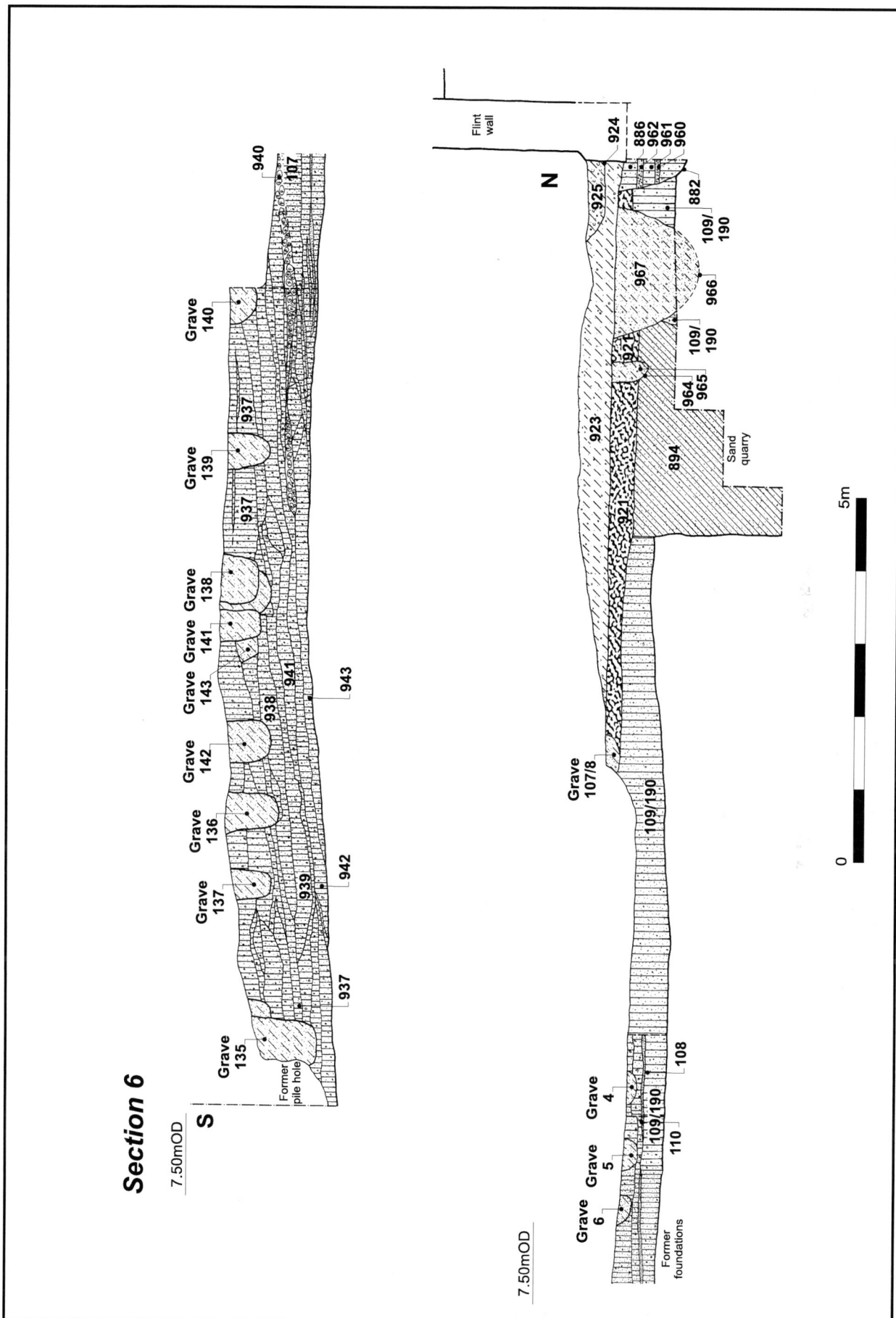

Figure 13 Section 6, graveyard and later deposits (south-north)

Three burials had their mouths deliberately packed with ash (graves *87*, *103* and *132*, all adult males: Pl. VII). This curious rite, seemingly not recorded archaeologically elsewhere, is discussed below.

## IV. Phase 4: Post-medieval garden soils

### Summary
The post-medieval use of the site for gardens may have been a respectful gesture in recognition of its former use as a cemetery. A series of dumps of soil were laid down. Surviving landscaping features of this period were confined to the edges of the excavation area, and comprised the mortar bed of a northern and eastern perimeter path and a small, vaulted brick cellar of 19th-century date. Former garden bedding trenches were noted.

The machine-removal of modern floors and foundations, comprising brick/concrete strips and concrete bases for steel stanchions, cellar floors, together with drains and manholes, had taken place during demolition works to clear the site prior to new foundation piling. This had caused deep localised damage to these deposits, as well as lowering the existing ground level.

### The excavated evidence
The archaeological brief did not prioritise investigation of the post-medieval use of the site, since desk-based assessment and evaluation had shown the presence of widespread garden layers. However, in some areas understanding the development of post-medieval build-ups was important to reconstructing the site sequence in detail, and appreciating how its secular history had taken into account the existing topography and former use. It seems reasonable to suggest that new owners might have seen a challenge or a problem in taking over a site which had just previously been a cemetery. However, 16th-century economic upheavals might have meant that the relatively secluded location off Tombland and down St Faith's Lane obviated any urgent pressure for redevelopment. It was not a prime location, nor was space at a premium.

It seems that the possible pentice represented by foundation slot *964* at the northern edge of the plot was retained at least into the 17th century: the possible drainage ditch (*307*) may have been backfilled earlier, but not until after 1550–74. With any pentice now gone the way would have stood open to reordering, and there may have been immediate work to the perimeter wall. A new surface of sand loams (*923*) was laid down: this was up to 0.50m thick and seems to have been quite extensive, stretching right up to the wall and across to the central areas of graves which it may have been designed to mask. A 1.3m-wide channel, *924*, filled with crushed chalk and mortar (*925*), had been dug against the wall and formed a path whose line was traced during the watching brief at various points right around the inside of the wall on the north and east sides of the plot. It mirrored, and possibly extended, the line of the former pentice. The Phase 3 revetment wall foundation *106* was robbed out at this time. The backfill of the trench (*104*, *105*) contained elements of medieval masonry, including a broken mullion/transom in Caen Stone and flint nodules and cobbles (identification by Dr Diana Sutherland, University of Leicester). This constituted the only possible Dissolution-related structural material on the site, with all other evidence of this kind relating to earlier construction programmes.

A trench extension at the extreme south-eastern corner of the site appears to have found the eastern limit of the medieval cemetery. Above medieval pits lay the ubiquitous former occupation soil *109/190*, into which the graves had subsequently been excavated elsewhere. The surface of the grave-earth hereabouts appeared to have been very flat; perhaps it had originally been grassed over. Soil had been dumped on top of it to raise the level by *c.* 0.30mm. A further layer of soil had either accumulated or was deliberately introduced and then turned over by cultivation: the profile of the underlying layer displayed regular scalloped cuts indicating planting trenches up to 0.80mm wide. One of these trenches contained a distinct grittier fill, suggesting that it might have been enriched when planted up. There was no dating evidence from these features. Further soil layers accumulated before the modern tarmac and other hard-standings were laid on top. Detailed records of these features are included in the site archive.

## V. Summary of dating evidence for key contexts

All Phase 1 and 2 features were cut into natural sand and sealed by layer *109/190*. The occurrence of 10th–11th century pottery in some features allowed contexts of Phase 1 to be distinguished from those of Phase 2. This latter phase was identified initially after the discovery of 12th–13th century pottery in some features, and distinctive differences in artefactual and ecofactual studies confirmed the distinction between two discrete phases.

With regard to Phase 3 and after, the key dated contexts are as follows:

*109/190:* former occupation surface, later grave-earth: coins of 1180–9 (very worn) and 1248–50
*529/893:* sand quarry backfill: 14th-century pottery
*195:* track base/dump below cart ruts: 14th-century pottery
*148:* dump sealing cart ruts: 14th-century pottery
*937:* builders' dump sequence: 14th-century pottery
*944:* fill of grave *138*: 15th-century pottery
*307:* ditch: jetton, 1550–74
*967:* pit sealing former sand quarry: 16th-century pottery
*965:* robbing of former pentice slot: 17th-century pottery.

# 3. The Human Skeletal Material
## by the late Trevor Anderson
## with E. McMullen Willis, J. Andrews and I. Hodgins

## I. Overview

One hundred and twenty-four graves dating from the 13th to the 16th centuries were excavated from the Franciscan cemetery at St Faith's Lane. The majority, 93.5% (116 out of 124) contained a single inhumation but five multiple burials were also present, including two doubles (graves *36*a–b; *121*a–b), two triples (graves *30*a–c; *141, 143* and *145*) and one quadruple (graves *8* and *9*a–c). Osteological examination indicates that graves *73, 112* and *135* each contained sufficient disarticulated bone to be considered double burials (*73*a–b; *112*a–b; *135*a–b). The multiple burials were not restricted to any particular area within the cemetery. Their presence gives a total of 136 discrete inhumations, all of which were laid extended and supine with their heads to the west.

While there is evidence for intercutting graves, and for burials overlying one another, the cemetery layout appears generally orderly, and distinct north-to-south rows of graves can be identified. The skeletal material was relatively undisturbed and as a result the assemblage collected for study is very complete in osteological terms. Over three-quarters of the sample burials are in excess of 80% complete, with only eighteen burials represented by less than 40% of the skeleton. Ground conditions were similarly conducive to good bone preservation. Over 60% of the skeletons could be classed as good and solid, whereas less than 7% of the sample was fragmented or highly fragmented. There was no difference between the completeness and condition of the adult and the sub-adult bones. A total of 72 abdominal samples were taken and their contents sieved for the presence of bony concretions such as abdominal stones.

Stature, based on complete long bone length (Trotter and Gleser 1958), could be calculated for over 93% of the adults (86/92). The mean stature of males (74/80) was 1.694m (5' 6¾"), with a range from 1.558m (5' 1½") to 1.811m (5' 11½"). Mean female stature, based on only twelve individuals, was 1.568m (5' 2"), with a range of 1.454m (4' 9½") to 1.652m (5' 5¼"). Study of a dataset of 1442 male and 930 female skeletons from various British sites suggests the mean medieval male and female stature is 1.709m (5' 7½") and 1.580m (5' 2¼"), respectively (Anderson and Andrews forthcoming, tables 57 and 58).

Detailed examination of British height statistics from the mid-18th century to the present suggests that stature attainment is related to childhood nutritional status (Floud *et al.* 1990), with stunting occurring before five years of age (Floud *et al.* 1990, 232). As such, it appears sensible to suggest that short stature in archaeological material may be related to relatively lower social status and poor nutrition, especially during the first years of life. However, there was no definite evidence that taller or shorter individuals were being buried in specific areas of the cemetery.

Full metrical data and other detailed anatomical analysis of the human skeletal material from the site are retained in archive. In the following summary of results the abbreviation SK (=skeleton) is interchangeable with the grave number referred to elsewhere and depicted on the relevant plans (Figs 9–12, with age and sex distributions shown in Figs 10 and 11 respectively). Multiple burials bear an alphabetical suffix.

## II. Demography

The skeletons have been aged and sexed on the basis of generally accepted criteria presented in the osteological literature (Bass 1987; Brothwell 1981; Ferembach *et al.* 1980). Due to the difficulties and problems involved in ageing adult skeletal material accurately, the adult remains have been subdivided into three main age categories: young adult (20–30 years); adult (30–40/45 years); mature (over 40/45 years). Before the onset of puberty, skeletal remains do not generally display definite sexual dimorphism and consequently it is not considered possible to sex child skeletons. However, accurate ageing may be achieved using dental development records and long bone lengths (Ferembach *et al.* 1980). The sub-adult burials have been subdivided into four age groups: infant I (under 1 year); infant II (1–6 years); infant III (6–12 years); juvenile (12–20 years).

Just over two-thirds of the sample (92/136) reached adulthood. All of these individuals were sexed and 76 (82.6%) were classed as male; females therefore represent only 17.4% of the adult sample. There is no evidence, however, that they were restricted to any particular area within the cemetery.

Among the adult men and women that could be aged, over 40% died before they were 30 years old, with approximately equal numbers of adults (30–40/45 years) and mature individuals (over 40/45 years old) noted. Approximately half the males were under 30 years old and less than a fifth survived into old age. Within the sample of females, two-thirds were classed as elderly. A chi-square test indicated that the difference in numbers of elderly males and females is statistically significant at the 0.001 level ($X2 = 14.377$, $df = 1$).

Almost a third of the sample (44/136) failed to reach adulthood. No children under the age of 8 years were buried within the cemetery. The majority of sub-adults, almost 80%, were classed as juvenile. All of the children, except one, were buried in the northern part of the cemetery, with four (SK *30*c, *33, 84, 119*) in close proximity in the same row. The only child burial in the southern part of the cemetery excavation area was SK 51. Juveniles appear to be scattered throughout the cemetery with no obvious clustering.

The osteological evidence indicates that this was not a cemetery open to all but one from which all infants and young children, as well as the majority of women, were excluded. Similar high frequencies of males have been noted at other medieval monastic sites (Anderson and Andrews forthcoming, table 55), most noticeably the Cistercian Abbey of Stratford Langthorne (males 98.9% [93/94]: Stuart-Macadam 1986) and the Greyfriars at Oxford (males 97.9% [47/48]: Harman 1985). However, the presence of sixteen females at St Faith's Lane represents an altogether larger proportion, and prevents this being regarded as an exclusively monastic cemetery on the basis of gender alone. Our inability to divide prepubescent skeletons along gender lines also introduces uncertainty on this point.

The absence of children under the age of 8 years also supports the view that only children who were old enough to be taught in the monastic environment were permitted burial at St Faith's Lane. A sub-adult mortality of approximately one-third would not be unusual in an urban medieval cemetery in which infants and young children were buried as well as adults (Anderson and Andrews forthcoming, table 56). However, the fact that such a large sample size died between the ages of 8 and 20 years indicates an extremely high level of fatal childhood illnesses with no skeletal manifestations. If these children were living together in dormitory accommodation, fatal diseases could have spread rapidly and reach epidemic proportions.

Few obvious family groupings were recognised, but two young adult males buried in close proximity in the southern part of the cemetery each display an abnormal sternal fusion and may have been related (SKs *56* and *94*), as could three separate individuals with bifid ribs (SKs *96*, *101* and *122*). Four females with metopism (SKs *23*, *38*, *113* and *143*) may have been members of a particular family who were permitted burial in the cemetery. Such a trait might occur over several generations, and it may be significant that the women were not buried in close proximity and probably occupied graves of different dates. The social origin of the few females remains unknown. It is not possible to estimate the sex of the children.

Squatting facets occur in forty-two individuals; interestingly, two adult males (SKs *81* and *90*) display hyperdorsiflexion of the toes, possibly caused by repeated kneeling (*cf.* Ubelaker 1979).

## III. Pathology

The most frequently observed pathological condition was osteoarthritis, with the spine and shoulder most affected. In one case, degeneration was secondary to chronic dislocation of the mandible (SK *74*). Another individual displayed marked spinal scoliosis, or side-to-side curvature of the spine, possibly due to congenital malformation (SK *61*).

A high percentage of 17.6% of the total adult sample — all males — displayed ante-mortem fractures. Ribs were the most frequently broken bones. In three cases (SKs *22*, *81* and *109*), costal fractures had occurred not long before death and were still in the process of healing. Another male (SK *67*) displayed fracture of the left clavicle and two left ribs each with double fractures, suggestive of a serious fall with crushing injury. A 9–11 year-old child had a healed femoral fracture (SK *30*c) and two juveniles presented with less serious clavicular (SK *120*) and metatarsal (SK *65*) fractures. All the fractures appear to have been due to accidents, perhaps including falls and injuries caused by dropping heavy objects. The standard of healing is very good.

Levels of bone infection and metabolic (nutritional) disease, including cribra orbitalia, were relatively low. A probable bladder stone was found in the grave of a mature male (SK *43*). The fact that the individual was also suffering from chronic bone infection and cranial porosis, suggestive of a diet lacking in iron, supports suggestions that bladder stone formation is directly related to lower social status and inadequate diet (Batty Shaw 1970; Green and Batty Shaw 1981).

Two juveniles displayed cystic cavitation of the knee region denoting a metaphyseal cortical defect, possibly associated with vascular disturbance (SKs *79* and *98*). Although this condition is well known in clinical practice, especially in children, these examples appear to represent the first recorded evidence for it in British archaeological material. There is no evidence, however, that the individuals were related.

No malignant bone tumours were detected amongst the skeletons but a possible case of meningioma, represented by cystic cavitation of a meningeal artery, was noted in a mature female (SK *66*).

The standard of adult oral health was very poor, with 36.4% of males and 57.1% of females displaying high ante-mortem tooth loss. In two mature females over twenty teeth had been lost during life (SKs *67* and *73*a) and in the most serious case (SK *73*a) only three mandibular teeth were present at the time of death. The most extensive male loss, of seventeen teeth, also occurred in a mature individual (SK *17*). By contrast, the standard of sub-adult oral health was relatively high, with low levels of caries and enamel hypoplasia.

Caries was present in 58.8% of the adult dentitions with no sexual variation. In one male (SK 109) cavities were restricted to the incisal edge of the maxillary anterior teeth: this is characteristic of bakers and plasterers, being related to high exposure to airborne flour and plaster. All but ten adults displayed some evidence of calculus and over two-fifths (42.5%) of adult dentitions presented with abscesses, with 2.3% of tooth positions involved. Only 7.5% of adults, comprising just six males, presented with enamel hypoplasia. They included a young adult (SK *18*) with partial anodontia, or congenital absence of several teeth, a condition that was also seen in another three males. Over a quarter of the juvenile and adult sample (27.7%) displayed congenital absence of a third molar, such as occurring in a fifth to almost a third of larger medieval samples (*cf.* Dawes 1986, table 4; Stroud and Kemp 1993, 197).

## IV. Conclusion

The findings from St Faith's Lane are in strong contrast to those from the nearby cemetery of St John de Berstrete, excavated in the context of the Castle Mall Project (Shepherd Popescu forthcoming) where levels of chronic bone infection, leprosy, iron deficiency and enamel hypoplasia are among the highest recorded from medieval England (Anderson 1996). In comparison, the adult population buried in the Franciscan cemetery appears to have enjoyed a healthier lifestyle and evidence of childhood growth problems, typified by enamel hypoplasia, was rare. On the other hand, they appear to have been more accident-prone and their oral health was poorer. Furthermore, fatal childhood disease was rife. Whilst the high standard of fracture repairs indicates some access to good quality medical care, no adequate treatment would have been available for the patient suffering from the excruciating pains of a bladder stone. The object is estimated to have been $c.$ 40mm in diameter, and is the earliest evidence in England for a condition which was to become endemic among the lower social classes in 18th- and 19th-century Norfolk (Batty Shaw 1970).

# 4. The Finds
## by Paul Blinkhorn, Andy Chapman and Tora Hylton

## I. Post-Roman pottery
by Paul Blinkhorn
(Figs 14 and 15)

The pottery assemblage from St Faith's Lane comprised 6256 sherds with a total weight of 73,132g. The minimum number of vessels (MNV) was 57.45. Details of the occurrence per context by number and weight of sherds per fabric type are retained in archive. Apart from two sherds of Romano-British Grey Ware, all the pottery was post-Roman. The material is typical of Late Saxon and medieval assemblages from the city of Norwich, largely comprising Thetford-type and local medieval wares in association with a wide range of regional and continental imports.

### Analytical methodology
The pottery was initially bulk sorted and recorded on a computer using DBase IV software. The material from each context was recorded by number and weight of sherds per fabric type, with featureless body sherds of the same fabric counted, weighed and recorded as one database entry. Feature sherds such as rims, bases and lugs were individually recorded, with individual codes used for the various types. Decorated sherds were similarly treated. In the case of rimsherds, the form, diameter in mm and the percentage remaining of the original complete circumference were all recorded. This figure was summed for each fabric type to obtain the minimum number of vessels (MNV).

The terminology used is that defined by the Medieval Pottery Research Group's *Guide to the Classification of Medieval Ceramic Forms* (MPRG 1998). All the statistical analyses were carried out using a Dbase package written by the author, which interrogated the original or subsidiary databases, with some of the final calculations made with an electronic calculator. All analyses were carried out to the minimum standards suggested by Orton (1998–9, 135–7).

### Fabrics
The following fabric types were noted.

**Early/Middle Saxon hand-made wares**
c. AD 450–850. 3 sherds, 77g, MNV = 0.04 (all jars).
Simple, handmade forms in a variety of sandy fabrics. Finds of hand-made pottery of this type are generally rare in the city. Jennings 1981, 12, notes that less than ten sherds of such pottery had been found in Norwich, since when very few sites in the city have produced any finds of the material. The exception is the excavation at Fishergate (Ayers 1994), which produced a relatively large group of 31 sherds. The sherds from this site are all similar to fabric 1 from Fishergate (Dallas 1994, 20).

The sherds from this site are similar in form to a vessel from Fishergate (Dallas 1994, fig. 14.5) and it is possible that it may be of early Middle Saxon (*i.e.* 7th-century) date. Dallas noted that such wares have been found in association with Ipswich Ware at several sites in Norfolk, that the forms are more 'developed' than is usual for Early Saxon pottery, and that stamped vessels have not been found (Dallas 1994, 28). These traits have been noted elsewhere. The form of the rim sherd from this site (Fig. 14, no 20), which is closed with a perfunctory everted rim-bead, is similar to that of vessels from the Lincolnshire fens which may be of 7th-century date (Blinkhorn forthcoming b). The same traits were not noted amongst the material from Norfolk, but very little hand-made pottery was noted from those excavations, with most recovered from fieldwalking. However, the small amount of excavated material was as common in contexts which produced Middle Saxon pottery as those which did not.

*Illustrations*
Fig. 14, 20 Jar rim, context *377*. Dark grey sandy fabric with brown outer surface. Inner surface very evenly smoothed.

**Ipswich ware**
c. AD 720–850 (Blinkhorn forthcoming a). 21 sherds, 372g, MNV = 0.44 (all jars).

Regional import. Slow-wheel made ware, manufactured exclusively in the eponymous Suffolk wic. The material probably had a currency between AD 725–40 and the mid-9th century at sites outside East Anglia. There are two main fabric types, although individual vessels which do not conform to these groups also occur.

*Group 1:* Hard and slightly sandy to the touch, with visible small quartz grains and some shreds of mica. Frequent fairly well-sorted angular to sub-angular grains of quartz, generally measuring below 0.3mm in size but with some larger grains, including a number which are polycrystalline in appearance. 10 sherds, 128g, MNV = 0.29.

*Group 2:* Like the sherds in Group 1, they are hard, sandy and mostly dark grey in colour. Their most prominent feature is a scatter of large quartz grains (up to *c.* 2.5mm) which either bulge or protrude through the surfaces of the vessel, giving rise to the term 'pimply' Ipswich ware (Hurst 1959, 14). This characteristic makes them quite rough to the touch. However, some sherds have the same groundmass but lack the larger quartz grains which are characteristic of this group, and chemical analysis suggests that they are made from the same clay. 2 sherds, 29g, MNV = 0.06.

None of the sherds is decorated other than with the common finger-grooving on the shoulders. The rims were classified using the system devised by West (1964) as follows:

I.A: 2 vessels, MNV = 0.16
I.C: 1 vessel, MNV = 0.03
II.F: 1 vessel, MNV = 0.13
III.I: 1 vessel, MNV = 0.06
III.J: 1 vessel, MNV = 0.06.

All the Ipswich ware was found redeposited in later contexts. The material is found throughout Norfolk, with around 500 findspots known (Blinkhorn forthcoming a), but is relatively rare in Norwich itself. Small numbers of sherds occur on many sites in the city (Jennings 1981, 264–73; Dallas 1994, 27–8), but large stratified groups remain elusive. This group is one of the largest known from Norwich, although the biggest is that from Fishergate (119 sherds: Dallas 1994, 20), which yielded a total greater than that from all other excavations in the city. At Fishergate all the sherds were redeposited in later contexts (as is usually the case in Norwich). In addition, six rims at this site were noted which were not classified as Ipswich Ware, but from the form and fabric appear likely to be of that type (Dallas 1994, fig. 14, 13–18). The Fishergate site also produced considerable quantities of Middle Saxon imported wares and a Middle Saxon coin (Gregory and Metcalf 1994) and it is thought to indicate that a Middle Saxon settlement lay nearby (Ayers 1994, 82).

**Thetford-type ware**
10th/11th century (Atkin *et al.*, 1983). 4539 sherds, 55,880g, MNV = 40.02.

Jars = 33.83, bowls = 0.82, pitchers = 0.31, storage jars = 3.59, crucibles = 0.18, ginger jars = 0.84, lamps = 0.45.

Local ware. Produced at several known locations in the city. Hard, wheel-thrown grey sandy fabric. Range of vessel types includes jars, bowls, storage jars, pitchers, 'ginger jars' and lamps.

Thetford ware, as is commonly the case in Norwich, completely dominates the Late Saxon and medieval pottery assemblages at this site, even from deposits that date to periods long after the material had long fallen from use. The range of vessel types is very typical of the tradition and few vessels are worthy of further comment. Decoration, other than the thumbed and/or stamped applied strips usually noted on storage jars and 'ginger jars' (*e.g.* Jennings 1983, figs 36–41), is entirely restricted to rouletting, and this largely on jars with just a single bowl being so treated. Two types of rouletting, diamond-notched and square notched were noted, as follows:

Diamond-notched rouletting: 12 sherds, 266g, MNV = 0.29 (Jars = 0.23. bowls = 0.06);

Square-notched rouletting: 2 sherds, 23g, MNV = 0.

This is very typical of Norwich Thetford-type ware. Both types are known from the recorded kiln sites (Jennings 1983, fig. 41). A sherd with a row of stamped imitation rouletting was also noted (Fig. 15, no. 29).

*Illustrations*
Fig. 14, 23  Rouletted jar rim, unstratified. Smooth, pale grey fabric with slightly darker surfaces.
Fig. 14, 24  Storage jar rim, *601*. Very hard light grey fabric with darker surfaces.
Fig. 15, 28  'Ginger jar' rim, *100*. Uniform dark grey fabric.
Fig. 15, 29  Stamped 'ginger jar' rim, *190*. Uniform dark grey fabric.

**St Neots ware**
*c*. AD 900–1100 (Denham 1985). 22 sherds, 333g, MNV = 0.44 (Jars = 0.38, bowls = 0.06).

Regional import. Moderate to dense finely crushed fossil shell, with varying quantities of quartz and/or ironstone. Usually purplish-black, black or grey, with fairly fine dense inclusions. Main forms small jars with sagging bases, although a few lamps are known.

All sherds appear to be of Denham's T1 (1) fabric. At least some of the pottery from Norwich classified as 'shelly ware' (*e.g.* Dallas 1994, 21) is of St Neots type, and sherds have been positively identified as such (*e.g.* Bown 1987, fig 73, 105), but it would be helpful if the 'shelly wares' were classified by type where possible, as similar material from Lincolnshire is also present in the city (*e.g.* Blinkhorn forthcoming c).

*Illustrations*
Fig. 14, 13  Inturned rim bowl, *266*. Grey fabric with reddish-brown surfaces.
Fig. 14, 22  Jar rim, *109*. Uniform grey fabric.

**Stamford ware**
*c*. AD 900–1200 (Kilmurry 1980). 61 sherds, 478g, MNV = 0.73 (Pitchers = 0.10, crucibles = 0.63).

Regional import. Wheel-thrown. White, pink, buff or grey fabric, usually with sparse to dense quartz up to 0.5mm, occasional black or red ironstone up to 1mm. Often glazed with yellow, pale or sage green glaze. Jars bowls, Pegeaux pitchers, cups, crucibles, and candlesticks.

This assemblage is fairly typical of Stamford ware groups from sites outside the ware's 'heartland' of south Lincolnshire, north Cambridgeshire and north-east Northamptonshire, but also demonstrates a few traits worthy of comment. The fragment of a 'Crowland bowl' type vessel (Fig. 14, no. 21) with its complex carved decoration is one of only very few examples known. The technique was classified by Kilmurry as type M12 and this sherd is similar, although by no means identical, to a sherd from Stamford Castle (Kilmurry 1980, fig 77.4) and dateable to the second half of the 12th century (*ibid.*, 142). Sherds from two similar vessels are known from the excavations at Chalk Lane in Northampton (Gryspeerdt 1981, figs 181 and 182). Further sherds are known from Northampton Castle, Cathedral Green in Winchester, Thetford (Kilmurry 1984, 124) and also London (*ibid.*, 118). The sherd from St Faith's Lane is a little abraded and was redeposited in a 14th-century context.

The presence of the Stamford ware crucibles (*e.g.* Fig. 14 no. 1) is worthy of note and provides further evidence that metalworking was taking place on the site during the Saxo-Norman or early medieval period. Stamford ware crucibles are by no means rare and are found at many sites away from the production centre, often in considerable quantities. The particularly large group of 351 such vessels from Flaxengate in Lincoln (Gilmour 1988, 70–6) was associated with glass- and copper working (*ibid.*, 58), and vessels from Minstergate in Thetford revealed traces of gold and silver (Bayley 1991). The demand for Stamford ware crucibles in Lincoln could be due to the fact that the sandy and shelly wares were not suitable for producing crucibles which were able to withstand the high temperatures required for metal- and glass-working. Certainly only one crucible from Flaxengate was of Lincoln Sandy ware, with the majority either Stamford ware, along with a small number of re-used Torksey Ware and Roman sherds. Local wares, including shelly fabrics, were more commonly associated with glass working.

At Thetford, local Thetford-type ware included crucibles in the range of vessel types, and some show evidence of having been used in industrial processes (Rogerson and Dallas 1984, fig. 175). It may be that Stamford ware, which is particularly fine-grained, may have been especially suited for such a purpose but Kilmurry (1984, 124) has suggested that they may provide evidence of peripatetic metalworkers. Certainly, the Thetford sites at which they were noted produced a noticeably larger number than normal of Stamford ware jars and bowls, implying that they were personal possessions rather than traded pots (*ibid.*). This was not the case at St Faith's Lane, but the amount of Stamford ware present generally is not comparable with that from the Thetford sites.

Crucibles are known from other sites in Norwich, including the nearby Mann Egerton site (Emery 2007, 116–18). Two medieval vessels from unknown sources were noted at 15–17 Princes Street (Jennings 1981, 37). None are known from any of the published kiln sites (Atkin *et al.* 1983) and finds of such vessels remain generally rare in the city. St Faith's Lane produced rimsherds from five vessels, of which four were Stamford ware (MNV = 0.63) and one probably of Thetford-type (MNV = 0.18).

*Illustrations*
Fig. 14, 1   Crucible, *190*. White fabric, pale buff surfaces. Thick (?post-deposition) sooting on both surfaces.
Fig. 14, 9   Jug handle, *190*. Pale grey fabric with glossy yellow glaze on the outer surface of body and handle.
Fig. 14, 21  Bodysherd from 'Crowland bowl' type vessel, *304*. Pale orange buff fabric with thin orange glaze on both surfaces.
Fig. 15, 35  Pitcher rim, *123*. Pale buff fabric with glossy yellow glaze below the neck flange.

**Early Medieval Sparse Shelly ware (EMSS)**
11th–12th century (Jennings 1981, 39). 156 sherds, 1,447g, MNV = 2.04 (Jars = 1.92, bowls = 0.04, lamps = 0.08).

?Local ware. Grey to brown fabric, dense quartz inclusions, sparse to moderate calcitic material. All sherds are undecorated. The material is very much a minor ware and appears to be residual by Phase M1 (see below), which is in keeping with the known chronology of the material.

**Local Medieval Unglazed ware (LMW)**
11th–15th century (Jennings 1981, 22–5). 929 sherds, 7,844g, MNV = 9.81 (Jars = 8.75, bowls = 0.66, jugs = 0.40).

?Local ware. Hard sandy fabric similar to Thetford ware, although usually oxidized reddish brown and hand-made. Forms include jars, bowls and ginger jars, but fragments of at least two spike lamps (Fig. 15, nos 30 and 31) and a curfew (Fig. 15, no. 25) were also present. Seven decorated sherds were noted, with combed cordons and/or wavy lines and incised diagonal slashing being the only types. Seven sherds with post-firing piercing were also noted (*e.g.* Fig. 15, no. 33), as well as two sherds with thumbed applied strips.

*Illustrations*
Fig. 15, 25  Curfew fragment, *190*. Smooth light grey fabric with darker surfaces. Hole punched through pre-firing.
Fig. 15, 30  Fragment of lamp spike and bowl, *471*. Dark grey fabric with browner surfaces.
Fig. 15, 31  Fragment of lamp spike and bowl, *129*. Dark grey fabric with browner surfaces.
Fig. 15, 32  Decorated jar rim, *148*. Light grey fabric with darker surfaces. Combed wavy line on top of the rim bead.
Fig. 15, 33  Pierced decorated bowl rim, *148*. Light grey fabric with darker surfaces. Wavy line on top of the rim bead. Hole drilled post-firing. Light grey fabric with darker surfaces.
Fig. 15, 34  Jug handle, *148*. Light grey fabric with darker surfaces.

**Miscellaneous Early Medieval Sandy wares (EMSW)**
11th–12th century (Jennings 1981, 39). 120 sherds, 1,272g, MNV = 1.21 (Jars = 0.79, bowls = 0.10, 'ginger jars' = 0.32).

A range of quartz-tempered wares with similar fabrics, probably from a variety of East Anglian sources. All sherds were undecorated, other than two examples with thumbed applied strips.

**Grimston ware**
13th–15th century (Leah 1994). 271 sherds, 3,499g, MNV = 1.01 (Jars = 0.21, jugs = 0.60, storage jars = 0.20).

Regional import. Wheel-thrown. Dark grey sandy fabric, usually with grey surfaces, although orange-red and (less commonly) buff surfaces are known. Manufactured at the eponymous production centre near King's Lynn, Norfolk. Mainly glazed jugs, plain or highly deco-

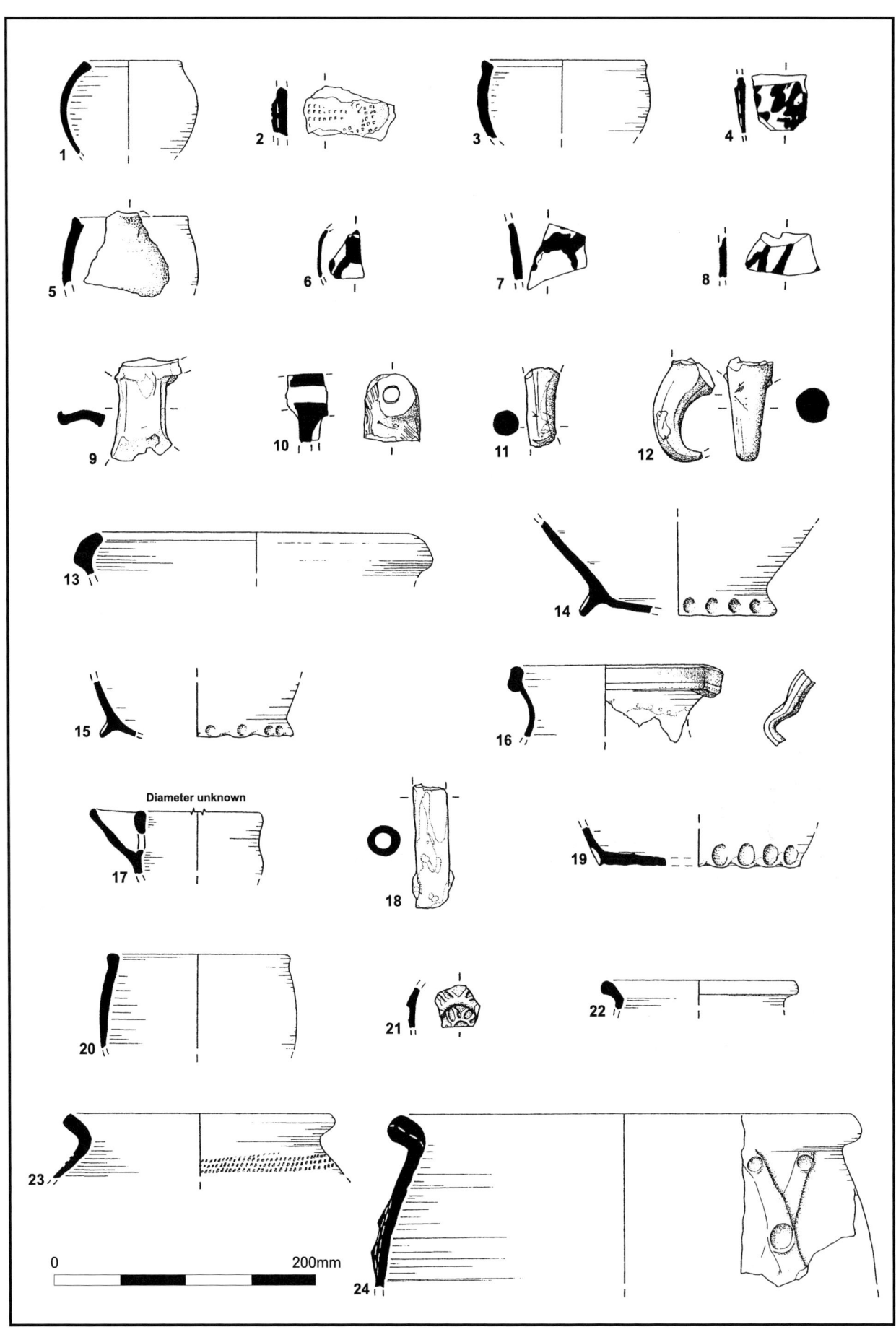

Figure 14 Medieval pottery, nos 1–24

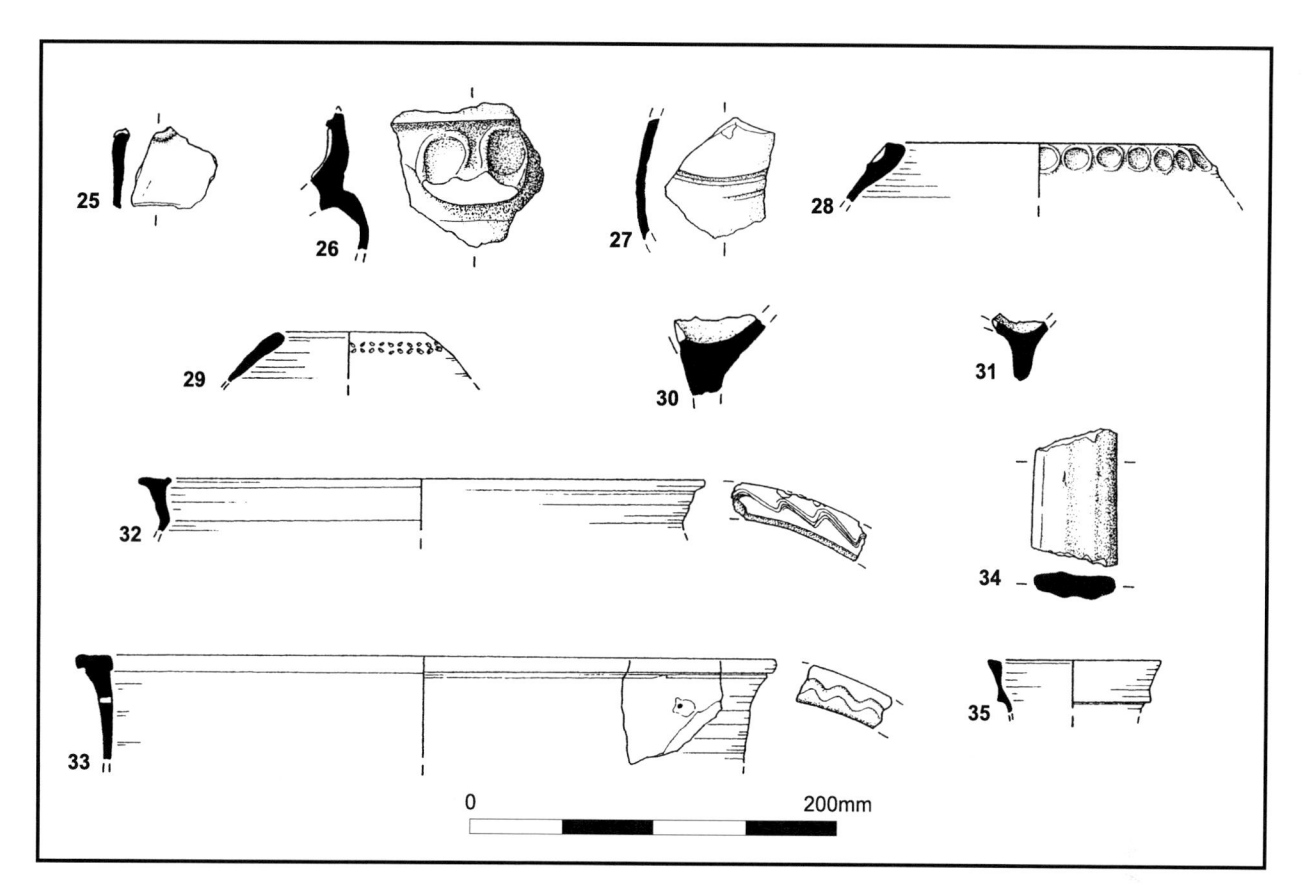

Figure 15  Medieval pottery, nos 25–35

rated, the former 13th century, the latter 14th. Face jugs a speciality, and the highly decorated vessels often have painted and applied strips and scales with iron slip.

A single very small fragment of a possible face-jug was noted in context *190*; two sherds with applied plastic decoration were also noted and 33 sherds with trailed slip decoration were present. The rest were undecorated other than by glazing and therefore likely to be of 13th-century date, although such vessels were still being made in the 14th century. A long tubular spout with the scar from a support strut (Fig. 14, no. 18) is somewhat unusual and can only be paralleled by a vessel from King's Lynn (Clarke and Carter 1977, fig. 91.12). That vessel has two anthropomorphic arms grasping the end of the spout, and the position of the scars on the present piece suggests it may once have been of a similar type.

*Illustrations*

Fig. 14, 17  Large bridge spout, *190*. Grey fabric with orange-buff surfaces. Dull green glaze on outer surface.

Fig. 14, 18  Long tubular spout with support-strut scar, *129*. Grey fabric with orange surfaces, patches and runs of dull green glaze.

Fig. 14, 19  Thumb-frilled base *471*. Dark grey fabric with dark reddish brown outer surface. Glossy olive glaze with kiln scar on base.

Fig. 15, 26  Jug rim and handle terminal, *118*. Darker grey fabric with orange outer surface, poor quality dirty green glaze on outer.

**Developed Stamford ware**

Late 12th–mid 13th century (Kilmurry 1980). 10 sherds, 73g, MNV = 0.1 (all jugs).

Regional import. Wheel-thrown. White, slightly sandy fabric, vessels usually highly-decorated and with a bright, copper-green external glaze. Usually jugs. Small quantities of this material occur at sites all over East Anglia and the south and east Midlands. One sherd from this site (Fig. 14, no. 10) is worthy of comment, being a somewhat unusual form, *i.e.* a fragment of a long tubular spout with a wide, strap handle-like support strut. A very similar vessel is known from the School Street kiln site, Stamford (McCarthy and Brooks 1988, fig. 146, no. 825).

*Illustrations*

Fig. 14, 10  Fragment of long tubular spout and support strut, *190*. Pale grey fabric with bright green, copper-spotted glaze.

Fig. 15, 27  Sherd from shoulder of jug, *596*. White fabric with glossy green, copper-spotted glaze on outer surface.

**Scarborough ware**

Late 12th–14th century (Farmer and Farmer 1982). 11 sherds, 179g, MNV = 0.17 (All jugs).

Regional import. All sherds 'Phase II' type. Sandy wheel-thrown glazed ware, mainly highly decorated jugs, although other forms occur. Small quantities of the material are found at ports all along the east coast of England and Scotland. This assemblage appears fairly typical, comprising entirely glazed jug fragments.

**London-type ware**

Late 12th–14th century (Pearce *et al.* 1985). 1 sherd, 17g, MNV = 0.

Regional import. Reddish brown sandy fabric with occasional sandstone, shell, organic and iron ore fragments. Vessels mainly glazed jugs, some highly decorated. The material is found in small quantities throughout eastern southern England, especially in the earlier medieval period, when many local glazed ware industries had yet to be established. The single sherd from this site is glazed but otherwise undecorated, which is slightly unusual although it may simply be that it is from a plain part of a decorated jug.

**Cambridge Sgraffito ware**

14th–15th century (McCarthy and Brooks 1988, 424–5). 2 sherds, 19g, MNV = 0.

Regional import. Fairly hard, smooth red fabric, outer surface of vessels covered in a white slip through which designs were incised to reveal the body clay, the whole covered in a yellow glaze which occasionally has green copper-spotting. Fairly common in Cambridgeshire, although the production source is as yet unknown. Occurs in small quantities throughout eastern England and other examples are known from Norwich (*e.g.* Jennings 1981, fig. 11, no. 242).

**Badorf-type ware**

9th–11th century (Jennings 1981, 22–3). 2 sherds, 54g, MNV = 0.

Continental import. Smooth, hard buff fabric with few visible inclusions except for sparse iron ore up to 0.5mm. Vessels typically relief-band amphorae with thick applied strips, often rouletted. Both sherds from this site are from such vessels (*e.g.* Fig. 14 no. 2). As with Ipswich ware, small numbers of sherds of this type occur at many sites in Norwich, with the Fishergate group again one of the largest.

*Illustrations*
Fig. 14, 2   Relief-band amphora fragment, *203*. Uniform (?burnt) light grey fabric.

**North French/Low Countries wares**
*c.* 9th–11th century (Jennings 1981, 32–3). 19 sherds, 201g, MNV = 0.1 (All jars).

Continental import. Commonly known as 'Beauvais' type, although many sources in northern France and the Low Countries are likely. Fine white fabric with sparse large quartz grains up to 1mm. Red-painted decoration common (*e.g.* Fig. 14, nos 4 and 8). Finds of the material from Norwich are relatively common and the material, like many other of the imported wares, occurs at many sites in the city. This assemblage comprises entirely bodysherds apart from a single rim and a single handle.

*Illustrations*
Fig. 14, 4   Bodysherd and handle terminal from red-painted jug, *102*. Buff sandy fabric with reddish brown painted slip decoration.
Fig. 14, 8   Painted bodysherd, *190*. Buff fabric with red-painted decoration.

**Pingsdorf ware**
10th–13th century (Jennings 1981, 29; Keller 1995). 13 sherds, 297g, MNV = 0.

Continental import. Hard, buff to dark yellowish-brown 'semi-stoneware'. Moderate to dense quartz up to 0.4mm, sparse red clay pellets. Vessels often red-painted (*e.g.* Fig. 14, nos 6 and 7). Commonly found in variable quantities at many sites in the city. All the sherds from this site were bodysherds or bases (*e.g.* Fig. 14, nos 14 and 15).

*Illustrations*
Fig. 14, 6   Painted bodysherd, *190*. Pale grey fabric with red painted decoration.
Fig. 14, 7   Painted bodysherd, *190*. Pale grey-brown fabric, orange outer surface with red painted decoration.
Fig. 14, 14  Thumb-frilled base, *266*. Grey fabric with yellowish surfaces.
Fig. 14, 15  Thumb-frilled base, *190*. Orange fabric with purplish brown surfaces.

**Andenne/Huy-type wares**
11th–15th century (Jennings 1981, 30). 5 sherds, 41g, MNV = 0.2 (All jugs).

Continental import. Buff to orange fabric, usually with a thick glossy yellow to orange external glaze, some vessels have applied strips of body clay. Commonly found in variable quantities at many sites in the city.

**Normandy Gritty wares**
11th–13th century (Jennings 1981, 33). 2 sherds, 63g, MNV = 0.1 (jug).

Continental import. Fine creamy white fabric with sparse to moderate quartz up to 2mm. Some vessels have a patchy, poor quality yellow glaze. Vessels mainly jugs. Both the sherds from this site were unglazed and from the rim of a jug (Fig. 14, no. 5).

*Illustrations*
Fig. 14, 5   Rimsherd from jug, context 294. Pale pinkish-grey fabric with a pale grey core.

**Flemish Grey wares**
11th–12th century (Jennings 1981, 27). 16 sherds, 279g, MNV = 0.

Continental imports. 'Catch-all' category for the products of many centres in northern France, Belgium and Holland. Usually whitish grey sandy fabrics with grey outer surface. Jars and pitchers. All the sherds from this site were featureless bodysherds.

**Rhenish Grey wares ('Blaugrau')**
12h–13th century (Jennings 1981, 26). 8 sherds, 164g, MNV = 0.22 (ladles).

Continental import. Hard, bluish grey sandy fabric, usually with a white core. Plentiful angular white quartz inclusions. Jars known, but the best-known form is the distinctive handled ladles. Rims from two examples were noted here (*e.g.* Fig. 14 no. 3) together with a handle (Fig. 14, no 12).

*Illustrations*
Fig. 14, 3   Ladle rim, *651*. Rough white sandy fabric with grey surfaces.
Fig. 14, 12  Ladle handle, *244*. Pale grey fabric with darker surfaces.

**Low Countries earthenwares**
12th–15th century (Jennings 1981, 31–2). 30 sherds, 466g, MNV = 0.82 (jugs).

Continental import. Commonly called 'Aardenburg-type', although likely to be from a number of sources in Belgium and Holland. Sandy fabric with few visible inclusions, often highly decorated with slips, rouletting and glaze. The majority of the sherds from this site were plain other than glazing, and all appear to be from jugs.

*Illustrations*
Fig. 14, 16  Jug rim, *129*. Grey fabric with brick-red surfaces, glossy variegated bright green and orange glaze.

**'Frisian' ware**
8th–11th century. 3 sherds, 36g, MNV = 0.

Similar to pottery from Oldorf in Friesland (Stilke 1993). Hard grey fabric with sparse protruding grey quartz up to 2mm. Sherds are all from the same vessel, probably a globular jar typical of the tradition.

**Rouen ware**
13th–14th century (Jennings 1981, 35). 1 sherd, 31g, MNV = 0.

Continental import. White smooth fabric with few visible inclusions. Usually highly decorated glazed jugs with painted red slip decoration. The single sherd from this site is a rod handle from a jug (Fig. 14, no. 11).

*Illustrations*
Fig. 14, 11  Jug handle, *928*. White fabric with buff surfaces. Patchy yellow glaze, splash of red slip.

**German stonewares**
14th century + (Gaimster 1997). 3 sherds, 37g, MNV = 0.

Continental imports. A range of hard, grey, salt-glazed fabrics produced at numerous sites in the Rhineland and beyond. All the sherds from this site are plain bodysherds.

**Red earthenwares**
15th century +. 4 sherds, 45g, MNV = 0.

Fine sandy earthenware, usually with a brown or green glaze, occurring in a range of utilitarian forms. Such 'country pottery' was first made in the 16th century and in some areas continued in use until the 19th century. Numerous kiln sites known, such as Fulmodestone (Wade-Martins 1983). All the sherds from this site are plain bodysherds.

**Tin-Glazed earthenware**
17th–18th century (Jennings 1981, 187–216). 1 sherd, 3g, MNV = 0.

?Anglo-Netherlandish. Fine white earthenware, occasionally pinkish or yellowish core. Thick white tin glaze, with painted cobalt blue decoration, occasionally manganese purple and ochre. All the sherds from this site are plain bodysherds.

## Discussion

All the wares from St Faith's Lane are types which have been previously noted in Norwich. The lack of later medieval pottery, particularly early post-medieval wares, is likely to be simply a reflection of site function, the use of the area as a cemetery from the 14th century onwards effectively ending deliberate pottery deposition at the site. It also led to an extremely high level of redeposition of the Late Saxon and medieval pottery (see below).

The Late Saxon and medieval wares from the site are all of types well known in Norwich (Jennings 1981) and the amount of imported pottery, which would perhaps be considered highly unusual in many inland towns in the period, is typical of sites in the city and at the ports of the east and south coasts generally. For example, the excavations at 29–31 St Benedict's Street in Norwich produced only 244 sherds of stratified pottery, but this included four sherds of Andenne/Huy type ware and a fragment of Pingsdorf-type (Jennings 1982, 8).

The excavations at the Saxo-Norman and early medieval waterfront at Whitefriars Street car park in 1979 produced an even wider range of material, but including a range of local and imported pottery similar to that from the present site (Ayers and Murphy 1983). The assemblage was dominated by Thetford ware, with small quantities of Ipswich, Stamford and local medieval wares comprising the local and regional English assemblage, each with a similar representation to that seen at St Faith's Lane. The range of imported wares is equally comparable: relief-band amphorae, Andenne/Huy types, Normandy Gritty wares, Paffrath ware, Low Countries wares and Pingsdorf-type vessels were all noted, with the latter comprising slightly more than 9% of the sherd count from the excavation, although this is due to the fact that two highly fragmented vessels were particularly well represented (Ayers and Murphy 1983, table 1). The level of residuality seen at St Faith's Lane can also be paralleled at the Whitefriars car park, where the Period IV (?13th century) phase was dominated by Thetford ware — although residual it comprised nearly 74% (by sherd count) of the period assemblage. Thetford ware is as dominant at St Faith's Lane in its earlier phases at it was at Whitefriars car park, despite the fact that the site was in decline from the immediate post-Conquest period (Whitefriars Period III broadly equates with pottery period 'EM' at this site).

The Late Saxon/Saxo-Norman assemblage from the north-east bailey of Norwich Castle (Ayers 1985) shows a somewhat more restricted range of imported wares than seen at the present site, but the local assemblage has the same general characteristics as here. Again, Thetford ware dominates, comprising 95% of the total assemblage (by sherd count). A single sherd of Ipswich ware and small quantities of Stamford and St Neots wares were present, with local medieval wares forming only a minor component due to the chronological character and nature of the site. The imported assemblage was limited to Rhenish, Pingsdorf and Andenne wares, and some fragments of medieval Rouen ware were also present.

Many small-scale excavations within the Greyfriars precinct have been carried out previously, with the general range of pottery types produced echoing that from this excavation, site-to-site variations notwithstanding. Salvage work at a building site at 33–41 King Street/2–4 Rose Lane (Norwich Survey, Site 76N: TG 2341 0850) produced a similar range of Saxon and medieval local wares, along with Paffrath, Pingsdorf and Andenne/Huy wares, as well as a wide range of post-medieval material (Jennings 1981, 248; Wilson and Hurst 1965, 173). All the pottery found at Greyfriars Road in 1962 (Site 65N: TG 2342 0858) was post-medieval with the exception of sherds of Thetford and Grimston ware (Jennings 1981, 247). Material of similar date was recovered from building sites in the vicinity of 21–23 King Street in 1913 and 1934 (Site 74N: approx. TG 2339 0858). Further salvage work within the precinct at 36 Prince of Wales Road in 1946 (Site 102N: TG 2348 0867) produced small quantities of local wares and a sherd of Aardenburg-type, although a similar action at 39–41 Prince of Wales Road in 1964 (Site 103N: TG 2552 0861) produced only Late Medieval Transitional and post-medieval material (Jennings 1981, 249). This assemblage resembled that salvaged from yet another building site at 6–22 Rose Lane in 1967 (Site 111N: TG 2343 0851). Local wares accounted for the entire assemblage from building sites at 90 St Faith's Lane (Site 239N: TG 2353 0861) in 1973 and 1974 (Jennings 1981, 255), as well as that from another site in the vicinity in 1974/5 (Site 270N: TG 2357 0867) although a sherd of Saintonge ware was also noted (Jennings 1981, 257).

The assemblages from Norwich that appear most similar to that from St Faith's Lane are those from the excavations at St Martin-at-Palace Plain in 1981 (Ayers 1987) and Fishergate in 1985 (Ayers 1994). Both of these had an almost identical range of Saxon and medieval pottery, imports and local wares, with all the Middle Saxon material redeposited in later contexts. The former site was located on a gravel spur on the edge of the River Wensum (Ayers 1987, fig. 1). The Fishergate site is thought to have been marshland before the 10th century (Ayers 1987, 80). In both cases, the pottery assemblages appear to be the result of refuse disposal from activity nearby, rather than direct occupation of the site. It is possible that the early component of the present site assemblage may be the result of similar activity: the location of St Faith's Lane, on the very edge of the Saxon marshlands on the western edge of the city, may have meant that similar refuse disposal patterns prevailed. However, the possibility remains that evidence for Middle Saxon occupation here has been obliterated by later activity, notably extensive pit-digging.

The status of imported medieval pottery has been given some consideration previously: where it was once seen as being indicative of status, it now seems more likely that it merely reflects consumer choice. Brown (1997) has examined the pattern of distribution of imported (mainly French) pottery in the port of Southampton and has noted that the evidence in this regard was generally inconclusive. This was a time when there was a large influx of people of French origin into the port and while there appeared to be some nucleation in the distribution of the imported pottery (Brown 1997, fig. 7), the castle — which one might expect to have been largely peopled by Normans — did not produce a particularly large proportion of imported pottery, suggesting that the presence of imports (or the lack of them) cannot be taken as evidence of 'foreigners' or people of high status. His conclusions were similar for the high medieval period. It is interesting that the limited excavations at Norwich Castle prior to the Castle Mall project of 1989–98 have produced similar results. A partial section across the castle bailey defences in 1963 (Site 60N) produced a medieval assemblage entirely made up of local wares (Jennings 1981, 266). A second trench dug in 1973 (Site 150N) did produce sherds of Pingsdorf and Andenne wares, but the assemblage was otherwise entirely local (Jennings 1981, 268). Finally, the Period V well and ditches excavated in the north-east bailey of the castle in 1979 and dated to the post-Conquest period (Ayers 1985, 21) produced an assemblage that almost entirely comprised local wares, with just three sherds of Rhenish pottery present. Other features of the same period produced a few sherds of imported pottery but they appear to represent a miniscule component of the period assemblage (Ayers 1985, 39–40).

| Phase | Date | Defining ware | No | Wt (g) | MNV |
|---|---|---|---|---|---|
| SN | 10th–11th C | Thetford Ware | 653 | 9284 | 6.77 |
| EM | 11th–12th C | Early Med Coarsewares | 2006 | 25345 | 20.16 |
| M1 | 13th C | Glazed Grimston Ware | 190 | 2447 | 2.03 |
| M2 | 14th–15th C | Decorated Glazed Grimston Ware | 3119 | 32474 | 25.87 |
| LMT | 16th C | LMT wares | 6 | 43 | 0 |
| PM | 17th C | Post-med wares | 5 | 13 | 0 |
| U/S | | Unstratified | 277 | 3526 | 2.62 |
| | | Total | 6256 | 73132 | 57.45 |

Table 1  Ceramic phases, including the amount of pottery per phase, all fabrics

Thus, the presence of imported pottery in Norwich is unlikely to be an indicator of 'ghettos' of any kind within the city. Rather, it signifies that the settlement was, like Southampton, a port of international importance.

**Chronology**
Each context-specific assemblage was given a seriated phase-date based on the presence of major wares, as shown in Table 1. The totals per phase are after adjustment in relation to the stratigraphic matrix.

It can be clearly seen that, in terms of pottery deposition, the site goes into serious decline during the 13th century, presumably due to the establishment of the Greyfriars precinct having led to a more controlled regime of refuse disposal. During the 14th century pottery again occurs in quantity but the majority of the material is redeposited, presumably as the result of extensive grave-digging (see below)

**Pottery occurrence**
The data in Table 2 show how Thetford Ware dominates the Late Saxon and medieval assemblages, including the later phases when it had ceased to be made and used. Only 34.5% of the Phase M1 assemblage can be regarded as contemporary and it seems likely, given the high degree of redeposition, that at least a proportion of the assemblages of some of the more long-lived wares, such as Early Medieval Sandwich ware, are also redeposited. During Phase M2, when the site was largely used as a cemetery, only 30% of the assemblage can be regarded as contemporary and this figure again supposes that all the current wares were not residual. The fragmentation

| Fabric | SN | EM | M1 | M2 | %Total | Total |
|---|---|---|---|---|---|---|
| E/MS Handmade | 0 | 0.2% | 0 | 0.1% | 0.1% | 77g |
| Ipswich Ware | 0.5% | 0.3% | 0.7% | 0.6% | 0.5% | 321g |
| Thetford Ware | 98.5% | 86.6% | 58.3% | 64.9% | 77.1% | 53597g |
| St Neots Ware | 0.5% | 0.1% | 1.8% | 0.5% | 0.4% | 247g |
| Stamford Ware | 0.6% | 0.5% | 0.6% | 0.8% | 0.6% | 463g |
| EMSS | | 2.7% | 0.9% | 1.8% | 1.8% | 1274g |
| LMW | | 5.5% | 14.1% | 17.4% | 10.6% | 7388g |
| EMSW | | 2.5% | 2.6% | 1.7% | 1.8% | 1222g |
| Developed Stamford | | 0.1% | 0.5% | 0.1% | 0.1% | 73g |
| Badorf-type | | 0.1% | 0 | 0.1% | 0.1% | 54g |
| Andenne | | 0 | 0 | 0.1% | 0.1% | 41g |
| Pingsdorf | | 0.1% | 6.8% | 0.3% | 0.4% | 297g |
| 'Beauvais-type' | | 0.3% | 0.6% | 0.3% | 0.3% | 184g |
| Flemish Greyware | | 0.2% | 0 | 0.7% | 0.4% | 279g |
| Aardenburg-type | | 0.1% | 2.9% | 1.1% | 0.7% | 466g |
| Normandy Gritty ware | | 0.2% | 0 | 0 | 0.1% | 63g |
| Blaugrau-type | | 0.3% | 0 | 0.3% | 0.2% | 164g |
| Kugeltopf | | 0.1% | 0 | 0 | 0.1% | 36g |
| Grimston | | | 8.6% | 9.0% | 4.5% | 3129g |
| Scarborough | | | 0.3% | 0.3% | 0.2% | 117g |
| Rouen | | | 1.3% | 0 | <0.1% | 31g |
| London Ware | | | | <0.1% | <0.1% | 8g |
| Cambridge Sgraffito | | | | <0.1% | <0.1% | 16g |
| Total | 9284g | 25345g | 2447g | 32474g | | 69550g |

Table 2  Pottery occurrence per ceramic phase, expressed as a percentage of the weight of pottery (in g) per phase (shaded cells indicate residual material)

| Fabric | SN | EM | M1 | M2 | Site mean |
|---|---|---|---|---|---|
| E/MS Handmade | 0 | 27.0g | 0 | 23.0g | 25.7g |
| Ipswich Ware | 14.3g | 13.5g | 17.0g | 18.0g | 17.7g |
| Thetford Ware | 14.3g | 13.4g | 12.4g | 10.8g | 12.3g |
| St Neots Ware | 10.8g | 5.0g | 21.5g | 11.6g | 14.2g |
| Stamford Ware | 8.8g | 6.2g | 7.5g | 9.0g | 7.8g |
| EMSS |  | 10.6g | 7.7g | 8.1g | 9.5g |
| LMW |  | 10.4g | 21.3g | 9.8g | 10.6g |
| EMSW |  | 7.8g | 9.6g | 8.4g | 8.4g |
| Developed Stamford |  | 0 | 6.5g | 3.7g | 7.3g |
| Badorf-type | 0 | 17.0g | 0 | 37.0g | 27.0g |
| Andenne |  | 0 | 0 | 8.2g | 8.2g |
| Pingsdorf |  | 5.3g | 167.0g | 13.6g | 22.8g |
| 'Beauvais-type' | 0 | 15.6g | 15.0g | 8.3g | 10.6g |
| Flemish Greyware |  | 9.5g | 0 | 22.2g | 17.4g |
| Aardenburg-type |  | 15.0g | 14.0g | 15.9g | 15.3g |
| Normandy Gritty ware |  | 31.5g | 0 | 0 | 31.5g |
| Blaugrau-type |  | 11.8g | 0 | 46.5g | 20.5g |
| 'Frisian' | 0 | 12.0g | 0 | 0 | 12.0g |
| Grimston |  |  | 12.4g | 12.6g | 12.9g |
| Scarborough |  |  | 8.0g | 18.2g | 16.3g |
| Rouen |  |  | 31.0g | 0 | 31.0g |
| London ware |  |  | 0 | 7.0g | 7.0g |
| Cambridge Sgraffito |  |  |  | 9.5g | 9.5g |

Table 3 Mean sherd weight per fabric type per ceramic phase (site mean inc. unstratified material)

analysis (below) shows that this clearly was not the case and it seems likely that only a tiny proportion of the M2 assemblage is contemporary with that period.

**Fragmentation analysis**
The data in Table 3 show a fragmentation pattern which is largely that which might be expected, given the character of the site. The mean sherd weight of the major ware — Thetford-type — declines steady through time, with the lowest figure during ceramic Phase M2. The local medieval wares exhibit a broadly similar pattern, allowing for the small assemblage size of the ceramic Phase M1 material. This is despite the fact that at least some of these wares were current during ceramic Phase M2 and demonstrates that a large portion of that assemblage was residual.

**Vessel use**
The range of vessel types (Table 4) is fairly typical of Late Saxon and medieval sites in southern and eastern England, imported 'exotica' (or at least vessels which would be regarded as such at more westerly settlements) aside. The pottery for the Saxo-Norman and early medieval phases demonstrates the pattern well: jars dominate the earliest phases with bowls and jugs forming only a minor component of the assemblage, although these become more common with time. The complete absence of jugs from the M1 assemblage is almost certainly due to the small assemblage size and the high levels of residuality it exhibits. The pattern appears similar to that displayed by the pottery from St Martin-at-Palace Plain (Bown 1988, table 4) although this latter dataset was (apparently) tabulated by estimated vessel equivalent and not minimum number of vessels, as stated in that table heading, thus making comparison extremely difficult. Jug rims were absent from the assemblage from the north-east bailey of Norwich Castle (Ayers 1985, table 2), which is a little unusual but seems likely to be simply a result of the vagaries of archaeological sampling. Certainly, handles from such vessels were definitely present (*ibid.*, fig. 33. 112).

No vessel occurrence data has been published in reports from most of the larger excavations in the city, and detailed comparison and consideration of site function therefore cannot be considered further.

| Phase | Jars | Bowls | Jugs | Storage Jars | 'Ginger jars' | Lamps | Crucibles | Ladles | Total MNV |
|---|---|---|---|---|---|---|---|---|---|
| SN | 79.0% | 1.2% | 1.5% | 11.9% | 5.4% | 1.0% | 0 | 0 | 6.87 |
| EM | 77.2% | 2.3% | 2.1% | 11.7% | 2.7% | 0 | 2.9% | 1.1% | 20.06 |
| M1 | 97.0% | 3.0% | 0 | 0 | 0 | 0 | 0 | 0 | 2.03 |
| M2 | 82.1% | 4.6% | 8.1% | 1.7% | 0.9% | 1.2% | 1.4% | 0 | 25.87 |
| **Total MNV** | **44.12** | **1.78** | **2.62** | **3.59** | **1.16** | **0.46** | **0.88** | **0.22** | **54.83** |

Table 4 Vessel occurrence per ceramic phase, all fabrics, expressed as a percentage of each phase assemblage, MNV

## II. The small finds
by Tora Hylton
(Figs 16 and 17)

**Introduction**
The excavations produced a collection of finds spanning the Late Saxon to post-medieval periods. The presence of 28 flints and two sherds of Roman pottery extend this date range to the prehistoric and Roman periods. Although the majority of artefacts appear to be of Late Saxon and early medieval date, there are very few artefacts from 10th–12th century deposits (Phases 1 and 2), indicating that soil disturbance during extensive grave digging in the 14th century has resulted in much of this material being redeposited within the graveyard soils. The majority of artefacts were retrieved from 13th–16th century cemetery deposits (Phase 3). The range of finds provides a glimpse of some aspects of life on the site prior to its use as a cemetery, and forms an assemblage that can be compared to those from other excavations in Norwich. Viewed in tandem with the pottery evidence, it indicates a community with far-flung contacts. There is evidence for metalworking (of iron, copper alloy and lead) and domestic activities, while the presence of a small collection of tools attests to textile manufacture and woodworking. There is limited indication of antler- or boneworking. Of particular interest is the presence of a small group of domestic artefacts which display Anglo-Scandinavian stylistic characteristics. These include fragments from combs and a mica-schist bowl.

There were 315 individual or group-recorded small finds, providing a total number of 486 individual objects in nine material types. With the exception of the coffin nails, each individual object has been described and measured and a full descriptive catalogue is retained in archive. Bulk finds include fired clay, tile, architectural fragments, flints and a large quantity of metalworking debris, all of which have been recorded under the bulk-finds system. The majority of artefacts were recovered by hand, but the use of a metal-detector at regular intervals during the excavation increased the recovery of metal objects.

| Material | Total |
| --- | --- |
| Silver | 2 |
| Copper alloy | 62 |
| Iron objects | 168 |
| Lead | 36 |
| Stone | 9 |
| Bone/antler | 21 |
| Glass | 7 |
| Slag | 6 |
| Ceramic | 4 |
| **Total** | **315** |

Table 5 Small finds quantified by material type

A total of 69 iron objects (excluding nails and small fragments) were submitted to David Parish, Buckinghamshire County Museum Conservation Service, for X-ray analysis. This not only provided a permanent record but also enabled identification and revealed technical details not previously visible. Only one iron object is coated in a non-ferrous metal. One object was chosen for further investigation, which entailed selective cleaning to reveal features of interest. No stabilisation was necessary.

**Phase 1 (Late Saxon industrial and domestic occupation: 10th–11th century)**
There is little to characterise the nature of the buildings that fronted St Faith's Lane during the 10th and 11th centuries. The presence of rubbish pits suggests that a possible structure in the north-west part of the site (Building A) may have been for domestic use. To the north-east, large amounts of discarded metalworking debris and furnace lining suggest the presence of a forge (Building B), largely located outside the area of excavation.

The majority of artefacts were retrieved from the series of pits close to Building A. The excavated pits did not contain any concentrations of finds which might denote specific activity areas, although one large pit (*592*, Figs 4 and 8) contained up to seventeen individually recorded small finds. These included eight clench bolts, one spindle whorl, one knife, an assortment of nails and miscellaneous fragments. It is possible that the clench bolts relate to a cover for the pit. Clench bolts are known to have been used for covers, such as a medieval well cover from Lydford, Devon (Geddes 1980, 165, fig. 17).

With the exception of a small number of unidentifiable fragments and strips of a kind ubiquitous on a site such as this one, the range of material represents items of costume and jewellery, knives and a small group of items which allude to industry and craft. Costume and jewellery is represented by an iron buckle coated in a non-ferrous metal, closely associated with Building B (pit *433*), and a finger-ring from pit *613*. There are fragments from three knives, one characteristically Saxon in style.

In addition to the evidence for large-scale metalworking, the presence of a spindle whorl used for the basic activity of hand spinning and pieces of partially worked antler are suggestive of small-scale craft activities, most probably to fulfil domestic requirements. A single horseshoe also came from pit *613*.

**Phase 2 (early medieval domestic occupation: 11th–13th century)**
There were a larger number and wider range of small finds from this phase, which together with the pottery indicate wider trading connections. A variety of domestic objects represent household equipment, personal possessions and tools. Manufacturing activities include antler-working, textile manufacture (weaving and sewing), leadworking and woodworking.

The majority of finds were located in the northern half of the site. As in Phase 1, there did not appear to be any concentrations of finds which might denote specific activity areas. One very large pit (*644*) contained nine individually recorded small finds, including two knives, a quern fragment, a pin beater and a 'buzz-bone', all probably domestic items. To the east, a series of intercutting pits yielded an almost complete, single-sided composite comb, while the utilisation of lead is represented by driblets or melted fragments. Beam-slot *516* yielded a stone bowl, while to the west a scatter of pits contained a small axehead (Fig. 17, 19), a fragment from a comb and a knife. In the southern plot there was a small quantity of ironwork, including a sliding bolt (Fig. 16, 11) and a key (Fig. 16, 12) both attesting to the need for security.

## Phase 3 (medieval cemetery: late 13th–16th centuries)

The majority of finds came from Phase 3 deposits and include a large number of coffin nails and a small collection of shroud pins from the graves. However, most items are residual Late Saxon and early medieval artefacts displaced by pit- and grave-digging.

## Phase 4 (post-medieval garden soils)

Four objects were retrieved from Phase 4 deposits, all deriving from post-Dissolution contexts. They comprise a small annular brooch, a lace chape and two nails.

## Discussion

### Personal possessions

This category comprises small portable items which would have formed part of a person's clothing (costume fittings), had been worn as jewellery, or would have been held by an individual for personal use (toilet equipment and objects for recreational use).

### Buckles

There are five buckles, three of copper alloy and two of iron, and two copper alloy buckle plates. One of the iron buckles, rectangular in form, may have been for use on heavy-duty straps. Stratigraphically the earliest buckle is of iron with a D-shaped frame (Fig. 16 no. 1), found in pit *433* (Phase 1). The X-ray revealed that it retains patches of a non-ferrous coating, which would have visually enhanced the buckle and protected it from corrosion. The copper alloy buckles were retrieved from Phase 3 former occupation surface *190*. They are similar in style, with cast D-shaped frames furnished with decorative knops (Fig. 16 nos 2 and 3). They resemble a form of buckle common during the 13th century and, whilst not identical, are similar stylistically to excavated examples from Alms Lane, Norwich (Margeson 1985a, fig. 35, 6) and London (Egan and Pritchard 1991, fig. 46, 314).

One other buckle is post-medieval in date. Its exterior covered in silver, it dates to *c.* 1720–90.

There are fragments from two buckle-plates manufactured from sheet metal, both of them unstratified. One is decorated with a marginally placed line of rouletted indentations and was retrieved from the spoil heap. The other is plain and came from a Phase 3/4 cleaning layer (*102*).

### Lace chapes

Three lace chapes were found, each made from rolled copper alloy sheet and 24–87mm long. Two were found in Phase 3 deposits, one within a burial (grave *14*) just above the neck and the other in former occupation surface *190*. A further example came from Phase 4 (context *967*). Two measure no more than 25mm and were both manufactured with overlapping seams, like Margeson's Type 3 (1985, 211). The much larger example has an edge-to-edge seam, like the Margeson Type 1 chape from Pottergate, Norwich (Margeson 1985b, fig. 38, 7). Similar

| Functional Category | Ph 1 | Ph 2 | Ph 3 | Ph 4 | U/S |
|---|---|---|---|---|---|
| **Personal possessions** | | | | | |
| Costume and jewellery | 1 | | 20 | 2 | 7 |
| Personal equipment | | 2 | 2 | | |
| Recreational objects | | 1 | 2 | | |
| **Equipment and furnishings** | | | | | |
| Building equipment | | | | | |
| General ironwork | 8 | 3 | 5 | | 2 |
| Nails (inc. coffin nails in Ph3) | 5 | 13 | 200 | 4 | 4 |
| Window glass | | 1 | 4 | | 1 |
| **Household equipment** | | *1* | *1* | | |
| Locks and keys | | 2 | | | 1 |
| Knives | 3 | 4 | 5 | | |
| Hones and sharpeners | | | 1 | | |
| **Tools** | | | | | |
| Metal working (crucible) | 1 | | | | 1 |
| Textile working | 1 | 2 | 3 | | |
| Woodworking | | 1 | | | |
| Trade | | | 4 | | 1 |
| Coins | | | 3 | | 1 |
| **Horse furniture** | | | | | |
| Horseshoes | 1 | | | | |
| Nails | | | 1 | | |
| Querns | | 1 | 2 | | 2 |
| **Miscellaneous and unidentified** | | | | | |
| Copper alloy | 2 | 3 | 15 | | 5 |
| Iron | 10 | 9 | 16 | | |
| Lead | | 1 | 61 | | 12 |
| Antler and bone | 1 | 4 | 6 | | 1 |
| Ceramic | 1 | | | | |

Table 6 Finds ordered by functional category

| | |
|---|---|
| Description | Henry II (1154–89), quarter cut short-cross penny, class 1c (1180–89) |
| Mint | Possibly London |
| Condition | Very worn |
| Reference | (North 1991, 962–964) |
| Location | SF 281, Context 190, Phase 3, grave earth |
| Description | Henry III (1216–72), quarter cut long-cross penny, class 3 (1248–50) |
| Mint | Exeter or Northampton |
| Moneyer | Philip |
| Reference | (North 1991, 986–988) |
| Location | SF 279, Context 190, Phase 3, grave earth |
| Description | Nuremburg stock jetton |
| Obverse | Three open crowns and three lys arranged alternately around a rose within an inner circle of rope pattern. Legend: Illegible |
| Reverse | The Reichsapfel within a double tressure of three curves and three angles set alternately. Legend: HANS.SCHVLTES. ?OMI |
| Diameter | 23mm |
| Reference | Barnard 1916, 222, 82 |
| Date | *c.*1550–74 |
| Location | SF 84, context 307, Phase 3 boundary ditch infill. |

Table 7  Coins

large chapes are known from London but their function is uncertain (Egan and Pritchard 1991, 282).

**Mounts**
Mounts are fittings used to strengthen and/or visually enhance items of textile or leather. Two cast mounts were found within Phase 3 former occupation surface *190*, a bar mount with terminal lobes (Margeson 1993, fig. 23, 286) and a belt stud with lozenge-shaped head (scalloped) and integral shank.

**Bells**
A white metal rumbler bell found within Phase 3 former occupation surface *190* was probably used as an accessory for dress. Although damaged, it is possible to determine that it falls into the category of closed bells, which have a 'pea' inside. The bell, cast in one piece, has four petal-like tabs and a loop for suspension. During casting the lower end would have been left open, so that the pea could have been inserted; the tabs would then be folded in, encasing the pea. The exterior surface of the bell is decorated with a chevron motif resembling that on an example from London (Egan and Pritchard 1991, fig. 221, 1668). Stratified examples of this type of bell are generally found in deposits dating to the 13th century.

**Pins**
Ten copper alloy pins include eight located within the fills of graves *16, 18, 29, 76, 86, 91, 101* and *140*, where they would have been used to secure a shroud prior to burial. They are all drawn wire pins up to 45mm long. Although three are incomplete (head missing), it is possible to classify the remainder as comprising two pins with globular heads and five pins with heads of coiled wire. The latter group can be divided according to Margeson's classification (1993, 13) into one wire-round spherical head (Type 1) and four wire-round top of shaft (Type 3).

**Jewellery**
Objects for personal adornment are represented by two brooches and a finger ring, all manufactured from copper alloy. The brooches are cast, annular, with constrictions for retaining the pin (extant) and decorated. One unstratified brooch is decorated with two distinct zones separated by the lie of the pin. One side is plain and with a circular cross-section, while the other is twisted to give the appearance of cable and is decorated with a double line of opposing triangles (Fig. 16 no. 4). A similar example from London (Egan and Pritchard 1991, fig. 160, 1310) has been dated *c.* 1230–60 AD. The other brooch was retrieved from Phase 4 context *118* and is decorated with three panels of transverse grooves, which divide the brooch into quarters (Fig. 16 no. 5).

A plain penannular finger ring (Fig. 16 no. 6) was found in pit *613* (Phase 1). It displays similarities to an 11th-century silver finger ring from Norwich Castle (Margeson and Williams 1985, fig. 23, 1). Copper alloy finger rings of a similar form have also been excavated from Alms Lane, Norwich (Margeson 1985, fig. 35, 1) and at Thetford (Rogerson and Dallas 1984, fig. 110, 22; Goodall 1993, fig. 115, 5).

**Toilet equipment**
There are parts of three bone/antler combs, comprising two single-sided composite combs from Phase 2 pits (*552, 673*) and one residual side-plate from Phase 3 former occupation surface *190*. All display stylistic features reminiscent of Anglo-Scandinavian examples from York (Waterman 1959, fig. 16). The most complete example comprises bone segments (three extant — there would originally have been seven) supported in a row by two slightly curved connecting plates secured by iron rivets (Fig. 16 no. 7). One connecting plate is decorated with an incised linear motif similar to that on a comb from St Martin-at-Palace Plain, Norwich (Ayers 1987, fig. 79, 2) which is of 11th century date. The other fragments include an end tooth segment from Phase 2 (pit *673*) and a fragment of a connecting plate, from the fill of grave *55*. The end tooth segment is distinctive having a convex profile and decorated with shallow incised lines. It displays similarities to a comb from Thetford (Rogerson and Dallas 1994, fig. 187, 16). The connecting plate is decorated with a cross-hatched motif flanked by transverse grooves.

**Recreational objects**
Three objects may be regarded as having a recreational use. They include two 'buzz-bones', from pit *644* (Phase 2) and grave *27* (Phase 3) respectively, and a pipe or flute from grave *113* (Phase 3).

The two 'buzz-bones' were manufactured from pig metapodia and have been perforated laterally through the anterior and posterior surfaces. Whilst such finds are common on sites of Saxon and medieval date in Britain and the continent, there is some dispute as to their actual function. They are frequently interpreted as clothes fasteners or 'toggles' (Williams 1987, 104) but MacGregor (1985, 102, 3) suggests that they would have been mounted on a twisted string as a buzzing, spinning toy. This interpretation has gained support in recent years and an example from Beverley was found to be threaded with a knotted leather thong (Foreman 1992, fig. 84, 505). For a discussion see Lawson 1995.

Part of a musical bone pipe was found within grave *113* (Phase 3) and is most probably residual (Fig. 16 no. 8). It was manufactured from a goose humerus and although missing both terminals, the presence of three frontal, knife-cut perforations indicate that the type of pipe represented is one of the most common forms recorded in Britain and on the continent. As in an example from Winchester (Biddle 1990, fig. 205, 2267), the vestige of a knife-cut facet at the proximal end indicates the position of the blowhole. The size of the finger holes (3mm) and the distance between them (*c.* 7mm) suggest that the pipe would have been for use by a child. The exterior surface is highly polished, indicating that it had been used extensively prior to deposition. A number of musical pipes manufactured from bird bones have been excavated in the East Anglia region; for further examples see Lawson and Margeson 1993, 211–12.

**Building equipment**
There is little evidence to help characterise the nature of the buildings that fronted St Faith's Lane during the 10th–12th centuries. Small quantities of ironwork were recovered from Late Saxon and early medieval contexts but nothing that would allude to the function of the structures.

General ironwork is represented by two staples and fourteen clench bolts. The two U-shaped staples were residual in Phase 3 deposits. Both were manufactured from rods with square or sub-circular cross-sections and have tapered terminals; they are up to 67mm long. Staples would have been driven into timbers leaving the U-shaped end protruding to form a fixing point for chains, rings, hasps and the like.

Clench bolts with lozenge-shaped roves were recovered from all three phases, with eight from Phase 1 and two from each of Phases 2 and 3. Such objects have been found elsewhere in Norwich (Margeson 1993, fig. 108, 1098–9). Goodall (1990a, 329) has indicated that clench bolts were used in the construction of doors, hatches and covers. It is possible that the eight clench bolts found in a single Phase 1 pit (*592*) may relate to a cover, like the medieval well cover attested from Lydford, Devon (Geddes 1980, 165, fig. 17). The regular plan-form of pit *592* would have lent itself well to a permanent cover: with its uniform sides and base, it could have been for storage (Figs 4 and 8).

The majority of nails were from Phase 3 deposits, and have been identified as coffin nails. Small numbers were retrieved from Phase 1 (five) and Phase 2 (twelve) contexts also. They are represented by two types: wedge-shaped with tapering profile and no distinct head; and nails with flat circular heads. Both types would have been used in carpentry and hammered flush with the surface of the timber.

**Glass**
A total of fourteen individual fragments of window glass were retrieved from six contexts, one fragment from Phase 2 (Pit *651*) and the remainder from Phase 3 grave fills (graves *4, 47, 103*) or former occupation surface *190*. Two fragments have grozed edges, indicating that they are parts of quarries which would have been held in place by lead cames. The fragments are heavily abraded with blackened manganese surfaces and range in size from 3mm to 67mm across. None of the pieces appears to be decorated.

**Household equipment**
There is a distinct lack of domestic equipment. The scant assemblage comprises a bowl with iron fittings and fragments of lava quern. The stone bowl and a quern fragment came from Phase 2, the former from beam-slot *516* and the latter from a large pit (*644*); the remainder are all residual in Phase 3 (cemetery soil layer *351* and quarry pit *254*).

Of particular interest is the presence of a bowl manufactured from garnet-rich mica-schist (identified by Dr Diana Sutherland, University of Leicester), which most probably originated from Scandinavia or Scotland. Although incomplete, it is possible to determine that it is a hemispherical bowl measuring 220mm in diameter (Fig. 16 no. 9). The rim is upright with a flat top and a ferrous metal fitting is secured to the exterior edge just below the rim, where it is secured by a rivet/nail which passes through the side of the bowl and is visible on the inside. It is possible that the fitting may be part of a handle. The style of the bowl is not dissimilar to a hemispherical bowl from York, which was made from soapstone (MacGregor 1982, 36, 373). Although stone bowls are rare in this part of England, it is of interest to note that fragments from two other stone bowls dating to the 9th–10th centuries were found at the Mann Egerton excavations elsewhere in the Greyfriars precinct (Emery 2007, fig. 5.51).

There are fragments from three lava querns. One piece still retains a vestige of the central hole and one worn surface, while the rest are amorphous lumps. They may have originated from the Mayen-Neidermendig area of Eiffel, Germany (for alternative sources see Wright 1992, 72–3).

**Locks and keys**
The presence of a small number of locks and keys attests to the need for security. Unusually, iron barrel padlocks or their constituent parts are not represented, although there is an unstratified small copper alloy padlock. A sliding bolt and a key were retrieved from the southern part of the site (Phase 2). The copper alloy padlock would have been for use on a small casket or chest. The cast case is octagonal and has attached to it the remains of an integral L-shaped arm (Fig. 16 no. 10). Like an example from London, three faces of the case are decorated with double lines of opposed punched triangles (Egan 1998, fig. 66, 244). The bolt still partially rotates within the case, but it appears to have been inserted into the end where the key should enter, maybe in error — two recessed square apertures at the other end indicate where the bolt should be. It is possible to view the leaf springs through a small aperture adjacent to the arm. The bolt terminates in an end plate with loop attached, most probably to attach a chain. While similar padlocks from London pre-date the 14th century (Egan 1998, 93–4), a not dissimilar padlock from Winchester was retrieved from a 15th century deposit (Goodall 1990b, fig. 313, 3666).

Both the sliding bolt and the key would have been for use with mounted locks. The former (Fig. 16 no. 11) comprises a rectangular-sectioned bar with two projections protruding from the underside, like another example from Norwich (Margeson 1993, fig. 116, 1257) — it would have enabled the key to throw the bolt within the lock. The key (Fig. 16 no. 12) is distinctive because the plain bit and hollow stem have been rolled in one like examples from Winchester (Goodall 1990b, fig. 326, 3741), which have been given a 9th-century date, and Alms Lane, Norwich (Margeson 1985a, fig. 38, 46) which was found in an early 16th-century deposit.

**Knives and hones**
Eleven knives were identified, comprising ten whittle-tang knives and one scale-tang knife. The former type is characterised by a tapered prong, which would have been inserted into an organic handle of wood, horn or bone. The blades of scale-tang knives terminate with an integral, parallel-sided perforated strip, to which scales of wood or bone would be fixed. Three knives came from Phase 1 deposits, and included one with distinctly Saxon characteristics from a large pit, and four each from Phases 2 and 3. There are no complete examples and it was not possible to identify any specific uses. Five of the knives are sufficiently complete to determine variations in form, which include:

- back of blade rises then angles to tip; cutting edge horizontal (Fig. 16 no. 13);
- back of blade horizontal then angles to tip; cutting edge curved then angles to tip (Fig. 16 no. 14);
- the cutting edge and the back of the blade are parallel (not illus.);
- the cutting edge and the back of the blade taper to the tip (Fig. 16 no. 15).

The site produced one whetstone for sharpening metal knives and tools. This was residual within grave *61* (Phase 3).

**Tools**
A small collection of tools represents equipment for the manufacture of textiles and an axe for woodworking. Metalworking is represented by fragments of possible furnace lining and a small unstratified crucible with copper alloy deposits on its rim, but there are no tools which would have been used in the process of metal working.

Objects used in the manufacture of textiles include a hemispherical spindle-whorl from pit *592* (Phase 1), a pinbeater from pit *644* (Phase 2) and three needles, two of copper alloy (from Phase 2 stake-hole *366* and Phase 3 grave *17*) and one of bone (Phase 3 grave *100*).

The spindle whorl was formed from the proximal end of a bovine femur (Fig. 17 no. 16) and would have been used in hand-spinning. Elsewhere within Norwich, examples are known from St Martin-at-Palace Plain, Norwich (Williams 1987, fig. 82, 22) and Alms Lane (Margeson 1985a, fig. 38, 51). The pinbeater (Fig. 17 no. 17) is double-pointed and would have been for use with a warp-weighted loom. Pinbeaters of this type generally pre-date the 9th century. There are no examples of pinbeaters with spatulate terminals, which would have been used with a vertical two-beam loom. In addition to two copper alloy needles (Fig. 17 no. 18), a tiny fragment of a third was manufactured from bone and decorated with ring and dot (not illus.).

Considering the importance of wood, there is a distinct lack of tools relating to its use apart from a fragment of an axe (Fig. 17 no. 19). Given its small size, it is likely that it was used for shaping wood. It came from a small pit (*673*) to the west of beam-slot *516*.

**Coins and trade**
Four coins, a Nuremburg stock jetton and parts of three balances represent evidence for commercial activity. The coins, two silver and two copper alloy, were all found in Phase 3 former occupation surface *190*. The silver coins pre-date Phase 3 and are therefore residual (although the later one may be a late loss). The copper alloy coins are impossible to identify.

Fragments from three balances comprise two balance arms from Phase 3 deposits (SF 83 from *301* and SF 66 from pit *254*: Fig. 17 nos 20 and 21 respectively) and one unstratified balance fork (Fig. 17 no. 22). Balances would have been used for the accurate weighing of precious commodities. They are generally assumed to have been the

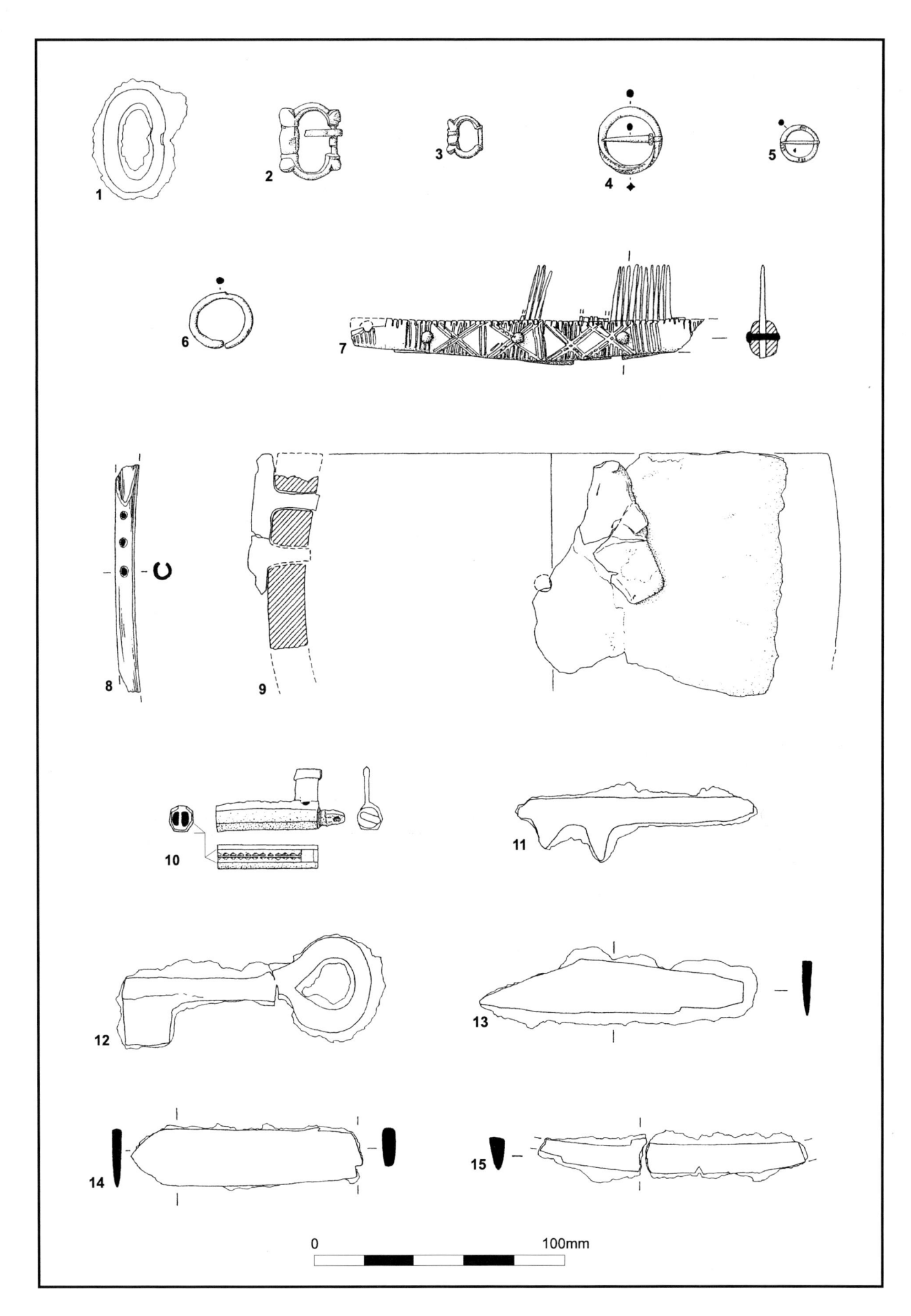

Figure 16  Small finds, nos 1–15

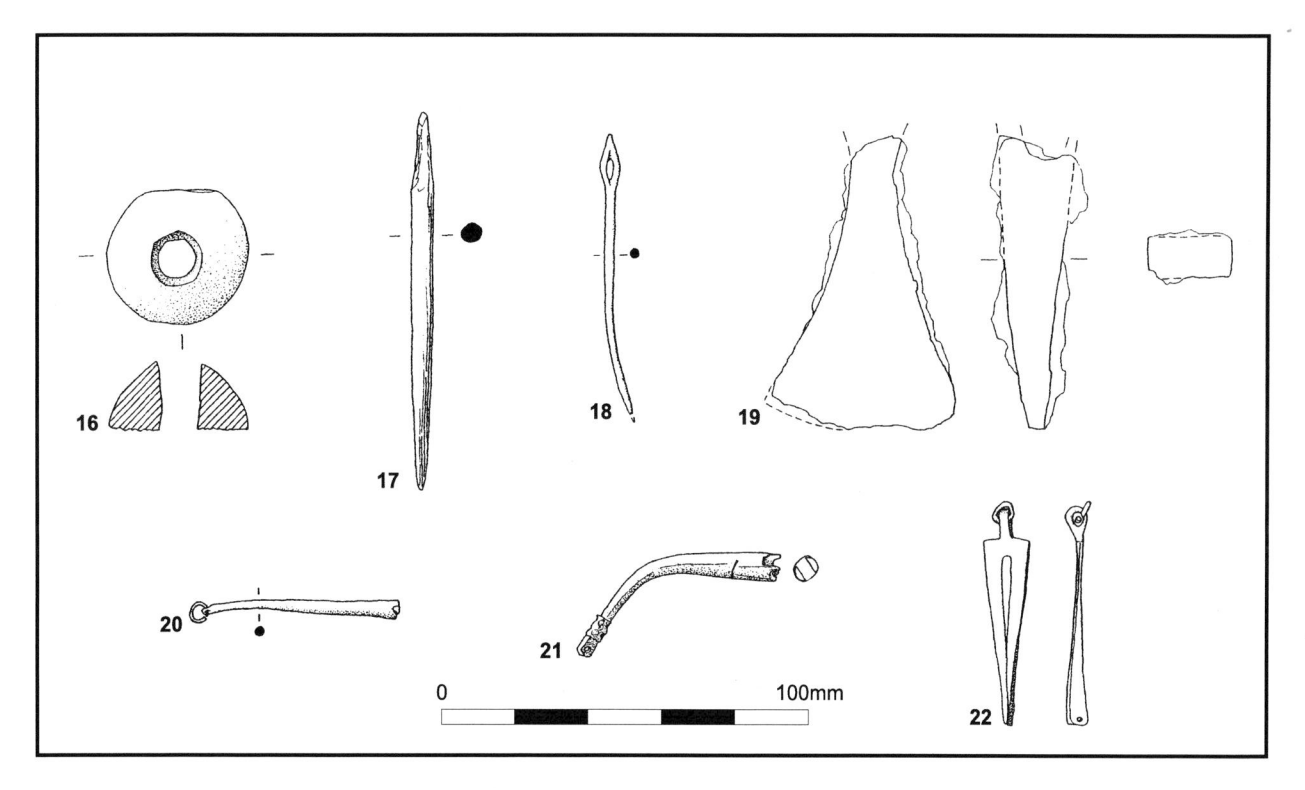

Figure 17 Small finds, nos 16–22

property of merchants and craftsmen, especially in urban contexts. They are often found in association with metalworking debris (Kruse 1992, 69). The balance arms from St Faith's Lane are all from hand-held folding balances which had broken at the point where the arms pivot. One is plain, tapered and terminates in a perforated loop, to which a small ring is attached. Its simple style recalls the terminals of early Anglo-Saxon fixed balances (Scull 1990) and a 9th-century example from Ipswich is not dissimilar (Kruse 1992, fig. 2 d). The other arm resembles 10th–11th century examples. It appears more robust and is tapered, with part of the beam still attached. The arm terminates in a squared loop with a 'chip-carved' type moulding set below (Fig. 17 no. 21). It displays similar characteristics to examples from Ipswich (Kruse 1992, fig. 4 b) and Thetford (Goodall 1984, fig. 113, 56–8).

The 'stirrup' or balance fork is complete and would have been used to suspend the balance arm and support the pointer. It is almost identical to a 10th–11th century example from the Butter Market site, Ipswich (Kruse 1982, fig. 4 d).

**Horse equipment**

There are only two objects associated with horses, a horseshoe and a horseshoe nail. The horseshoe was found in pit *613* (Phase 1) and has a sinuous/wavy outline with three rectangular countersunk depressions on each branch, pierced by circular nail holes. The horseshoe nail was residual in Phase 3. It is an unused 'fiddle-key' nail that would have been used with the type of shoe found in Phase 1.

**Catalogue of illustrated small finds**
(Figs 16–17)

1. **Buckle**, Fe. Incomplete, pin missing. D-shaped frame, bar to which strap would have been attached is slightly waisted; wear, probably caused by pin. Non-ferrous coating. L: 24mm H: 40mm. SF 211, *433*, Phase 1, pit.
2. **Buckle**, Ae. Cast D-shaped frame with offset bar; decorative knops on outside edge of frame. Pin incomplete, manufactured from a strip of sheet metal curled around the bar. L: 25mm H: 29mm. SF 283, *190*, Phase 3, former occupation surface.
3. **Buckle**, Ae Incomplete, pin missing. Cast D-shaped frame with offset bar; decorative knops on outside edge of frame. L: 14mm H: 16mm. SF 291, *190*, Phase 3, former occupation surface.
4. **Brooch**, Ae. Complete with pin attached. Annular brooch with two distinct zones; one side is decorated with a cable pattern punched with double lines of opposing triangles, the other side is plain with a circular cross-section. Pin circular sectioned, tapered to a rounded point and furnished with a square moulding at the base, the outer edges of which are decorated with a zigzag motif. D: 25mm. SF273, Unstratified.
5. **Brooch**, Ae. Complete, with pin attached. Circular cross-section with recess for the pin, which is flanked by equidistant panels of transverse grooves dividing the brooch into quarters. D: 15mm. SF 8, *118*, Phase 3, former occupation surface.
6. **Finger ring**, Ae. Complete. Penannular, with circular cross-section and slightly tapered terminals. Dimensions (external): 25 x 22mm; H: 2mm. SF 147, *593*, Phase 1, pit *613*.
7. **Comb**, antler. Incomplete, terminals and most of teeth missing. Single-sided composite comb; one connecting plate is decorated with an incised motif, the other side is plain. L: 140mm. H: 37mm (five teeth per 10mm). SF 131, *552*, Phase 2, *552*.
8. **Pipe/flute**, goose humerus. Incomplete, both terminals missing. Three frontally placed, knife-cut finger holes (7mm apart); a knife-cut facet (42mm from finger holes) indicates position of blowhole. The exterior surface is highly polished, suggesting prolonged use. L (incomplete): 89mm D: 8–9mm. SF 253, *335*, Phase 3, grave *113*.
9. **Stone bowl**, mica-schist/Fe. Incomplete, large rim/body sherd with iron fitting attached. D: 220mm. Th: 18mm (rim)–15mm. SF 127, *376*, Phase 2, beam-slot *516*.
10. **Padlock**, Ae. Octagonal case with integral L-shaped arm, cast in one piece. 40 x 10mm. SF 184, Unstratified.
11. **Sliding bolt**, Fe. Incomplete, one terminal missing. L (incomplete): 93mm Th: 10mm. SF 181, *853*, Phase 2, pit *880*.
12. **Key**, Fe. Pear-shaped bow; bit rolled in one with hollow stem; stem and bit in line. L: 100mm. SF 119, *526*, Phase 2, pit *504*.
13. **Knife**, Fe. Incomplete, most of tang missing. Tang almost in line with back of blade which rises and then angles down to the tip; cutting horizontal. Blade L: 96mm. W: 21mm Th: 3mm. SF 135, *377*, Phase 1, pit *592*.
14. **Knife**, Fe. Incomplete, part of blade and tang missing. Back of blade horizontal then angles to tip; cutting edge curved then angles to tip. Mineral-preserved organics visible on surface of corrosion. Blade W: 20mm Th: 3mm. SF 172, *667*, Phase 2, pit *504*.
15. **Knife**, Fe. Incomplete, part of blade and tang missing. The cutting edge and the back of the blade taper to the tip. Blade L: 68mm W: 12mm Th: 4mm. SF 318, *738*, Phase 2, pit *644*.

16. **Spindle whorl**, bone. Hemispherical whorl with large, waisted central perforation, indicating that it was drilled from both sides. D: 38mm. H: 19mm. Weight: 12g. SF139, *377*, Phase 1, pit *592*.
17. **Pinbeater**, bone. Incomplete, one terminal missing. Knife-cut facets evident at broken end; there is no sign of wear (surface not polished), therefore it may have broken during manufacture. L: 89mm. SF 159, *278*, Phase 2, pit *644*.
18. **Needle/bodkin**, Ae. Complete; circular sectioned shank tapered to a fine point; eye cut by hand. L: 77mm. D: 3mm. SF 93, *366*, Phase 2, stake-hole.
19. **Axe**, Fe. Incomplete. Blade from small axe with convex edge, collar missing. Blade W: 49mm L: 75mm. SF 163, *627*, Phase 2, pit *673*.
20. **Balance**, Ae. Arm, tapered with circular cross-section and widening to a square cross-section. The small end is perforated with a wire ring for suspending the balance pan. The other end is broken at the point where the folding arm would have pivoted. The remains of an iron rivet survive in the recess. L (incomplete): 55mm. SF 66, *254*, Phase 3, pit *254*.
21. **Balance**, Ae. Arm and part of beam, chip-carved decoration set just below perforated terminal. L (arm): 61mm. SF 83, *301*, Phase 3, spread of crushed stone under trackway.
22. **Balance forks (stirrups)**, Ae. Complete. L: 58mm. SF 6, *102*, Unstratified, residue of modern layers.

## III. The ironworking waste
by Andy Chapman with I. Mack and G. McDonnell

**Introduction**
A total of 131.7kg of iron slag was recovered. Of this, 13.9kg were retrieved as small quantities residual in forty-seven different contexts of later medieval date, including former occupation surface and grave fills. These contexts typically produced less than 0.5kg each, although two contained larger pieces of 1.4kg and 4.5kg. A further 45.8 kg were recovered from seventy-one contexts of Saxo-Norman/early medieval date, where the slag was mixed with quantities of domestic waste. These contexts typically contained less than 1.5kg, although there were three contexts with 2.2kg, 2.7kg and 3.4kg respectively. Finally, a total of 72.0kg was recovered from fifteen contexts as primary dumps of slag, largely from the pit group in the north-eastern corner of the site. The quantity of slag per context in this primary group ranged between 1.06kg and 14.6kg, with pits *561*, *712*, *433*, and *686* producing 6.7kg, 8.3kg, 14.6kg and 6.4kg respectively. An assessment of this material was carried out by I. Mack and Dr G. McDonnell from the Ancient Metallurgy Research Group, Department of Archaeological Sciences, University of Bradford.

The assemblage of slags from this site was very unusual. An estimated 80% of the sample could be identified as hearth or furnace lining. Hearth lining is typically deposited within metres of the ironworking activity and is readily destroyed by later disturbance. The survival of such a quantity of lining material must indicate that the working occurred within metres of the excavated area. There is little variation between the slags, most of which have a very fluid morphology and are predominantly high silica. The presence of proto-hearth bottom forms suggests that the slag derived from smithing processes, although the high fluidity would suggest predominantly high-temperature operations — i.e. welding.

The recommendation arising from the assessment was that little could be done with the material other than to record the tuyere mouths and the size of the tuyere plates. The present report provides the results of this analysis.

**Tuyere plates**
Tuyere plates are formed within the hottest zone of a smithing hearth near the blowing hole, where air is forced in by bellows to raise the temperature to the required level. The plates are typically roughly circular or oval in form and are characterised by their vitrified, glassy, surfaces. Towards the base there will be a circular aperture, the blowing hole or tuyere mouth, where the actual tuyere or nozzle entered the furnace, although this is often damaged or lost (English Heritage 2001, 13–15, fig. 10).

All of the material recovered from the primary contexts was examined in detail. All large fragments of tuyere plates and tuyere mouths were extracted for measurement, while the presence of small fragments was noted. Ten of the primary contexts produced fragments of tuyere plates, with a major group of four or five plates coming from *421*, a fill of pit *712*. The recovered pieces represent a minimum of thirteen tuyere plates. Five plates retain part of the tuyere mouth. In four instances these had broken horizontally, the lower half separating from the larger upper part of the plate, while a single example has a near-vertical break. The plates range from 95mm to 120mm in diameter, but only four are sufficiently intact to be measurable. The five tuyere mouths are respectively greater than 20mm, 23mm, 24mm, 26mm and 30mm in diameter. The vitrified plates are from 40–100mm thick, with pieces of dark red to bright orange burnt clay lining adhering to their back surfaces.

**Hammerscale**
The fine dust derived from the primary contexts was tested with a magnet and the majority produced at least some hammerscale. In particular, pits *712*, *433* and *686*, all of which also produced multiple fragments of tuyere plates, contained substantial quantities of hammerscale and samples have been separated out and retained in archive. Pits *561*, *712*, *430*, and *754* produced smaller quantities.

Examination of the recovered samples under low (x10) magnification indicates that it largely comprises flake hammerscale including pieces measuring up to 2–3mm, but spheroidal hammerslag was also present in small quantities.

# 5. Economic and Environmental Evidence
by Philip L. Armitage and Wendy J. Carruthers

## I. Faunal remains
by Philip L. Armitage

### Introduction

*Numbers of bones and species represented*
A total of 3972 hand-collected animal bone elements and fragments from site occupation Phases 1 and 2 were submitted for full analysis, using standard archaeozoological methodological procedures as described in a previously published report (Armitage 1999). From this analysis, 3060 bone specimens (77% of the total) have been identified to species and part of skeleton, and 912 (23%) remain as unidentified fragments. Of the 3972 identified bones, 2656 (86.8% of the total) are mammalian, 315 (10.3%) bird, 85 (2.8%) fish, and four (0.1%) amphibian.

In addition to hand-collected material, bones obtained from sieved soil samples were also submitted for analysis and yielded important further remains of the fish eaten (comprising 2489 identified fish bone elements and fragments), including evidence of species lacking in the hand-collected samples.

A summary of the numbers of bone elements and fragments (NISP) by species/taxa and site phase is presented in Table 8 (Phases 1 and 2 combined).

*Preservation*
The overall state of preservation of the bones from both Phases 1 and 2 is good with only moderate numbers of bone elements exhibiting modification due to sub-aerial weathering/erosion or biological degradation. It would therefore appear that the inhabitants disposed of and buried their food and other bone refuse in a timely manner soon after discard, and that only a relatively small proportion of such waste was left scattered or exposed. This interpretation is supported by the low incidence of bones gnawed by dogs. Rapid burial of household refuse would have denied dogs any opportunity of scavenging food debris. The relatively low frequency of burnt bone in each phase indicates the inhabitants did not regularly burn food debris as a sanitary measure. Perhaps the relatively small numbers of burnt specimens present had resulted from the casual throwing of table waste into kitchen/cooking fires.

### Descriptions of the main livestock species

#### Cattle
A single horn core from context *278* (pit *644*: Figs 5 and 7) is identified as a medium-horned bull (classification system of Armitage and Clutton-Brock 1976, 331–2). Gender in five other animals may be determined from anatomical features in their innominate bones (based on the criteria of Grigson 1982, 8), allowing the recognition of one female and one castrate from Phase 1 and three females from Phase 2. Stature (withers heights) in seven of the cattle represented in Phase 2 by complete metapodia may be calculated (using the factors of Fock in von den Driesch *et al.* 1974) from the measured greatest lengths (GL) in these bones. The calculated values (mean 107.7cm, range 103.0–111.2cm) compare well with the withers heights of Saxo-Norman/early medieval cattle from other East Anglian sites but are on average noticeably shorter than their 9th–10th century predecessors. The continuing diminution in the size of cattle from the post-Conquest/early medieval period onwards culminated in the late 12th–13th centuries in a preponderance throughout Britain (as well as in continental Europe) of dwarf cattle with withers heights under 1m. Such small cattle are reminiscent of those found in pre-Roman Iron Age Britain and are clearly indicative of a severe deterioration in livestock husbandry, which among other factors resulted from the restrictive conditions imposed by the manorial (common grazing) system of farming (as discussed by Armitage 1980 and 1982). British cattle do not show any marked improvement until the late 14th century, when in south-eastern England taller and more robust cattle (some with relatively massive long horns) first appear.

#### Sheep
In Phase 1 horned sheep are represented by five detached (chopped) horn cores whose sex is determined as follows (using the criteria of Armitage 1977, 82-88; Hatting 1975; and Armitage in Clutton-Brock *et al.* 1990): three males, one female and one castrate. So-called 'thumb-print' depressions are seen in the horn cores of the castrate (from context *593*, pit *613*). This condition is thought by Hatting (1975) and Albarella (1995) to indicate a period of malnutrition in the life of a sheep. In addition to these five sheep, another seven horned animals are represented in Phase 1 by cranial portions that have had their horn cores

| Mammalian species/taxa | |
|---|---|
| Horse | *Equus caballus* (domestic) |
| Cattle | *Bos* (domestic) |
| Sheep | *Ovis* (domestic) |
| Goat | *Capra* (domestic) |
| Pig | *Sus* (domestic) |
| Dog | *Canis* (domestic) |
| Cat | *Felis* (domestic) |
| Brown hare | *Lepus* sp. (capensis) |
| Red/fallow deer | *Cervus elaphus* or *Dama dama* |
| **Bird species/taxa** | |
| Grey-lag/domestic goose | *Anser anser*/domestic |
| Domestic fowl | *Gallus gallus* |
| Mallard/domestic duck | *Anas platyrhynchos*/domestic |
| Teal | *Anas crecca* |
| White-tailed eagle | *Haliaeetus albicalla* |
| ?Crane | ?*Grus grus* |
| Swan | *Cygnus* sp. |
| *cf.* Rockdove/domestic pigeon | *Columba livia*/domestic |
| Blackbird | *Turdus merula* |
| **Fish species/taxa** | |
| Cod | *Gadus morhua* |
| Whiting | *Merlangius merlangus* |
| Sea bass | *Dicentrarchus labrax* |
| Herring | *Clupea harengus* |
| Mackerel | *Scomber scombrus* |
| Flatfish *cf.* plaice | *cf. Pleuronectes platessa* |
| Thornback ray | *Raja clavata* |
| Freshwater eel | *Anguilla anguilla* |
| **Amphibian species** | |
| Common frog | *Rana temporaria* |

Table 8 Faunal species

chopped off using an axe or cleaver. In four of the crania the size and appearance of the surviving basal part of the horn core identifies each as male. Phase 1 also yielded evidence of a polled (naturally hornless) sheep, represented by crania from context *426* (pit *712*), whose sex is indeterminate.

No polled examples came from Phase 2, where all the sheep are horned, represented by seventeen detached horn cores (chopped through their bases: thirteen male and four castrates, all adults or young adults) and eleven adult crania whose horn cores had been removed (chopped off close to the base). Only one of these crania can be sexed (male); the others are fragmentary and indeterminate.

Slaughter pattern evidence from 45 sheep of Phases 1 and 2, based on stages of eruption and wear in their lower mandibular cheekteeth (method of Payne 1973), reveals that most animals in each phase were killed between their second and sixth year, with few killed as lambs. This kill-off pattern suggests the sheep in both phases came from a mixed economy aimed at the production of meat and wool. Albarella *et al.* (1997) recorded a similar kill-off pattern for the sheep from Late Saxon–early medieval contexts (Periods 1–3) at Castle Mall, Norwich.

A pooled reconstructed withers height for the sheep (Phase 1 and Phase 2 combined) based on lengths of four radii and nine metapodia (method of Teichert, 1975) gives a mean value of 60.9cm (SD 5.2) and size range of 49.1–68.0 cm. These data compare well with the thirteen sheep documented by Albarella (2004) from 11th–12th century Mill Lane, Thetford, whose mean withers height was 59.4cm (SD 3.3) with a range of 55.0–67.8cm. Similar mean values have been recorded in other early medieval sheep from regions outside East Anglia, including those from Flaxengate, Lincoln (mean 59.5cm (SD 3.6), range 50.0–72.2cm, N=170: O'Connor 1982) and Falcon House, City of London (mean 59.3cm (SD 3.1), range 54.0–64.1 cm, N=23: Armitage 1998).

### Goat
This animal is represented only in Phase 2, by two horn cores (1R and 1 L; a pair?) from pit *644*. The shape of each core may be described as long and straight with a well-developed keel along the anterior edge, as seen in the horn of the Old English goat. On the basis of their size and general appearance, both cores are recognised as female and compare well with those from the medieval (13th century) tannery refuse at 's-Hertogenbosch, Netherlands (Prummel 1978, 403, fig. 2). In the absence of any recognizable post-cranial goat elements from the site, it may be suggested these particular horn cores are not from an animal (or animals) that had been slaughtered/butchered locally as a meat source but instead may have originally been in the form of detached horns (with their cores still inside) imported into the town specifically for the purposes of hornworking. Alternatively, these cores may represent discarded waste from imported goat skins (with their horns still attached) used in leather-making.

### Pigs
Using the criteria of Mayer and Brisbin (1988) nine canine teeth (tusks) are sexed as follows.

Phase 1: lower canines, 2 males; upper canines, 2 females.
Phase 2: lower canines, 3 males; upper canines, 2 females.

Pooling these identifications gives an overall ratio of 1 female: 1.25 males. Their ages, based on dental eruption in the lower jawbones of nine individuals, are given in Table 9 (using the criteria of Bull and Payne 1982).

From these data it is seen that the majority of pigs were slaughtered before the end of their second year, as is commonly reported from other medieval sites throughout Britain.

Special mention should be made of a complete adult metacarpus IV from context *593*, pit *613* (Phase 1) whose size (GL = 83mm) matches exactly that of a modern wild boar documented by Noddle (1980, 407). While this specimen may indeed represent a wild pig it could be from an extra-large domestic male, or perhaps even a domestic/wild hybrid. In respect of the latter suggestion, reference can be made to the statement made by Clutton-Brock (1976, 378) that 'It is possible ... Anglo-Saxon pigs still freely interbred with the wild boars which were living in the forest' — a situation arising from the commonplace pre-Conquest system of keeping domestic pigs not in the farmyard but free range in woodlands (see Trow-Smith 1957, 53–5). Large pigs also feature in Saxon/early medieval contexts from elsewhere in Britain, including North Elmham (mean 72.4mm (SD 6.67), range 63–85mm, N=15: Noddle 1980: 407) and Middle Saxon (8th–10th century) Melbourne Street, Southampton (Hamwih) (mean 70.1mm (SD 3.7), range 62.8 – 81.0, N=25: Bourdillon and Coy 1980).

### Household pets
Canid bone elements recovered from both Phases 1 and 2 show that dogs featured in the lives of the St Faith's Lane inhabitants. Of special interest is the adult jawbone from context *278*, pit *644* (Phase 2) which has a cheektooth row length (P1–M3) of 53mm: this value falls well below the size-range of Anglo-Saxon dogs documented by Harcourt (1974, 168: mean 77.5mm (SD 5.25), range 71–87 mm, N 13). Albarella (2004) however reported the presence of 'some very small dogs' from 10th–12th century deposits at Mill Lane, Thetford. Together with the present example, these are best interpreted as lap- or house-dogs kept as ladies' or children's companions rather than as working animals used in guarding property or hunting. An indication that dogs kept locally were fed horseflesh (perhaps obtained from a nearby knacker's yard) is provided by a gnawed calcaneum. It is of interest that apart from this particular calcaneum and a metacarpus from pit *644* (Phase 2) all of the other horse bones from St Faith's Lane are phalanges ('pastern bones': five phalanx I and a single phalanx II) representing remains of the extremities of fore and hind legs. Perhaps these derived from horse skins being processed by leatherworkers nearby.

Evidence for the presence of cats is limited to an isolated subadult humerus from context *652* (pit *864*, Phase 2) in which the distal epiphysis is fully fused while that at the proximal end is fusing/partially fused, indicating an age at death of *c.* 20–24 months (criteria of Smith 1969). This cat was either a household pet or a feral animal living freely as a scavenger in the area.

## Descriptions of the fish species
Lists of identified bones of the predominate fish species represented at the site (cod and herring) are retained in archive. Measurements taken from selected fish bone elements allow the following reconstructions of size in individuals and groups.

### Cod
Estimates of size (TL = total length) of the cod were made using measurements taken from three dentaries, one premaxiilla and two cleithra (using the formulae of Wheeler and Jones 1976 and Rojo 1986) and by comparison (one vertebrate) with modern comparative specimens of known size. The results of the calculations are summarised in Table 10.

These data may be compared against other Norwich fish bone assemblages. Apart from one small fish (TL 45cm) the cod from Alms Lane documented by Jones and Scott (1985, 226) were of 'respectable size' (90–105cm) while those from the Magistrates' Courts reported by Locker (1987, 115) ranged from 40cm to 100cm (N=11): the latter assemblage is interpreted as cod supplied by an inshore fishery. Beyond Norwich at King's Lynn, Wheeler (1977) recognised two size groupings in the cod from medieval contexts: smaller sized cod of TL 60–80cm, which he believed derived from a winter inshore fishery, and a group of larger fish of TL 88–137cm from a distant water fishery. Based on the criteria of Wheeler and Locker it is suggested that the cod consumed by the St Faith's Lane inhabitants had been supplied by both inshore and deep-water fisheries (probably based at Great Yarmouth). By comparison, the cod eaten by the Saxo-Norman/early medieval inhabitants at the Falcon House site, City of London, had apparently been supplied entirely by a distant water fishery, as evidenced by the preponderance of larger fish (TL 90–149cm: Armitage 1998).

| *Suggested age range* | *Number of pigs* | |
|---|---|---|
| | *Phase 1* | *Phase 2* |
| Neonate/sucking pig | | 2 |
| 1 – 1½ yrs | 3 | 2 |
| 2 yrs and over | 1 | 1 |

Table 9  Pig remains

| | *TL range (in cm)* | *No. specimens* |
|---|---|---|
| Phase 1 | 81 – 109 | 4 |
| Phase 2 | 87 – 100 | 3 |
| Overall | 81 – 109 | 7 |

Table 10  Details of cod remains

**Whiting**

Based on the depth of the ramus (3.7mm) in the dentary of a whiting from context *711* (pit *754*, Phase 1; sieved sample 30) the total length (TL) is estimated at 35.5cm (using the regression formula of Jones and Scott 1985: MFT 26). According to the descriptions given in Wheeler (1997, 48) the average size recorded in modern whiting is 40cm, which compares well with the value calculated for the St Faith's Lane specimen. Other authors have documented the size of whiting from other medieval contexts in Norwich: those at Alms Lane were mostly between 30cm and 45cm TL, with a range 25–60cm (Jones and Scott 1985, 226), while those at the Magistrates' Court were found to be 29–36cm TL (Locker 1987, 115).

**Sea bass**

Context *667* (pit *504*, Phase 2) yielded a complete preoperculum identified as sea bass. From the measured chord length (71.2mm) this bone is believed to come from a fish whose standard length (SL) is estimated as 55–60cm (based on the graph given in Sternberg 1992, 18, diagram 62, showing the relationship between chord lengths and SL values in a sample of modern sea bass). The size of the St Faith's Lane sea bass compares well with the average size (60cm) recorded in modern catches (Wheeler 1997, 92).

## Interpretation and discussion

### Site environment

Pit-derived deposits of organic household refuse generated by medieval activity in the vicinity of St Faith's Lane would have supported high densities of invertebrates, whose presence in turn undoubtedly attracted scavengers. Among these opportunists may have been the blackbird represented in context *667* (pit *504*, Phase 2) by a complete tarsometatarsus. Especially 'ripe' piles of refuse would have swarmed with flies which may have also attracted frogs onto the site — as suggested by the presence of four frog bone elements (one humerus, one femur and two tibio-fibulae) in context *531* (pit *562*, Phase 2). None of these frog bones exhibits mechanical damage or erosion from digestive juices, as would be expected had they represented the remains of a regurgitated food pellet of an avian predator. The bones from context *531* therefore appear to be skeletal parts of at least one frog that died at the site, rather than of an animal living elsewhere whose remains had been imported onto the site by a visiting raptor such as a kestrel or a barn owl. Casually discarded food debris from local households may also have been responsible for attracting white-tailed eagles, whose skeletal remains are represented in both Phases 1 and 2, to the site. Although today regarded as a 'sea eagle' this species is believed to have had a much more widespread inland distribution in Britain from Roman times and throughout the Middle Ages (Baxter 1993, 80) and its occurrence in Norwich, away from the coast, would not have been out of the ordinary during the Late Saxon/post-Conquest/early medieval period. Its role as a 'carrion feeder' explains its inclusion in Anglo-Saxon epic poems where, under the name of 'earn' and as a companion of the wolf and the raven, this bird is linked to the aftermath of battles when animal scavengers feasted off the human dead (Baxter 1993, 78).

The above interpretations are based on the detailed reviews published by O'Connor (1993 and 2000a) of the animal species which are believed to have been associated in the past with the urban scavenger niche. Alternative explanations are considered below for the presence at the St Faith's Lane site of blackbird (possibly as food debris) and white-tailed eagle (possibly as craft waste).

### Diet

In each of the bone assemblages representing site occupation Phases 1 and 2, the bulk of the material is recognised as discarded food debris from all stages of meat preparation and consumption (on-site slaughtering, primary/secondary and tertiary butchering, as well as kitchen and table waste). Analysis of these food bones therefore provides useful insights into the diet and food procurement strategies of the site inhabitants during the Late Saxon and post-Conquest/early medieval periods.

Considered in broad terms, there are remarkable similarities in the dietary profiles of both phases. In each, beef clearly predominates as the staple meat, followed by mutton and lesser amounts of pork. Even with respect to the grades of meat cuts represented there are striking similarities between Phase 1 and Phase 2. This may be illustrated with reference to the beef. Based on the developed methodology of West (in Armitage and West 1985) an assessment of the cattle bones from each phase reveals that the majority (over 85%) represent a combination of the choicest (*i.e.* more meaty) cuts and medium-grade cuts, with proportionally smaller amounts of the inferior (less meaty) cuts and offal making up the balance. Irrespective of grade, however, all of this beef would be considered by modern standards coarse and unappetizing since it almost exclusively derives from culled working/draught cattle slaughtered well past their prime age. Veal apparently was very rarely eaten by the St Faith's Lane inhabitants, as evidenced by the very few bone elements from this age recovered from the excavated contexts: these were limited to an isolated femur from Phase 1 and a single mandible and one metacarpus from Phase 2.

Likewise, relatively small amounts of lamb appear to have been eaten and much of the meat that the inhabitants purchased in the market probably came from culled stock kept primarily for their value as wool- rather than meat-producers. As a consequence, much of the mutton eaten was probably somewhat coarse.

Only the pigs, slaughtered at a relatively younger age than either the cattle or sheep, would have yielded meat of reasonable prime quality. The presence of the remains of sucking pigs in Phase 1 also points to the possibility that breeding sows were being kept on or near the site for home provisioning.

Backyard farming in the locality is additionally indicated in both phases by the presence of immature domestic fowl, with the relatively high ratio of hens to cocks suggesting that egg production was as important as meat production (criteria of Albarella *et al.* 1997, 48). Geese may also have played a part in home provisioning, supplying not only meat but also feathers (an important commodity in medieval times).

In order to test objectively whether subsistence backyard farming had indeed been established at the St Faith's Lane site during the occupational phases under review, the methodology devised by O'Connor (1994, 145) was applied to the bone assemblages. This method involves calculating frequencies of the combined NISP counts of the pig + fowl + geese bones (in each phase) and expressing these values as a percentage of the total (combined) NISP values for all the principal meat-yielding species (namely, cattle + sheep + pig + fowl + geese). Applying such analysis to the St Faith's Lane faunal material gives results as indicated in Table 11.

| Phase | % |
|---|---|
| 1 | 23.1% |
| 2 | 21.8% |

Table 11 Percentage of 'backyard farmed' animals present

Both of the calculated frequencies compare favourably with the value (26.3%) documented by O'Connor (1994, 145) for late 10th–early 11th century York, and they confirm the presence of backyard (small livestock) farming activity at St Faith's Lane during occupation Phases 1 and 2. Where the site's inhabitants differ from their contemporaries in York, however, is in the relative degrees of exploitation of the wild food resources of their respective rural hinterlands. In York, there was evidence that the inhabitants greatly diversified their diet through the procurement of both hunted wild game and wildfowl. By comparison, similar evidence from St Faith's Lane is extremely limited and includes an isolated hare radius from context *377* (pit *592*, Phase 1) and a few bones of wild ducks (teal) from Phases 1 and 2. Furthermore, there is no comparable evidence for the consumption of venison.

The dietary food resource base at the St Faith's Lane site therefore appears relatively narrow, with high reliance on traditional farm-produced meat resources (beef, mutton and pork) obtained through the urban market place, supplemented by meat from home-reared small livestock (pigs, fowl, geese and perhaps also domestic ducks). It is open to question whether the blackbird represented by the tarsometatarsus from context *667* (pit *504*, Phase 2) contributed to the dietary variety of the inhabitants. What is known, however, is that poulterers in medieval towns frequently sold blackbirds along with other small wild birds as food (Wilson 1976, 109).

The single coracoid identified as swan from context *384* (part of quarry *893*) seems somewhat out of place in a dietary regimen which otherwise may be described as one of 'solid sufficiency' rather than one of wide variety or extravagance. Swans, despite their oily, tough and somewhat unappetizing flesh, were frequently sold by medieval poulterers. However, swan was always the most expensive bird on sale (Wilson 1976, 109) and for this reason was generally purchased only by the wealthier classes for presentation at banquets where a swan was 'favoured more for its looks than for its eating quality', according to Tannahill (1973, 224). The chopping observed in the swan coracoid from St Faith's Lane, which has sheared completely through the bone, might indeed indicate home butchering in preparation for cooking this particular bird. However, it is equally plausible that this is evidence that the wings of a swan captured and killed outside the town had been removed in preparation for transport as a source of feathers, making the bird remains craft-related waste as much as food waste.

*The fisheries supplying Norwich*
Modern anglers are familiar with the abundance of freshwater fish species present in the rivers in the Norwich area. Wilson (1978, 1406–7) stated that the River Wensum has roach, bream, large dace, perch, chub and pike 'in plenty', while below Norwich in the upper and lower reaches of the River Yare there are 'good stocks' of dace, roach, bream, perch and chub. It comes as a surprise therefore to note that in Late Saxon/early medieval times the inhabitants of Norwich do not appear to have fully exploited these abundant freshwater species, as indicated by the relative paucity of fish bone assemblages excavated elsewhere in the city at the Magistrates' Courts (Locker 1987), Fishergate (Locker 1994) and Alms Lane (Jones and Scott 1985) sites. St Faith's Lane provides further evidence for the predominance of marine over freshwater fish species in the Late Saxon–early medieval diet in Norwich.

A similar fish consumption pattern apparently prevailed throughout early and later medieval Britain and also in continental north-western Europe, where it has been suggested that the decline in freshwater fish in the diet may have coincided with a deterioration of riverine ecosystems. Such deterioration may have been due to overfishing, water pollution and destruction of freshwater habitats, all of which would have been especially pronounced in rivers associated with the more densely populated urban settlements (van Neer and Ervynck 1996, 160). In the case of Norwich, however, such ecological factors may not have been of great significance. Documentary sources indicate that there were still substantial numbers and a great variety of freshwater fish in the Wensum as late as the 13th–14th centuries (Jones and Scott 1985, 228). However, these same historical sources further indicate that such local fish stocks were not freely available to all the inhabitants of Norwich (*ibid.*). It is significant that fishing in the city was considered important enough to offer as a quantifiable gift in respect of the Dallingflete in 1405 (Kirkpatrick 1845, 115–17).

As a consequence of strict local laws controlling the fishing of rivers throughout Britain during the medieval period, access to and exploitation of freshwater fish stocks were usually vested in the hands of a few wealthy individuals, placing this food resource (with the notable exception of freshwater eels!) beyond the purchasing power of ordinary folk (Woolgar 2000, 39). The lowest strata of medieval urban society, however, would have been able to obtain affordable supplies of marine fishes, principally in the form of dried cod and salt herring — indeed, these items were often relatively cheaper than meat, especially before 1350 (Woolgar 2000). The proximity of the major fishing port of Great Yarmouth meant that preserved fish was readily available in the region and could be transported directly up river to Norwich. Supplies of herrings would have been especially abundant as Great Yarmouth had already become well established as the East Coast's premier herring fishery by the time of the Norman Conquest. It continued to prosper in this capacity until the mid-15th century when — faced with a severe loss in its home and overseas markets in the face of foreign competition (particularly from the Low Countries), as well as a harbour that was silting up — the industry experienced a marked decline. (Childs 2000, 21 and Locker 2001, 44 provide a more detailed discussion of this later history.) During the Late Saxon/early medieval period, however, the Great Yarmouth herring fishery was at its zenith, and this is reflected in the predominance of this species in the Phase 1 and 2 fish bone assemblages from St Faith's Lane.

Analysis of the herring remains from the site revealed the presence of cranial bone elements, indicating that these herring had been supplied in the form of complete fish with their heads still attached. This discovery fits well into our knowledge of the food-preservation techniques of that period, which in the case of herring simply involved salting of the whole (ungutted) fish (Wilson 1989, 23). It is of interest that the St Faith's Lane cod remains from both Phase 1 and Phase 2 also include cranial elements (Table 8); unlike in the case of the herring, however, their presence probably indicates that the fish were supplied fresh. Preservation of cod generally involved removal of the head in order that the body could be split lengthways for salting and drying: the presence of remains of processed/stored cod in archaeological assemblages would therefore be recognised from the absence of cranial bone elements (criterion of Perdikaris 1996). Given the proximity of Great Yarmouth to Norwich it would not seem unreasonable to accept that fresh cod could have been transported to the city overland or by river without spoilage becoming a significant problem.

The sea bass among the food refuse in Phase 2 could also have been supplied by the Great Yarmouth sea fishery or caught by baited line in the River Yare (either in its estuary or in its lower reaches). The geographical distribution of bass encompasses the southern waters of the North Sea as far north as Lincolnshire, particularly along the shoreline (where it especially favours shelving beaches of gravelly sand). In the summer months, however, this fish will ascend rivers for some distance, entering brackish and even nearly fresh water (Kennedy 1954, 85–6).

*Craft/industrial activities*

Hornworking
Apart from an isolated tine from pit *644* (Phase 2), which may be residual or redeposited material on account of its abraded/weathered appearance, there is a notable absence of sawn/offcut pieces of deer antler among the craft/industrial debris. Instead, hornworking waste predominates in both Phases 1 and 2. The total absence of evidence for antler-working from this part of Late Saxon/early medieval Norwich supports the suggestion by MacGregor (1989, 113) that from the late 10th century onward such crafts were rendered obsolete by urban craftspeople's increased distance from the rural resources which had been available more freely to their Early–Middle Saxon predecessors. The access to supplies of antler would have been disrupted by the extension in the forest laws governing the hunting/exploitation of deer, which under Norman rule became especially harsh and included blinding as a punishment for transgressors.

Craftsmen specializing in hornworking therefore took the place of the itinerant antler-workers who had played an important role in the Middle Saxon economy. They moved permanently into urban centres throughout Britain in order to exploit the increasing abundance of cattle and sheep horns made available by the slaughter of ever-increasing numbers of livestock required to feed rapidly growing urban populations. At St Faith's Lane excavated evidence of horn-working activity is provided by the presence in the faunal assemblages of chopped sheep horn cores, as well as sheep crania with their horn cores removed or chopped off. Features yielding this sort of evidence were of both Phase 1 (gullies *515* and *530*, pits *592*, *613* and *618*) and Phase 2 (pits *589*, *644*, *728*, *777* and *950*). It may be noted that one of the horn cores, in addition to exhibiting evidence of chopping at the base, was also sawn through transversely approximately half way along its length, providing evidence that the horn sheath had been cut up into sections whilst still attached to its core.

Evidence of hornworking activity using cattle horns is limited to context *278* (pit *644*, Phase 2) which yielded two horn cores chopped through the base, one identified as a juvenile castrate and the other an adult medium horned bull, and to context *568* (pit *861*, Phase 2) which yielded an isolated piece of sawn horn core of indeterminate age and sex.

Fletching
It may be highly significant that in contexts of both Phases 1 and 2 white-tailed eagles are represented exclusively by wing-bone elements (Tables 6 and 7). This situation parallels that found at many early medieval sites throughout western and central Europe, which has prompted the suggestion by Reichstein and Pieper (1986) that detached eagle wings were imported into medieval towns as sources of feathers for fletching arrows (*cf.* O'Connor 2000b, 78). Other sources of feathers for this purpose may have included the wings from swans and geese, both species that are also represented among the bird bones from St Faith's Lane. Presumably in Late Saxon/post-Conquest Norwich such an enterprise, which drew on resources outside the town, was carried out by established skilled craftsmen, rather than by ordinary townsfolk as an occasional domestic craft/'individual activity' in the home.

Boneworking
Hylton (above, p.34–40) has discussed the evidence for the working of animal bone.

## II. The charred and mineralised plant remains
by Wendy J. Carruthers

**Introduction**
Environmental samples were taken during excavation, primarily from pits, and were processed by Northamptonshire Archaeology staff using standard methods of flotation (using a 500-micron mesh for the flots and a minimum mesh of 1mm for the residues).

Thirteen samples from Phase 1 to Phase 3 features were previously assessed by the author (Carruthers in Soden 2000b). Residuality was a problem in many of the samples and some produced large amounts of charcoal but very few fruits and seeds. Therefore, following assessment full analysis was focussed on three Phase 2 pits which had produced well-preserved charred and mineralised plant remains. Reserve soil samples from some of these deposits were processed by Northamptonshire Archaeology staff and the additional flots and residues were sent to the author for analysis.

This report, therefore, discusses the results from analysing seven samples from three mid 11th–12th century pits, *473*, *504* and *644*. These features pre-date

| Sample no. | habitat | 25 | 9 | 20 | 24 | 26 | 27 | 28 |
|---|---|---|---|---|---|---|---|---|
| Context |  | 624 | 524 | 522 | 643 | 690 | 738 | 645 |
| Taxa  Feature |  | 473 |  | 504 |  |  | 644 |  |
| **Grain** |  |  |  |  |  |  |  |  |
| *Triticum aestivum*-type (bread-type wheat grain) | * | 5 |  | 8 |  |  |  |  |
| *Triticum* sp. (tetraploid-type wheat) | * | 2 |  |  |  |  |  |  |
| *Avena* sp. (wild/cultivated oat grain) | *A | 59 | 6 | 8 |  | 63 | 16 | 6 |
| *Cf. Avena* sp. (*cf.* oat grain) | *A | 5 |  |  | 1 |  |  |  |
| *Hordeum* sp. (hulled barley grain) | * | 28 | 3 | 1 |  | 61 |  | 3 |
| *Cf. Hordeum* sp. (cf. barley grain) | * |  |  |  | 1 |  |  |  |
| *Secale cereale* L. ( rye grain) | * | 2 | 1 | 3 |  | 1 | 1 |  |
| Indeterminate cereals | * | 65 | 11 | 18 |  |  | 5 |  |
| **Chaff** |  |  |  |  |  |  |  |  |
| *Hordeum* sp. (barley rachis frag.) | * | 3 | 1 |  |  |  |  |  |
| *Secale cereale* L. (rye rachis frag.) | * | 1 |  |  |  |  |  |  |
| Cereal-type culm nodes | * | 6 |  |  |  |  |  |  |
| **Weeds *etc.*** |  |  |  |  |  |  |  |  |
| *Urtica urens* L.(small nettle achene) | CD | 1 |  |  |  |  | [1] |  |
| *Corylus avellana* L. (hazelnut shell frags) | HSW* | 4 |  |  |  | 39 | 9 | 10 |
| *Chenopodium album* L. (fat-hen seed) | CDn | 1 |  | 4 |  |  |  |  |
| *Atriplex patula/prostrata* (orache seed) | CDn | 2 |  |  |  |  |  |  |
| Chenopodiaceae (embryo) | CD | 1 |  |  |  |  | [14] |  |
| *Agrostemma githago* L. (corn cockle seed) | A | 7 |  | 1 |  |  | 1[56] |  |
| *Stellaria media* (L.)Villars (common chickweed seed) | CDn | 2 |  |  |  |  |  |  |
| *Spergula arvensis* L. (corn spurrey seed) | Aas | 1 |  |  |  |  |  |  |
| *Cf. Persicaria maculosa* (*cf.* redshank achene) | Cwo |  |  |  |  |  |  |  |
| *Fallopia convolvulus* (L.) A.Love (black bindweed achene) | AD |  |  |  |  |  | 1 |  |
| *Rumex acetosella* L. (sheep's sorrel achene) | CEGas | 3 |  |  |  |  |  |  |
| *Rumex* sp. (dock achene) | wide | 4 |  |  |  |  | 2[8] |  |
| *Malva* sp. (mallow nutlet) | DY | 1 |  |  |  |  |  |  |
| *Brassica/Sinapis* sp. (charlock, mustard etc. seed) | CD* | 3 | 3 | [1] |  |  | [29] |  |
| *Raphanus raphanistrum* L. (wild radish capsule frag.) | CD | 1 |  |  |  |  |  |  |
| *Erica* sp./*Calluna vulgaris* (ericaceous fruit) | E |  | 13 |  |  |  |  |  |
| *Malus sylvestris/Pyrus communis* (apple/pear seed) | HSW* |  | 2 |  |  |  | [3] |  |
| *Prunus spinosa* L.(sloe stone) | HSW* |  |  |  |  |  |  | 1 |
| *Trifoilum /Lotus* sp. (clover/trefoil seed) | CDG | 3 |  |  |  |  |  |  |
| *Vicia faba var. minor* (broad bean) | * | 1 |  | 1 |  |  | 3 |  |
| *cf. V. faba* (*cf.* bean frag.) | *? |  | 2 |  |  |  |  |  |
| *cf. Pisum sativum* L.(cf. pea) | *? | 2 | 5 |  |  |  |  |  |
| *Vicia/Pisum* sp.(large legume frag., pea/bean) | *? | 7 | 3 | 1 |  |  |  |  |
| *Vicia/Lathyrus* sp. (small seeded vetch/tare) | CGY | 3 | 1 |  |  |  |  |  |
| Umbellifer *cf. Daucus carota* L. (*cf.* wild carrot mericarp) | DGc |  |  |  |  |  | [5] |  |
| *Galeopsis tetrahit* L. (common hemp nettle nutlet) | ADWod |  |  |  |  |  | [1] |  |
| *Sherardia arvensis* L. (field madder nutlet) | AD | 1 |  |  |  |  |  |  |
| *Galium aparine* L. (cleavers nutlet) | ACHSo |  |  |  |  | 1 |  |  |
| *Sambucus nigra* L.(elder seeds) | HSW* | <4> | <20> | <1> | <4> |  | <71> |  |
| *Centaurea cyanus* L.(cornflower achene) | AD | 1 |  |  |  |  |  |  |
| *Lapsana communis* L. (nipplewort achene) | DHWo |  |  | 1 |  |  |  |  |
| *Anthemis cotula* L. (stinking mayweed achene) | ADdh | 22 |  | 3 |  |  |  |  |
| *Tripleuropspermum inodorum* (L.)Schultz-Bip. (scentless mayweed achene) | CD |  |  | 1 |  |  |  |  |
| *Eleocharis* subg. *Palustres* (spike-rush nutlet) | MP | 5 | 1 | 2 |  |  |  |  |
| *Cladium mariscus* (L.)Pohl (great fen-sedge nut) | MPc | 2 | 1 |  |  |  |  |  |

| Sample no. | habitat | 25 | 9 | 20 | 24 | 26 | 27 | 28 |
|---|---|---|---|---|---|---|---|---|
| Context | | 624 | 524 | 522 | 643 | 690 | 738 | 645 |
| Taxa　　　　　Feature | | 473 | | 504 | | | 644 | |
| *Carex* sp. (sedge nut) | GMP | 6 | 1 | | | | | |
| Cyperaceae (indeterminate Cyperaceae nut) | GMP | 10 | 2 | | | | | |
| *Lolium temulentum* L. (darnel caryopsis) | AD | 15 | | | | | | |
| *Bromus* sect. *Bromus* (chess caryopsis) | ADG | 8 | 1 | | | | 2[25] | |
| Poaceae (grass caryopsis) | CDG | 18 | | 1 | | | [2] | |
| Poaceae (culm frag.) | CDG | 13 | | | | | [2] | |
| **Total** | | 328 | 77 | 54[1] | 6 | 165 | 111[146] | 20 |
| Sample volume (litres): | | 20 | 20 | 20 | 5 | 20 | 20 | 20 |
| Frags per litre: | | 16.4 | 3.9 | 2.8 | 1.2 | 8.3 | 12.9 | 1 |
| Charred Grain : Chaff : Weed seed ratio | | 17:1:12 | | 61:1:36 | | | 22:0:1 | |

Plant remains are charred apart from <> = uncharred [ ] = mineralised * = crop plant/edible; A = arable; C = cultivated; D = disturbed/waste; E = heath; G = grassland; H = hedgerow; M = marsh/fen; P = ponds/ditches/streams; S = scrub; W = woods; Y = waysides; a = acidic soils; c = calcareous/base-rich; d = damp; h = heavy; n = nutrient-rich; o = open; s = sandy

Table 12 Charred and mineralised plant remains

the use of the plot as a cemetery by the Franciscan Friary from *c.* 1291 onward, and probably pre-date 1226.

## Methods and Results

Because mineralised plant remains were observed in some of the flots, both the flots and residues were fully sorted under a microscope. The table below presents the results of the analysis. Nomenclature and most of the habitat information follow Stace 1991.

*Some notes on identification*

Two taxa are noteworthy from an archaeobotanical point of view. Two grains of wheat from pit *473* recorded as 'tetraploid-type' were long, narrow and deep-keeled, resembling spelt wheat. Spelt is occasionally found in small amounts in medieval samples but is generally considered to have been replaced by free-threshing bread-type wheats by the Middle Saxon period at the latest. Many of these occasional records of spelt in medieval contexts may be due to residuality, and this could be a possibility for the St Faith's Lane grains since some Romano-British residual material was present on the site. However, a waterlogged spelt spikelet was recovered from a medieval deposit at Fishergate (Murphy 1994), so it is possible that relict plants survived in some fields. The other possibility is that the grain was from a free-threshing tetraploid wheat such as rivet (*Triticum turgidum*). These grains tend to be deep-keeled and more oval than bread-type wheat, but grain morphology is too variable to provide a definite identification. Free-threshing tetraploid wheats are increasingly being recorded from medieval sites across Britain (Moffett 1991). However, they are not commonly recovered from archaeobotanical samples from Norwich (Peter Murphy, *pers. comm.*). Since no rachis fragments or glume bases were recovered to confirm the identification of these grains, they have simply been recorded as 'tetraploid-type wheat'.

The second taxon of note is broad bean, *Vicia faba*. Although two well-preserved beans from pits *473* and *644* were of the cylindrical shape, usually identified as field bean or Celtic bean (*V. faba* var. minor), they were particularly large specimens according to the author's past experience (11.6mm x 6.9mm and 9.1mm x 6.0mm, respectively). The evolution of broad beans into the large, flattened form that is grown today is not fully understood, with no clear genetic differences being present between the varieties (Simmonds 1976). Medieval *V. faba* are usually of the field bean type, and it is likely that these were two particularly large beans from *V. faba* var. minor.

## Discussion

The seven samples from the three features examined during this analysis produced fairly high concentrations of charred and mineralised (mainly in sample 27, context *738*, pit *644*) plant remains. Uncharred elderberry (*Sambucus nigra*) seeds were recovered from five of the samples and may be contemporary with the deposits rather than being contaminants. The tough seed coats of this taxon can survive for centuries, even in aerobic soils. Uncharred elder seeds have been recovered from many other sites excavated in Norwich.

The three features were all 11th–12th century pits (Phase 2) which are thought to have been dug in the backyards of buildings fronting the lane. The plant assemblages from the pits are likely, therefore, to provide information about the occupants of this plot.

**Pit *644***

The most northerly pit, *644*, was the largest, deepest and most complex of the features (Fig. 7). The three samples examined for this study came from the lowest level excavated, *738*, and from two layers higher up the soil profile. Context *738*, although possibly not the primary fill, was the lowest layer that it was safe to excavate. It was rich in mineralised plant remains, fish bones, slag and charcoal. The recovery of mineralised plant remains and fish bones in this type of context usually suggests that faecal waste had been deposited in the feature. The principal taxon in the mineralised assemblage, however, was not an edible species but the toxic arable weed corn cockle (*Agrostemma githago*, 56 seeds). These were primarily whole seeds rather than fragments, suggesting that they had not been ground into flour and consumed accidentally. The only edible remains recovered from this deposit were three mineralised embryos from apple/pear seeds (*Malus sylvestris*/*Pyrus communis*) and 29 seeds from a species that may have been used as a flavouring or may alternatively have been a weed, *Brassica*/*Sinapis* sp. (includes mustard, charlock, cabbage, etc.). *Brassica*/*Sinapis* sp. seeds are very common and often very frequent in mineralised seed assemblages, suggesting that they are readily mineralised, but corn cockle seeds are less common. No concretions containing cereal bran fragments were recovered, as are usually frequent in cesspit-type deposits. The other mineralised seeds were common ruderal/segetal weeds such as dock (*Rumex* sp.) and chess (*Bromus* sect. *Bromus*). A few charred oats grains (*Avena* sp.), a rye grain (*Secale cereale*), three broad beans (*Vicia faba var. minor*), hazelnut shell fragments (*Corylus avellana*) and a few charred weed seeds were also recovered.

Since other types of waste such as fish bones, slag and charcoal were frequent in this deposit, it is possible that the corn cockle seeds were derived from mixed domestic waste that had been thrown onto a midden, rather than human faeces or dung. The fact that mineralisation (calcium phosphate replacement) had taken place, however, is indicative of the highly organic, moist nature of the waste in which the seeds were preserved (Green 1979; Carruthers 2000a).

The large black seeds of corn cockle must be hand-picked from a cereal crop, as they are a similar size and weight to the grain and so cannot be sieved or winnowed out. Corn cockle appears to have been a problematic weed during the medieval period, particularly in rye crops. Contamination levels exceeding *c.* 0.5% in bread or gruel are said to have a debilitating effect on the consumer (Wilson 1975) and to make them more susceptible to leprosy. Chronic or rapid poisoning of livestock resulting in death can occur if they are fed with contaminated grain or screenings. It is unlikely therefore that the remains represent crop-processing waste that had been fed to livestock and became mineralised in a dung heap.

The other two samples, from layers higher up the fill profile, produced lower concentrations of remains (1 fragment per litre (fpl) and 8.3 fpl compared with 12.9 fpl). Deposit *645* was greenish in colour, which usually indicates the presence of cess. This sandy layer produced a few charred oats, barley, hazelnut shell fragments and a sloe stone, whilst the assemblage from a few layers above (context *690*) consisted primarily of charred oats, barley and fragments of hazelnut shell.

The overall ratio of cereal grains to chaff fragments to arable weed seeds was 22:0:1, suggesting that the charred assemblages consisted of cleaned grain. Crop-processing waste is usually scarce on medieval urban sites, presumably because cereals would have been processed closer to the point of cultivation and brought into town as cleaned crops. Some hand-picking of noxious weed seeds may have been done at home whilst preparing the grain for human consumption, hence the presence of the mineralised corn cockle seeds in this feature. Charring may have occurred whilst drying the grain prior to grinding, or through the burning of animal bedding, floor sweepings and other domestic waste.

**Pit *473***

This sample came from the middle layer (*624*) of a *c.* 1.4m-diameter, circular pit (Fig. 8, Section 4). This sample produced the highest density of charred plant remains (16.4 fpl) and the highest ratio of chaff and arable/cultivation weed seeds to grain (G:Ch:W = 17:1:12). It is clear that crop-processing waste was present in this sample, since the weed seeds were almost as frequent as the cereal grains. Chaff fragments are never very numerous in free-threshing cereal assemblages for the reason given above and because differential preservation brought about by charring favours cereal grains as opposed to chaff (Boardman and Jones 1990).

The predominant cereal in this sample was again oats (*Avena* sp.). Although no well preserved oat florets were recovered to confirm the presence of cultivated (as opposed to wild) oats, the dominance of oats in six out of seven samples makes clear that cultivated oats were being used by the occupants of this site. Oats are a high-energy cereal that has long been valued as a fodder crop for draught animals. Their frequent occurrence with barley (another fodder crop) in these samples could indicate the disposal of burnt waste fodder and animal bedding in these pits, rather than human domestic waste. However, Peter Murphy (*pers. comm.*) has found that oats and barley usually predominate in charred assemblages from medieval Norwich. This is probably due to the use of whole grains for malting. There is evidence for oats being used for malting in the 11th century (Murphy in Shepherd Popescu forthcoming) with a shift to barley later. Wheat and rye would mainly have been consumed as bread and other products made out of flour, so whole grains would have been less likely to be burnt in urban sites. A few rye and bread-type wheat grains were present in this sample but the ratio of oats:barley:wheat:rye was 32:14:4:1. A bean, a few possible peas and hazelnut shell were the only other charred remains of food plants.

The arable weeds were typical of the period, including corn cockle (*Agrostemma githago*), cornflower (*Centaurea cyanus*) and darnel (*Lolium temulentum*). The frequent occurrence of stinking mayweed achenes (*Anthemis cotula*) suggests that heavy damp soils were being cultivated, and the recovery of corn spurrey (*Spergula arvensis*) is evidence for the acidity of the local sandy soils. Very similar ranges of weed seeds have been recovered from other sites in Norwich (Murphy 1983, 1985, 1991, 1994).

Cereal straw is usually one of the first materials to be lost on combustion (Boardman and Jones 1990) but six large cereal-sized culm nodes ('joints' in the straw) were present in this sample. In addition, the number of wetland plant remains was relatively high, including spike-rush (*Eleocharis* subg. *Palustres*), great fen-sedge (*Cladium mariscus*) and sedges (*Carex* sp. and other *Cyperaceae*). Charred grass-type stem fragments were also recovered. This suggests that burnt animal bedding and fodder, including hay cut from wet meadows, had been deposited in this feature.

**Pit *504***

Three samples from the middle and upper levels of this *c.* 1.6m-diameter, deep circular pit were examined (*643*, *524* and *522*: Fig. 8, Section 5). They produced fairly low concentrations (1.2–3.0 fpl) of charred plant remains in the ratio of 61:1:36 cereal grains:chaff:weed seeds. Oats were again dominant, although bread-type wheat grains were the next most frequent cereal. However, only 61 cereal grains in total were recovered, so the results are not very significant.

Two charred apple pips (*Malus sylvestris*) and a few possible broad beans and peas were present in one of the upper levels of the pit, suggesting that burnt domestic waste had been deposited. This sample also produced several wetland plant seeds and thirteen ericaceous fruits (heather or ling, *Calluna vulgaris/Erica* sp.), indicating the burning of hay from wet meadows and vegetation gathered from heathland. Murphy has recovered charred heathland remains from a number of sites in Norwich and suggests that fuel was probably collected from nearby Mousehold Heath overlooking Norwich (Peter Murphy, *pers. comm.*). Heather is a useful fuel for industrial purposes because of the high temperature at which it burns. The presence of large quantities of charcoal and slag in many of the pits on this site suggests that industrial activities were taking place locally.

## Comparisons with other sites and conclusions

Norwich has produced a wide range of archaeobotanical information relating to settlement during the Saxon and medieval periods. Waterlogged, mineralised and charred plant remains have been examined by Peter Murphy over the last two decades, providing information about diet, agriculture, trade and the environment (Murphy 1983, 1985, 1991, 1994). The charred and mineralised plant remains from St Faith's Lane fit well with the overall picture for the Norwich environment during the 11th–13th centuries, and add more specific information regarding the range of activities taking place behind the street frontage.

One very notable feature of the charred cereal assemblages from Norwich is the predominance of oats and barley in many of the samples. Reasons for this have been given by Murphy in various publications and have been referred to above. There was no evidence from this site that the fairly small quantities of oats, barley or other cereals had been used for malting, *i.e.* no sprouted grains were present. However, if these crops were being brought into the town in large quantities as whole grain for malting, they would also have been freely available at market for use as animal fodder in the backyards of the properties on St Faith's Lane. Armitage (above) has suggested that the faunal assemblages from the site are indicative of backyard farming activities.

Armitage also notes that the range of meat resources used by the occupants was quite narrow, with very few wild game and wildfowl being consumed. Fish were predominantly marine rather than freshwater, again possibly reflecting the lower status of the inhabitants of St Faith's Lane. Although it is not clear whether human faecal remains were preserved in pit *644*, no evidence for imported exotic food plants was recovered from these samples. In the experience of the author, the plant foods represented are more typical of a rural or 'low-status' diet than an urban one, with legumes and wild fruits such as apples and hazelnuts appearing to be of some importance alongside cereal-based foods. It should be noted that the apple seeds could have come from orchard-grown fruits, since the seeds of cultivated and wild apples cannot be told apart.

The three features studied in depth produced evidence for the use of damp meadow hay and heathland vegetation for fodder, bedding and fuel. Both resources would have been available fairly locally, with Mousehold Heath overlooking the town and the River Wensum flowing close to the site. Evidence for the use of heathland vegetation for fuel and/or floor covering has been recovered from other medieval sites in Norwich, *e.g.* Calvert Street (Murphy 1991). Murphy has also provided evidence that the valley floor of the River Wensum provided a habitat for wetland vegetation such as open reedswamp and meadows. However, conditions at the nearby site at Fishergate (Murphy 1994) were much drier by the 10th century and during the 10th–11th centuries large-scale dumping of organic refuse took place there.

In conclusion, activities represented by the burnt and mineralised waste deposited in the three pits may be summarised as follows:

- industrial processes (slag, frequent charcoal and fuel plants such as heather);
- crop-processing and hand picking of cereal contaminants prior to cooking (charred crop processing waste, mineralised corn cockle seeds);
- the deposition of highly organic and burnt household waste (charred and mineralised food plants, fodder and bedding).

The crop-processing waste may have been used as a fuel or fed to livestock. It is uncertain whether human faecal material was deposited in pit *644* or the remains had become preserved in a midden-type deposit. It is also uncertain what proportion of the charred cereal remains was from animal bedding/fodder and how much had originally been destined for human consumption. The plant and bone evidence, however, support the suggestion that backyard farming was taking place.

# 6. Discussion

## I. Pre-Friary

**Street origins and street/plot layout**
The area of the excavation was clearly occupied as early as the 10th century, although no more specific date may be established. Occupation in the vicinity may go back earlier, as attested by a notable copper alloy buckle plate and frame found in the evaluation works (Emery 1997). Attention should also be drawn to the relatively large quantity of Ipswich ware from the site (twenty-one sherds) which, together with three hand-made Saxon sherds, may indicate occupation in the area in the 9th century. As so often the case in Norwich, however, this material was all residual in later features.

St Faith's Lane has long been thought to have origins in the Late Saxon period, but recent reconstructions of this early phase have been unclear about its precise course (see Emery 2007). The present discoveries imply not only that this end of the street was in existence by the 10th century, but that it had already adopted the course which survives today: the early buildings appear to align and relate exactly to the carriageway. This accords well with the broadly rectilinear street plan that is thought to have existed in Late Saxon Norwich within an area between King Street to the west and a putative road alignment 200m to the east (Emery 2007, fig. 2.24). Excavations to the south-east at the Mann Egerton site found a north–south and an east–west road, both thought to be minor elements of this gridded street plan, but which were closed in the 13th century as part of the development of the friary (*ibid.*, 36–9). The track found on the current site was located on a similar alignment to the north–south lane, but was a new creation of the 14th century, intended to serve a specific and unrelated purpose.

It has been rightly pointed out that the noxious character of iron smelting meant that such industrial areas were located at the edge of settlement (Atkin 1985, 3). To this may be added the very real risk of fire, especially in towns where thatch was ubiquitous and wooden shingles a precursor of tile. It has been suggested that the increasing pressure for space for a growing population pushed such undesirable industries increasingly further outwards (Atkin 1985, 3; Atkin *et al.* 1983, 96). In this case, however, the industry seems not to have been widespread but was composed of specialist craftsmen: the iron industry of St Faith's Lane might be considered as tucked away from the public focus but not on the fringes of the 10th-century settlement. Specialist smiths congregating within other towns during this period, as at York (Ottaway 1992), and a similar grouping in Norwich may be indicated by the evidence of more widespread metalworking from the Mann Egerton site nearby (Emery 2007). Metalworkers of all sorts may have gathered together to share resources and expertise, but also to keep out of other people's way. As the Phase 2 remains do not include metalworking, it may be that commercial activity such as metalworking suffered a general decline in the years following the Conquest, or that, given that the area was opposite the newly created Cathedral Close, such industries were moved away. The new regime may also have made continued trade on the old terms unviable. Some artisans may have found trade restricted or curtailed.

Too little evidence survived to permit estimation of the size of the 10th–12th century plot with any certainty. It is only in Phase 2 that some signs of demarcation appear. The surviving features indicate a conjectural plot about 20m deep and 18m wide (*c.* 66 x 59 feet) if the entrance-gap in the southern boundary ditches lay at the midpoint of the rear boundary. The extent of pit digging makes the identification of plot alignments almost impossible at the eastern end of the site, beyond which disturbance intensifies as suggested by previous archaeological evaluation (Emery 1997). However, extensive documentary research undertaken for the Mann Egerton site suggests that the plots ran from east to west backing onto the dog-leg, giving plots *c.* 45m deep and 22m wide (Emery 2007, 39–40).

The development of the Franciscan Friary effectively formalised the alignment of the existing frontage, although the buildings that stood here had probably already gone. Certainly any plot subdivision was swept away in the creation of the cemetery: with the construction of the substantial precinct boundary wall, probably early in the 16th century, the buried foundations and features of the former street-facing wall were lost. What survived into the post-medieval, post-Reformation world was therefore essentially monastic, with the line of the street being the sole survivor of an earlier age. This persists today, little changed from the 16th century and perhaps an approximation of the alignment of the 10th century.

**Cultural exchange and trade**
The site in the pre-Conquest period has a paucity of distinctive finds to indicate anything other than a broad similarity with many other sites in the city, with a pottery assemblage dominated by Thetford-type ware and a range of imported wares. In common with many other places in East Anglia and the East Midlands, there is little or nothing in the archaeological record at the site to attest to the ebb and flow of specifically Anglo-Saxon or Danish fortunes. As at other Norwich sites, the pottery indicates a strong pre-Conquest connection with France and the Low Countries — a relationship that grew from proximity and endured throughout the medieval period. The continental link would have been strengthened after 1066 through the Norman royal presence and the importation of Caen Stone, probably brought up-river by barge just as Barnack Stone from Northamptonshire was ferried eastwards to Peterborough, Ely and Bury St Edmunds (Jenkins 1993). Even at times when Danish influence is thought to have been stronger, this 10th–11th century east–west trade corridor is discernible in materials and products in the archaeological record as far inland as Northampton (Soden 2000a, 115). The start of construction of both a castle and a cathedral in Norwich, within a generation of each other, would only serve to strengthen links to France by sea.

Visible links with the wider hinterland, indicated by pottery in particular, are limited in the early periods by the small range of production centres that existed. What the local Thetford-type ware potters could not provide had to be sought elsewhere and initially in the Late Saxon period there were only Ipswich, Stamford and St Neots as alternatives. They are all represented in the archaeological record here. Little pottery deposition took place in the subsequent cemetery and later medieval regional imports to the site are confined to very small quantities of London-type ware, Cambridge Sgraffito ware and Scarborough ware (probably an import via Lynn or Yarmouth). The Franciscans had a major network of movement between urban houses but there may have been little need for many imports if their needs were catered for locally.

In ceramic terms, the St Faith's Lane site indicates Norwich's self-sufficiency within its region, with few links westward beyond the area of Stamford. Foreign imports are probably a straightforward but significant by-product of sustained overseas contact, rather than indicating any cosmopolitan affectations (Blinkhorn, Chapter 4, p.32). Norwich, with its insular location, looked largely to its own provision from local sources and augmented its material culture by imported luxuries, primarily through its relatively accessible coastal neighbours. This is consistent with the known origins of pottery published from the Norwich Survey (Jennings 1981).

The growing fishing industry was clearly a source of regular contact with the coast and beyond. Boats loaded with processed catches may have carried other goods from the ports where they had been landed, as was the case in early post-medieval Boston (Hinton 1956). There should be no presumption that the deep sea fisheries exploited were close to the Norfolk coast, not least because the predominant herring stocks are migratory. At some times of the year fleets would have to drop their nets throughout the North Sea as far as the southern tip of Norway. At other times the shoals would be beyond range, leading to a seasonal reliance even near the coast upon salted or smoked fish which was not just a matter of short-term fish preservation. Extreme winter weather at sea also would have limited the sailing season. Thus for much of the year foreign ports extending from Norway to France would have been as necessary a group of havens for Norfolk fishermen as their home ports. The late 12th-century town of Bergen was said to be awash with salt fish and the port crowded with Danes, Swedes, Germans, English, Irish and Greenlanders (Carus-Wilson 1962–3, 190). Such regular contact would have produced noticeable exchange. The trade in fish from Norfolk was probably imported far inland in large quantities, salted or smoked, but it is uncertain if Norwich directly engaged in extensive trade.

Any pastoral relationship with Norfolk's rural hinterland in the early period is hard to gauge from the assemblages. Bird bones, while indicating an unsurprising range of species available at table, do not point to widespread urban exploitation of the wetlands of East Anglia. Possibly the rural fowlers could only supply a purely local demand because of limits to the numbers they could catch by available means; alternatively there may have been tenurial limits to fowling activities on lands controlled by pre- or post-Conquest feudal lords. Any difficulty of terrain in getting stock to market while fresh would have been negated by the fact that such birds were generally imported live. As it is, the range of birds consumed seems actually less than some significant excavated town sites with a royal presence much further inland, such as Coventry and Northampton. A reduced availability of such goods in the marketplace may be the result of changes in the status of landowners and increased control over the resources of the land by the wealthy (Locock 2000; Soden 2000a, 117). Some kind of restricted access to natural resources could also explain the low incidence of certain small-scale industries in Norwich, such as antler-working, which is considered to reflect an increasing gulf between town and country (Armitage, above p.45, after MacGregor 1989, 113). Such division would have been given permanence by Norman foresting laws. The evidence for small-scale antler-working on the Mann Egerton site elsewhere in the Greyfriars precinct, however, warns of the dangers of too generalised a view (Emery 2007, 43–4).

Analysis of the archaeobotanical remains also emphasises local provisioning, as seen on other Norwich sites (Carruthers, above p.49). The limited range of seed types suggests fairly low-status occupation during the early medieval period and it seems again that access to land and the variety of goods that it produces — the mark of true wealth — was strictly limited.

**Industry and craft**

In the Saxo-Norman period (Phase 1) the site was clearly linked to a metalworking industry, probably in an adjacent house-plot. It is not certain if the excavated buildings were connected directly with that process but the nature of the iron slag suggests that the furnaces were within metres of the excavated area. However, there were no finds of bar iron, scrap, blanks, or smithing tools comparable with those from metalworking tenements in 10th-century Coppergate, York (Ottaway 1992) and the range of finds gives no indication of what was being made. The high fluidity of the slag suggests that high-temperature operations were being carried out, possibly welding. An unstratified crucible fragment may indicate that copper was also worked nearby.

The presence of detached horn cores and sawn-off horn stumps in the pre-Friary phases indicates other craftwork but no finished items survive. It is possible that bone- and hornworking was linked with the iron industry to supply handles for tools and implements, or that the products were used in other ways. Theophilus, writing in the 12th century, describes how iron tools can be hardened into steel by sprinkling them with a mixture of burnt oxhorn and salt before heating to redness (Geddes 1991, 173); other animal products might have been similarly used.

The wing feathers of white-tailed eagles could have been used for fletching arrows, perhaps together with those from swans and geese (Armitage, above p.45). Both of these latter species would also have yielded perfectly acceptable meat.

The occurrence of parts of three separate Late Saxon or early medieval balances, albeit unstratified or as residual finds in cemetery contexts, adds weight to the evidence from the nearby Mann Egerton site that precious metals were worked in some parts of the area subsequently occupied by the Greyfriars precinct (Emery 2007, 42–3). These finds might indicate that assay or quality control of some kind took place at the site.

**Domestic arrangements: change and decay**
The structural remains of Phases 1 and 2 were truncated by the later use of the site as a cemetery and artefactual evidence of the early occupation was limited to refuse pits within pits. Since no floors survived the specific uses to which buildings, or parts of buildings, were put cannot be ascertained. It seems clear, however, that a number of industries or craft activities were pursued from these premises over a period of up to 200 years. The domestic debris suggests that the occupants were a family unit: a spindle-whorl and a pin-beater betoken the traditionally female activity of small-scale textile manufacture, while the bull-roarer and flute could reflect the presence of children.

There is little in the food bone to indicate changing patterns of meat consumption from Phase 1 to Phase 2, suggesting that the status of the occupants remained largely unchanged over a period of 300 years, despite the ending of the site's industrial function at the end of the Saxon period. Such stability might be the result of the nature of the site, which might have seemed almost incapable of any form of gentrification. What had been a noisome backstreet then looked out onto the fledgling Benedictine precinct, in a quarter soon to be dominated by the nearby castle. Its appeal, therefore, might have been limited to those who were prepared to inhabit the old properties despite the disadvantages of their location. The wealthy in medieval society were increasingly encouraged to display their riches by moving to more fashionable areas, such as the former settlement and burgeoning mercantile suburb of Conesford (King Street). For a location such as St Faith's Lane, such a situation was a prescription for, at best, 'like for like' redevelopment, at worst, for stagnation. The lowly status of the properties on St Faith's Lane throughout Phase 2 seems confirmed by the archaeobotanical evidence for backyard farming, with its emphasis on exploitation of a limited range of resources for food, bedding, fodder and fuel (Carruthers, above p.49).

The demise of the buildings in Phase 2 seems to have taken place long before the construction of the Franciscan Friary precinct. Indeed, there is no artefactual indication that the buildings, and even previous levels of occupation, survived into the 13th century. By this later date, the level of pit-digging had fallen away quite markedly. This is in keeping with the situation observed at the Mann Egerton site (Emery 2007).

The reason for final abandonment is unclear. Dr Margot Tillyard (*pers. comm.*) considers that the area became generally run down, as denoted by documentary evidence for wider depopulation and abandonment (*cf.* Emery 2007, 11). This may have been precipitated by the Norman marginalisation of Tombland and the relocation of the marketplace to its present, more distant, position (Andy Hutcheson, *pers. comm.*). In addition, unrest in 1136, 1174 and 1216 may have contributed to swathes of the city becoming disadvantaged to the point of failure (Campbell 1975, 9). It is possible therefore that the plot, once deprived of its Phase 1 industrial base, was simply no longer attractive to stable, long-term occupancy.

Whatever the reality, the Franciscans inherited a less than desirable site. This may have been a deliberate acquisition on their part, helping them to augment their precinct in the only way their Rule allowed (by the addition of contiguous plots). Alternatively, it may have been a gift of dubious value, bestowed upon the only recipients who could make good use of it at the time.

## II. The Franciscan Friary

**Church-planting and expansion**
The arrival of the Franciscans was greeted with acclaim by an English populace hungry for religious and monastic reform. The popularity of the Greyfriars was immediate and lasting. However, in establishment circles the welcome was at best guarded — at worst the friars were treated with open hostility in numerous urban centres, where they came up against the previously unchallenged Benedictines, giving rise to some very uncomplimentary responses by such as Florence of Worcester (Thorpe 1848).

The spread of the Franciscan Rule in England was rapid, aided by their fresh, inclusive appeal and their overtly mendicant lifestyle. Their vows of poverty were seen to be far closer to the monastic ideal than the complacency in the old orders of black monks who sat at the head of wealthy estates and businesses, and whose worship in ostentatious luxury and unholy lifestyles were harangued from *c.* 1124 by St Bernard of Clairvaux (Migne 1849–55 vol 182, 914–16) — though to little avail. There had long been room for a monastic wind of change. It has been remarked that the mendicant orders 'were responsible for perhaps the last really distinctive and decisive transformation of the traditional institutional and ideological patterns of church and town in late medieval England' (Dobson 1984, 110). It is therefore regrettable that 'no source at all exists to tell us in any detail how most of the friars of medieval England actually spent their time, let alone what was uppermost in their minds' (*ibid.*).

The likely circumstances of the Franciscans' acquisition of this part of their precinct fit into one of three patterns observed previously across the country (Butler 1984, 123; 1993, 80):

- acquisition by gift of 'rejected' premises in otherwise densely occupied towns (such as here at Norwich);
- settlement on open ground (often by communities overtly in need of help);
- piecemeal acquisitions by gift or purchases.

It is certain that the new friaries as foundations benefited from an atmosphere of dissipating goodwill towards the old orders, combined with a thirst for the kinds of ideas the mendicants espoused. The friars took Christ's Great Commission to 'make disciples of all nations' (*Matthew* 28, 19–20) quite literally. The Franciscan passion for preaching was, however, yet another subject for debate and disagreement and their sermons were seized upon as examples of poor teaching by various angry cathedral authorities across England, who felt that their influence was set to be undermined. They continued to press their carping criticism at every turn despite the clear knowledge that such open disunity harmed the whole Church and ran counter to biblical teaching (*1 Corinthians* 12; *Colossians* 3, 12–17). This attitude also flew in the face of Papal endorsement of Norwich Greyfriars as a place of learning (Tanner 1984, 11).

As the friaries grew and became, inevitably, urban institutions with complicated interactions within a network of friaries, the Franciscan Order in particular developed a reputation as one given to learning. Norwich was a prime example of such specialisation and became a study centre for the Order, housing many foreign visitors (Hale and Rogers 1991, 17–18). The *studium* or pre-university college at the Norwich Greyfriars was one of seven in England whose status was ratified by an ordinance of Pope Benedict XII in 1336 (Tanner 1984, 34). In fact, the school at Norwich had been in operation since as early as 1250, upon a transfer from the Cambridge *studium* which served the Cambridge Custody or administrative region that included the Norwich house (Doucet 1953, 86 and n2; *cf.* Roest 2000, 23 and 72, n245). The quality of teaching became such that it attracted novice friars from all over Europe prior to their ordination as 'Friars of Norwich' (Doucet 1953, 34–5) and its popularity continued until the Dissolution. As well as a set curriculum there seems to have been a practice of mentoring, as shown by a letter in 1460 from the well-known and politically aware Friar Brackley (d. 1467) to Sir John Paston I (1421–1466), in which he details an unknown young friar's pupilage which continued through the ill-health of his own declining years (*ibid.*, 34).

During the later 15th century the Norwich school became entitled to receive lectorate students from all order provinces (Roest 2000, 40–1, n145). The school did not officially bestow degrees: this role was left to the nearby Cambridge house with its *studium universitarium*, described by Doucet as an '*ecole universitaire*' linked to the University (Doucet 1953, 86). However, it is difficult to see how the Norwich school could have gained its international reputation if it was not able to grant degree honours. Within each Franciscan Custody young friars might be taught courses in the arts by the best *lectores*, such as Adam Wodeham and Ralph Pigaz who were at Norwich in the 1320s (Roest 2000, 71–3). Later teachers included Roger Roseth, Haverel, and Bartholomew de Repps (from Cambridge after 1332–3), as attested by Nicholas of Assisi who was a student in 1337–8 (Doucet 1953, 88, 95). Another student of that year, Adam Hely (d'Ely) went on to become master of the Cambridge *studium* in 1346–7 (Doucet 1953, 92). Such eminent scholars may have benefitted from a library of secular sciences at Norwich — a rare distinction possibly only shared by Oxford and Cambridge (Roest 2000, 214).

**Burial rights and rites: the dead of the cemetery**
The excavated part of the Friary cemetery constitutes an archaeologically significant, but ultimately unknown, proportion of the burials made by 1538. Subsequent redevelopment, particularly in the later 19th to mid-20th centuries, means that the original resource has been denuded to an unknown degree and only the eastern limit of burials can be certainly identified. Apocryphal tales of the discovery of bones during building works and other better documented disturbances may relate to gaps in the area excavated, or to areas further west (Emery 1997; Emery 2007, table 1). The land rises westward towards Upper King Street, and the blanket of overburden and made ground that once existed here has been severely truncated by extant buildings. Examination of levels across the area suggests that the westernmost line of excavated burials probably marks the furthest westerly extent that is likely to have survived later destruction. To the north the former Friary precinct wall and the carriageway of St Faiths Lane, together with an earlier boundary, indicate the natural edge of any possible cemetery, while to the south the extent of the cemetery was probably defined by the southern boundary wall of the site, a feature known to be in existence by the 17th century but which also contained medieval material (see Emery 2007, 49–53). Any demographic conclusions drawn from the skeletons must be qualified by this knowledge.

The presence of seventy-six males among the ninety-two adult skeletons recorded, and an unusually high proportion of juveniles aged *c.* 8–20 years (one third of the total), may indicate that this was a specifically monastic cemetery. Given the background of a Franciscan community, lay benefactors and an international *studium*, it might be expected that burials of scholars (in medieval terms not solely children) would predominate. The low number of females and an absence of children under *c.* 8 years of age otherwise requires explanation since both should be highly represented in an open, 'unrestricted' cemetery. Segregation of different kinds of interment within a larger cemetery seems unlikely, because the assemblage does not conform rigidly to any specific criteria of age or sex. The burials were not solely of juveniles, nor solely of males (Figs 10 and 11). Similarly, there is no evidence of segregation of adult from juvenile, or male from female, in the distribution of excavated graves. The cemetery merely seems to have an unusual age and sex bias but without any focal groupings based on either.

Previous research, based upon the survival of eight wills (Emery 1997), has suggested a bias towards the burial of richer, more prominent members of society. This, however, is felt to be an erroneous premise since documented requests for burial are biased towards intramural interment, a preferred site for richer members of society. The burial rites afforded the individuals in the cemetery indicate no special rites that can be attributed to specific Franciscan custom. Apart from a few instances of post-mortem acts of penance, in the form of the mouth being packed with ash, there is nothing in the archaeological record to indicate the status of particular individuals.

The conflict between the Greyfriars and Norwich Cathedral has been highlighted. One of the reasons for this has often been stated as the struggle for burial fees, which were traditionally claimed by the parish church: in many Norwich parishes, the Cathedral was the parish patron. Tanner (1984, 12) considers the struggle to have been in part justified, since between 1370 and 1517 the numbers of lay testators requesting burial in any of the friaries (not merely Greyfriars) remained fairly constant at around 10%. It fell sharply from 1518 to around 4%. A similar drop occurred in testamentary bequests as support faltered on the eve of the Dissolution. He concedes that the testators were drawn disproportionately from the upper echelons of Norwich society, but balances this by stating that 'the paucity of wills known to have been made by members of the lower ranks of society in Norwich makes it impossible to draw meaningful comparisons between the rich and poor regarding their choice of place for burial' (Tanner 1984, 12).

There is an obvious reason for the lack of wills amongst the poorer classes. It is clear that bequeathing a range of gifts to a variety of churches and monastic institutions was a normal mortuary practice for the truly wealthy. In the words of Daniell (1997, 32–4): 'It has been suggested that the primary function of the will may have been to pass on property. The will itself was not given much spiritual efficacy, but acted as a sign of the testator's willingness to pass on property and goods and sever links with the material world.' If one owned very little, therefore, there was very little to pass on, so there was no point in making a will. Concerning the Norwich Greyfriars in particular, there were thirty-nine lay and two clerical requests for burial out of 1804 wills examined, being those from the period 1370 to 1532, making a total of only 2.27% (Tanner 1984, 189).

Friar John Brackley may have played a part in securing particular bequests from richer citizens in the middle of the 15th century when he was named as executor in various wills, despite a clear Franciscan directive against friars acting in this capacity. He went on to influence Sir John Fastolf to favour his patron and friend John Paston I. Others followed, strengthening family ties of patronage by asking for burial in the Greyfriars church (Tanner 1984, 15). Many more people are known to have left small mortuary gifts to monasteries or friaries — often a raft of such gifts to each order locally, and sometimes stating *cum corpore meo sepeliendo* (with my body for burial). This was slightly higher in Norwich (44–47%) than at York (33%) or London (36%). Elsewhere — at Coventry, for example — the friaries, and in particular the Franciscans attracted regular bequests (Fretton 1882). In Norwich a total of forty-six lay and forty-four clerical testamentary bequests were made to the Franciscans between 1370 and 1532, out of 904 wills where other monastic beneficiaries are also recorded (Tanner 1984, 222–3). Any pattern which might be discernible may be distorted by a movement in the early 15th century away from funereal pomp and ceremony, even amongst the upper classes, perhaps under the influence of Lollardy (Daniell 1997, 51). The simplest of graves might therefore be expected generally, regardless of the status of the interred

At any time in the medieval period burial in an open cemetery was less sought after than inside a church, despite the latter being discouraged by the Papacy: between 1370 and 1378 Pope Gregory XI tried to ban it (Litten 1992, 199). There was, however, an unwritten concentric hierarchy of burial places emanating from the high altar, with the furthest reaches of the churchyard being the least important (Daniell 1997, 95). There might also be segregation based upon social standing within a churchyard, with burial places sometimes clustered around a churchyard cross (*ibid.*, 99).

There has been a suggestion that the area might contain the remains of a mortuary chapel (Phil Emery, *pers. comm.*). No such structure was observed, although it is possible that this was a relatively ephemeral building such as a timber structure represented by now-lost ground sills or post-holes. Although there was considerable evidence of nearby medieval building works, these could equally relate to any major 14th-century building (or rebuilding) project within the precinct.

Two apparent graves contained no skeletons (graves *6* and *25*: Figs 7, 9 and 10). Similar absences have been noted at St Anne's Charterhouse, Coventry (Carthusian: Soden 1995, 67), Sandwell Priory, West Midlands (Benedictine/Cluniac: Hodder 1991, 97) and St James' Abbey, Northampton (Augustinian: A. Chapman, *pers.*

*comm.*). Whilst it was not uncommon for remains to be exhumed and moved elsewhere (Daniell 1997, 88) there was no evidence for any re-cut within the grave fill, although the removal of the body could have required a wider excavation. Alternatively, these instances may be examples of the practice of *mos teutonicus*, following the death of a foreigner: in the absence of suitable embalming techniques, the flesh would be boiled off so that the bones could be packed up to be sent home for burial. Despite attempts to outlaw the practice by Pope Boniface VIII at the end of the 13th century, it continued into the 15th century (Litten 1992, 37). The burial of the soft tissue (accorded a full grave) would leave no physical remains unless the ground conditions were wholly conducive to preservation. Such an interpretation seems feasible given the international reputation of Norwich's Franciscan *studium*.

In general burial practice appeared uniform, with very little variation. The use of simple wooden, wedge- or lozenge-shaped coffins was noted. The type appears widespread during the medieval period and preserved or reconstructable examples (from nail plots) are known from Norwich Whitefriars, Coventry Charterhouse and ordinary country churchyards (Litten 1992, pl. 8, fig. 42; Soden 1995, 75; Hayward 2001). Many of the deceased at St Faith's Lane, however, were probably buried only in a winding sheet or occasionally a shroud, attested in eight instances by the presence of simple copper alloy pins. The combination of coffin and shroud was clearly also acceptable, given its depiction in the Luttrell Psalter (Hadley 2001, pl. 17). Single planks could also be used as 'beds' within the grave, as preferred by the Carthusian Order. These might have been new or re-used, which may explain the occurrence of odd nails in several graves. Pegged coffins, on the other hand, would leave behind no nails and, in the absence of any clear coffin line within the grave fill, no trace whatsoever. The patterning of individual foot-bones is not considered a reliable guide to coffin/winding sheet presence due to the soft sandy soils and vagaries of collapse during the decomposition of organic matter. The presence of confirmed coffins and shrouds is summarised in Fig. 12.

The absence of stone coffins may be date-related, since their use had largely ended by the time the Greyfriars' cemetery began. Alternatively, the use of expensive materials could have been viewed as extravagant by all except the wealthiest families. Stone coffins might therefore largely be expected in intramural locations where familial or even monastic recognition was a factor and the grave would be seen by impressionable lay folk as well as clergy. Their use in a more informal and secluded outdoor cemetery, beyond public gaze, would serve little purpose.

Three burials of adult males had their mouths deliberately packed out with ash (graves *87*, *103* and *132*). The Franciscan rites of burial are not dissimilar to those of the Dominicans from the mid-13th century, for which written requirements survive. The use of ashes was widespread but generally as a bed on which the friar would prepare for death as a sign of his contrition (Berthier 1950, 308). There is some evidence that this practice was extended to lay persons (Weatherley 1936, 235), and its symbolic extension from deathbed to grave is attested by a Carmelite example from Northampton (Serjeantson 1911, citing earlier sources).

Whilst the placing of ashes could have been carried out at the prior request of the deceased it might equally be associated with punitive penance. The reasons for this must remain a matter of speculation but it could be that words spoken in life were considered heretical. From the 13th century, with the establishment of the doctrine of purgatory, there would seem to be less scope for such ideas of penance being administered after death. This might suggest that the particular graves were earlier, primary interments. It may be significant that, along with a few other graves, they form a distinct, apparently deliberate cluster with a gap at either side to both north and south. They may therefore have been segregated from the wider cemetery; alternatively, others may have wished not to be buried nearby. Conversely, the clustering may indicate that the penance, if not punitive but merely an act of humility, made the burial site attractive to others who sought burial close by. For instance, at Coventry Greyfriars, where a long list of burials are known by name, one wealthy patron expressly wished to be buried in 1525 at the feet of his late spiritual mentor, Dr James Standysshe, a noted Franciscan preacher and Friar Provincial from 1506 (Soden 2005, 77).

## Enclosure of the precinct and the use of space

While the layout of graves was for the most part orderly, their individual depth varied considerably by as much as 2.3m. At the extreme west the cemetery ground surface had not survived but at the east the greater thickness of surviving grave-earth afforded the graves more protection from subsequent development.

Close to the northern edge the burials were not dense enough to have raised local ground levels noticeably either before or after the building of the Friary precinct wall, perhaps around 1500. In fact, the thickness of the former occupation surface (*109/190*) into which the graves were dug denotes a north- and eastward progression of burials over time, moving away from the most desirable plots closer to the Upper King Street frontage at the west and the church to the south. Indeed, the precinct might have been walled off along the St Faith's Lane frontage in response to burials approaching the road. Urban monastic precincts with apparently incomplete boundary walls are not unknown, as at the Coventry Charterhouse which was still apparently unenclosed by 1506 (Soden 1995, 8). Alternatively, the wall in St Faith's Lane could have replaced an earlier boundary that has left no trace.

So long as a cemetery contained mounded-up graves, the space available for future burial could be appreciated easily. As individual graves sank and mounds were flattened, however, it became necessary to maintain order by means of grave-markers or a drawn plan. No grave-markers were identified during excavation and the initial orderly plan seems to have disintegrated quickly, with earlier graves damaged by secondary interments. Daniell (1997, 145–6) sees this kind of organisational decay as reflecting nothing more than pressure upon space. The later lines of graves, which would have been dug while at least some of their predecessors were still discernible, lack the regularity of the initial burials.

Most rows of graves were originally laid out with just enough space around them to avoid encroachment upon adjacent burials. However, the depths of individual burials suggests that some bodies lay only a few centimetres below the ground surface and the space between rows seems to have been barely enough to prevent people walking over them, as certainly became the case with the secondary interments. This might indicate that graves were not expected to receive visitors after the funeral. The increased space between the second and third rows from the east may denote the presence of a path or hedge dividing the groups of rows into larger blocks (*cf.* Rahtz 1978, 2).

Previous study of grave orientation has highlighted its potential, in some circumstances, for indicating patterns of disease and plague (Rahtz 1978, 9–10). However, by the time that the Greyfriars cemetery was established, the layout of the nearby church would have provided an 'ecclesiastical' compass with its altar at the nominal eastern end. With the straight line of the road to the north, it would have been a simple matter to position graves without needing to observe the sun's movement. The cemetery plan shows that there were very few anomalous orientations. Only one grave has been dug haphazardly (grave *87* — also the deepest, at 4.15m above OD) but this may have been aligned to miss an existing feature, such as a tree, which has otherwise left no trace.

None of the gaps recorded in the lines can be firmly related to former built features; in some cases they are due to disturbance by later foundations. There is therefore no evidence of a structural focus for the burials in this part of the cemetery.

Nearby building works in the 14th century interrupted the progress of burials across the site. The digging of a large quarry pit at the northern edge of the area involved running heavily-laden carts over three existing graves. Burial was later resumed in this row but the graves in the next row to the west (the westernmost excavated) cut through building rubble and associated dumps that had begun to accumulate whilst the trackway was still in use and which raised the ground level quite considerably (Fig. 13). Burials must have continued during all this activity and it may be significant that the greatest incidence of intercutting and clustering of graves occurs just to the east, where the related skeletal analysis does not suggest any familial relationships between the buried individuals by way of explanation.

The westernmost line of graves was dug after dumping ceased and a wall had been erected to prevent the material from slumping eastwards and smothering the next row of graves. The imposition of such topographical changes, maximising the use of space for both spoil removal and burial, produced a distinctive terrace, later revetted at the west, together with flat grassplats which were punctuated by small mounds where repeated use of burial plots and intercutting had raised the ground locally.

## The Dissolution and beyond

The Crown's sale of the St Faith's Lane site and its immediate surroundings as a garden formed part of the much wider depradation of former monastic properties and interests. Reaction was mixed, and probably followed partisan lines that had been drawn long before the Dissolution actually came. Officialdom seems to have been caught up in a frenzy of destructive behaviour and resentment towards former monastic establishments; in Norwich, this particularly targeted the friars (*cf.* Hale and Rogers 1991, 25). Any impressions of anti-mendicant zeal, and of the Reformation within the city as a vendetta conducted against the friars alone, may however be biased, and fuelled to some extent by the manner in which so many buildings of the Benedictine Cathedral Priory have survived, in contrast with the friaries' almost complete obliteration.

Any continued use of the cemetery may have been problematic. Although the Dissolution did not de-consecrate monastic precincts, they were generally no longer regarded as a fit place to bury the dead. Indeed, there were still burial fees to be extracted, and this fell once more to the parish churches. A succession of Crown-related liturgical reforms meant that up to 1559 the protocols surrounding burial were confused and changed repeatedly (Litten 1991, 143ff).

At St Faith's Lane the presence of hundreds of bodies, possibly including recent burials of relatives of city residents, may have presented a problem. A garden was probably all that could be created within this northern part of the precinct where an alternative use might be viewed as unnecessary and potentially as wilful desecration. That is, if a choice ever arose, for Norwich was entering a period of social stagnation and it would be many years before there was any serious pressure for space in the new, post-monastic city.

## III. Envoi: site context and future research objectives

**Limitations of the evidence**
When considering the evidence from St Faith's Lane for any period, or with any archaeological theme in mind, much of the data appears at first glance to be of limited value. Critics of current practices in British archaeology would note that the excavation site was not selected for research reasons but because it came under threat from new development. The precise area chosen for excavation was decided on the basis of projected levels of damage that might occur to surviving archaeological deposits as conjectured from evaluation trenches, which had been constrained by existing physical barriers. The regional research framework *Research and Archaeology* refers to this as 'threat-led research' (Wade and Brown 2000, 53). The criteria currently used by the Department of Culture, Media and Sport match up poorly when applied to deeply stratified urban sites, where residuality, intrusion and the vagaries of responding to modern development detract from rather than contribute to the value of the resource and the prevention of further damage.

This circumstance is clearly less than ideal, and must be moderated by acceptance that no-one can ever really know what lies beneath the ground, so that too much selectivity may be disastrous (Wade and Brown 2000, 53). The production of a retrospective assessment of the resource (*e.g.* Glazebrook 1997) goes some way to reminding us of the overall value of what has been done so far and informs the research agenda and strategy for the future (Brown and Glazebrook 2000).

**Moderating factors and benefits**
Referring to monastic studies, Butler (1984, 84) reminds us that 'the danger of arguing from imperfect samples is always present, particularly when urban monastic sites are so prone to fragmentation of later ownership and consequent fragmentation of modern site development'. The best-preserved sites in any period or landscape enhance our knowledge to the greatest degree, whilst also best justifying current agendas and enabling their continued refinement and relevance.

The remains excavated at St Faith's Lane cannot be said to be well preserved in any phase, but gain significance in the wider context of the Norwich Greyfriars Project, and when placed alongside the results of larger-scale excavation elsewhere in the precinct (Emery 2007). The results complement this larger project and form a further contribution to an increasingly valuable body of evidence for a major urban planning block. Viewed in these terms, the contribution of the development-led work at St Faith's Lane is therefore considerable.

The denuded Saxo-Norman frontage, dating the creation of St Faith's Lane firmly to the 10th century, fits into our emerging understanding of pattern of growth of early Norwich. The Phase 1 and 2 assemblages provide a view of Saxo-Norman status, whether real or aspirant, in a minor industrial zone and help to address issues concerning the relationship between town and country in this period as well as Norwich's wider connections. Some of the results are consistent with those from elsewhere in Norwich, while others are not.

As a burial place, without clear restriction, the cemetery at St Faith's Lane has a comparative value to set against parochial burial environments in Norwich and it may in future be possible to compare the data from the St Faith's Lane skeletons with unpublished information from the parish churchyard of St Margaret in combusto, Magdalen Street, which was excavated in the 1980s (Stirland forthcoming). Comparison could be made, for example, between the type of medical care offered by the monastic orders and that which filtered into the secular world. A wider sample of comparative or contrasting cemetery sites from Norwich would be helpful.

At the present site the nature of the site stratigraphy and associated finds provided little evidence of internal phasing, and precluded detailed dating of individual burial events. Whilst systematic radiocarbon dating might help to develop a chronological sequence, this is expensive for a large sample and its potential is limited when dealing with a short time-span. Recourse to this dating method ought nevertheless to be considered by planning archaeologists as part of the potential recording strategy in future cemetery excavations.

It is as an element of the Franciscan Friary that the excavation contributes most, and the importance of the results goes far beyond what was probably conceived when the site became the subject of redevelopment. As one of seventy-eight such foundations in Britain, with forty of them established in England by 1250, the Friary was part of a national monastic system, for which modern research priorities are only now being reassessed. In 1984 a survey of work on monastic houses showed that between 1956 and 1980 the excavation of mendicant houses remained fairly constant (25%) but in almost every case the aim was to recover plans of churches and cloisters. The scope was therefore limited and few other questions were asked (Clarke 1984, 86–8, 103).

It was lamented some time ago that no friars' cemetery had ever been fully excavated (Butler 1984, 131); however, the casual reader might be forgiven for passing over the St Faith's Lane site as a potential candidate since, in omitting it from his principal list, Butler did not consider the Norwich Greyfriars 'worthy of attention' (*ibid.*, 129). Subsequently mourning the loss of the place reserved for monastic research after the seminal programmes of the early 20th century, Butler further noted that 'the effort once expended on monastic excavation and clearance is now absorbed into urban rescue archaeology in which the houses of the friars or of the nuns are but one element in the complexity of social landscapes and economic hierarchy ... [where] major sites need to be assessed for what evidence they provide upon social separation and change, diet and disease, market catchments and distant trade, religious economy and artistic patronage' (Butler 1993, 83). The results of the work at St Faith's Lane surely contribute to study of the very complexity of social landscape and economic hierarchy that Butler saw as detracting from a focus on monastic remains in their own right. The two are inseparable, especially in so far as a mendicant house could not (and should not) be separated from its flock, the city. To focus on the one without the other is to fail to understand the *raison d'être* of the Greyfriars.

In the same overview Butler set a challenge which few areas of archaeology could better: recognising the national standing of research upon an international monastic order. He pointed to 'the danger ... that monastic excavation will continue to be prompted by local pressure and considerations [rather] than by a national overview. Yet if excavation is perceived as answering primarily the local questions and as supporting local identity, then such an outcome is inevitable' (Butler 1993, 85). Research with such breadth of scope has been rare and continues to be missing after more than ten years of developer-led archaeology (Keevill 2001, 1–2). It is to be regretted that there is 'still a paucity of reports on anatomical research and burial practices', and a clear distinction needs to be drawn between the different groups likely to be buried on a monastic site (Greene 2001, 6). It is to be hoped that the excavations at St Faith's Lane have gone some way to redressing that paucity of reports.

# Bibliography

Albarella, U., 1995 — 'Depressions on sheep horncores', *J. Archaeol. Sci.* 22, 699–704

Albarella, U., 2004 — 'Mammal and bird bones', in Wallis, H., *Excavations at Mill Lane, Thetford, 1995*, E. Anglian Archaeol. 108, 88–99

Albarella, U., Beech, M. and Mulville, J., 1997 — *The Saxon, Medieval and Post-Medieval Mammal and Bird Bones Excavated 1989–91 from Castle Mall, Norwich, Norfolk*, English Heritage AML Rep 72/97

Anderson, S., 1996 — *Human Skeletal Remains from Timberhill, Castle Mall, Norwich (excavated 1989–91)*, English Heritage AML Rep 73/96

Anderson, T. and Andrews, J., forthcoming — 'The human skeletons', in Hicks, M. and Hicks, A., forthcoming, *St Gregory's Priory, Canterbury*

Armitage, P.L., 1977 — *The mammalian remains from the Tudor site of Baynards Castle, London: A biometrical and historical analysis* (unpubl. Ph.D. thesis, Royal Holloway College & British Museum)

Armitage, P.L., 1980 — 'A preliminary description of British cattle from the late twelfth to early sixteenth century', *The Ark* 7 (12), 405–13

Armitage, P.L., 1982 — 'A system for ageing and sexing the horn cores of cattle from British Post-Medieval sites (17th to early 18th century)', in Wilson, B., Grigson, C. and Payne, S. (eds), *Ageing and sexing Animal Bones from Archaeological Sites*, Brit. Archaeol. Rep. Brit. Ser. 37–54

Armitage, P.L., 1998 — *Report on the mammal, bird and fish bones from Alder/Castle/Falcon House (Site AES96)*, unpubl. rep., Pre-Construct Archaeology Ltd

Armitage, P.L. and Clutton-Brock, J., 1976 — 'A system for classification and description of the horn cores of cattle from archaeological sites', *J. Archaeol. Sci.* 3, 329–48

Armitage, P.L. and West, B., 1985 — 'Faunal evidence from a late medieval garden well of the Greyfriars, London', *Trans. London Middlesex Archaeol. Soc.* 36, 107–36

Atkin, M., 1982 — '29–31 St Benedict's Street (Site 147N)' in Carter, A. (ed.), *Excavations in Norwich 1971–1978 Part I*, E. Anglian Archaeol. 15, 5–10

Atkin, M., Ayers, B. and Jennings, S., 1983 — 'Thetford-Type Ware Production in Norwich' in *Waterfront Excavation and Thetford Ware Production, Norwich*, E. Anglian Archaeol. 17, 61–97

Atkin, M., 1985 — 'Excavations on Alms Lane (Site 302N)', in Atkin, M., Carter, A. and Evans, D.H., *Excavations in Norwich 1971–1978 Part II*, E. Anglian Archaeol. 26, 144–260

Ayers, B., 1985 — *Excavations within the North-East Bailey of Norwich Castle, 1979*, E. Anglian Archaeol. 28

Ayers, B., 1987 — *Excavations at St Martin-at-Palace Plain, Norwich 1981*, E. Anglian Archaeol. 37

Ayers, B., 1994 — *Excavations at Fishergate, Norwich, 1985*, E. Anglian Archaeol. 68

Ayers, B, 1996 — 'The Cathedral site before 1096', in Atherton, I., Fernie, E., Harper-Bill, C. and Smith, H. (eds), *Norwich Cathedral: Church, City and Diocese 1096–1996* (London), 59–72

Ayers, B, 2003 — *Norwich: a fine city* (Stroud)

Ayers, B. and Murphy, P., 1983 — 'A Waterfront Excavation at Whitefriars Street Car Park, Norwich 1979', in *Waterfront Excavation and Thetford Ware Production, Norwich*, E. Anglian Archaeol. 17, 1–59

Bailey, G., Charles, R. and Winder, N. (eds), 2000 — *Human Ecodynamics*, Symposia of the Association for Environmental Archaeology 19

Barnard, F.P., 1916 — *The Casting Counter and the Counting Board: a chapter in the history of numismatics and early arithmetic* (Oxford)

Bass, W.M., 1987 — *Human Osteology: A Laboratory and Field Manual of the Human Skeleton*, Missouri Archaeol. Soc. Specl. Publ. 2 (3rd edn)

Batty Shaw, A., 1970 — 'The Norwich school of lithotomy', *Medical History* 14, 221–59

Baxter, I.L., 1993 — 'Eagles in Anglo-Saxon and Norse poems', *Circaea* 10 (2), 78–81

Bayley, J., 1991 — *Crucibles from Minstergate, Thetford, Norfolk*, English Heritage AML Rep 15/91

Bennett, J.H.E., 1921 — 'The Grey Friars of Chester', *J. Chester Archaeol. Soc.* 24 (1), 5–85

Berthier, J.J. (ed.), 1950 — 'Humbert of Romans' De officiis servitor infirmarie', *Opera de vita regulari* 2

Blinkhorn, P.W., forthcoming a — *The Ipswich Ware Project: Ceramics, Trade and Society in Middle Saxon England*, Medieval Pottery Res. Grp. Monogr.

Blinkhorn, P.W., forthcoming b — *Pottery from the Fenland Management Project*, E. Anglian Archaeol.

Blinkhorn, P.W., forthcoming c — *Pottery from Wensum St, Norwich (Site 26585N)*, Archaeological Project Services Evaluation Rep.

Blomefield, F., 1806 — *An Essay towards a topographical history of the County of Norfolk; IV*

Boardman, S. and Jones, G., 1990 — 'Experiments on the effects of charring on cereal plant components', *J. Archaeol. Sci.* 17, 1–11

Bourdillon, J. and Coy, J., 1980 — 'The animal bones', in Holdsworth, P., *Excavations at Melbourne Street, Southampton 1972–76*, Counc. Brit. Archaeol. Res. Rep. 33, 79–110

Bown, J., 1987 — 'English wares', in Ayers, B., *Excavations at St Martin-at-Palace Plain, Norwich 1981*, E. Anglian Archaeol. 37, 74–96

Brothwell, D.R., 1981 — *Digging Up Bones: The Excavation, Treatment, and Study of Human Skeletal Remains*, 3rd edn (Ithaca, NY)

Brown, D.H., 1997 — 'The social significance of imported medieval pottery', in Cumberpatch, C.G. and Blinkhorn, P.W. (eds), *Not So Much a Pot, More a Way of Life*, Oxbow Monogr. 83, 95–112

Brown, N. and Glazebrook, J. (eds), 2000 — *Research and Archaeology: a framework for the eastern counties, 2. research agenda and strategy*, E. Anglian Archaeol. Occ. Pap 8

| | | | |
|---|---|---|---|
| Butler, L.A.S., 1984 | 'The houses of the mendicant orders in Britain: recent archaeological work', in Addyman, P.V. and Black, V.E. (eds), *Archaeological Papers from York presented to M.W. Barley* (York), 123–36 | Egan, G., 1998 | *The Medieval Household: daily living 1150–1450*, Medieval Finds from Excavations in London 6 |
| Butler, L.A.S., 1993 | 'The archaeology of urban monasteries in Britain', in Gilchrist, R. and Mytum, H., *Advances in Monastic Archaeology*, Brit. Archaeol. Rep. Brit. Series 227, 79–86 | Egan, G. and Pritchard, F., 1991 | *Dress accessories 1150–1450*, Medieval Finds from Excavations in London 3 |
| | | Emery, P.A., 1997 | Evaluation excavation at the former Wallace King premises, St Faith's Lane, Norwich, Norfolk Archaeological Unit Report 285 |
| Campbell, J., 1975 | *The Atlas of Historic Towns; 2: Norwich* (London) | Emery, P.A., 2007 | *Norwich Greyfriars: pre-Conquest town and medieval friary*, E. Anglian Archaeol. 120 |
| Carruthers, W.J., 2000a | 'Charred plant remains', in Soden, I., *A story of urban regeneration: excavations in advance of development off St Peter's Walk, Northampton*, Northamptonshire Archaeology 28, 85–91 | English Heritage, 2001 | *Archaeometallurgy*, Centre for Archaeology Guidelines |
| | | Evans, D.H. and Carter, A., 1985 | 'Excavations on 31–51 Pottergate (Site 149N)', in Atkin, M., Carter, A. and Evans, D.H., *Excavations in Norwich 1971–1978 Part II*, E. Anglian Archaeol. 26, 9–85 |
| Carruthers, W.J., 2000b | 'Mineralised plant remains', in Lawson, A.J., *Potterne 1982–5: Animal Husbandry in Later Prehistoric Wiltshire*, Trust for Wessex Archaeology, Wessex Archaeol. Rep. 17, (Salisbury), 72–84 | Farmer, G. and Farmer, N.C., 1982 | 'The dating of the Scarborough Ware pottery industry', *Medieval Ceramics* 6, 66–86 |
| Carus-Wilson, E.M., 1962–3 | 'The medieval trade of the parts of the world', *Medieval Archaeol.* 6–7, 182–201 | Ferembach, D., Schwidetzky, I. and Stloukal, M., 1980 | 'Recommendations for age and sex diagnoses of skeletons', *J. Human Evolution* 9, 517–49 |
| Childs, W.R., 2000 | 'Fishing and fisheries in the Middle Ages: the eastern fisheries', in Starkey, D.J., Reid, C. and Ashcroft, N. (eds), *England's Sea Fisheries. The Commercial Sea Fisheries of England and Wales since 1300* (London), 19–23 | Floud, R., Wachter, K. and Gregory, A., 1990 | *Height, Health and History: nutritional status in the United Kingdom, 1750–1980*, Cambridge Stud. Population Econom. Soc. Past Time 9 |
| | | Foreman, M., 1992 | 'Objects of bone, antler and shell', in Evans, D.H. and Tomlinson, D.G., *Excavations at 33–35 Eastgate, Beverley 1983–86*, Sheffield Excavation Rep. 3, 163–74 |
| Clarke, H., 1984 | *The Archaeology of Medieval England* (London) | | |
| Clarke, H. and Carter, A., 1977 | *Excavations in King's Lynn 1963–1970*, Soc. Medieval Archaeol. Monogr. 7 | | |
| Clutton-Brock, J., 1976 | 'The animal resources', in Wilson, D.M. (ed.), *The Archaeology of Anglo-Saxon England* (Cambridge), 372–92 | Fretton, W.G., 1882 | 'Memorials of the Franciscans or Grey Friars, Coventry', *Trans Birmingham Archaeol. Soc.* (for 1878–9), 34–53 |
| | | Gaimster, D.R.M., 1997 | *German Stoneware 1200–1900* (London) |
| Clutton-Brock, J., Dennis-Bryan, K., Armitage, P.L. and Jewell, P.A., 1990 | 'Osteology of the Soay sheep', *Bulletin British Museum (Nat. Hist.) Zoology Series* 56 (no. 1), 1–56 | Geddes, J., 1980 | 'Well cover', in Saunders, A.D., 'Lydford Castle, Devon', *Medieval Archaeol.* 24, 123–186, 165 |
| Dallas, C., 1993 | *Excavations in Thetford by B.K. Davison between 1964 and 1970*, E. Anglian Archaeol. 62 | Geddes, J., 1991 | 'Iron', in Blair, J. and Ramsay, N., *English Medieval Industries* (London), 167–88 |
| Dallas, C., 1994 | 'The pottery', in Ayers, B., *Excavations at Fishergate, Norwich 1985*, E. Anglian Archaeol. 68, 19–29 | Gilmour, L.A., 1988 | *Early medieval pottery from Flaxengate, Lincoln*, Archaeol. Lincoln 17/2 |
| Daniell, C., 1997 | *Death and Burial in Medieval England* (New York) | Glazebrook, J. (ed.), 1997 | *Research and Archaeology: a framework for the eastern counties, 1. resource assessment*, E. Anglian Archaeol. Occ. Pap. 3 |
| Davey, P. and Hodges, R., 1983 | *Ceramics and Trade: The production and distribution of later medieval pottery in Northwest Europe* (Sheffield) | Goodall, A., 1984 | 'Non-ferrous metal objects', in Rogerson, A. and Dallas, C., *Excavations in Thetford 1948–59 and 1973–80*, E. Anglian Archaeol. 22, 68–75 |
| Dawes, J.D., 1986 | 'The human bones', in Gilmour, J.J. and Stocker, D.A., *St Mark's Church and Cemetery*, Archaeol. Lincoln 13/1, 19–82 | Goodall, A., 1993 | 'The finds', in Dallas, C., *Excavations in Thetford by B.K. Davison between 1964 and 1970*, E. Anglian Archaeol. 62, 95ff |
| Denham, V, 1985 | 'The pottery', in Williams, J.H., Shaw, M. and Denham, V., *Middle Saxon Palaces at Northampton*, Northampton Dev. Corp. Archaeol. Monogr. 4, 46–64 | Goodall, I.H., 1990a | 'Building ironwork', in Biddle, M., *Object and Economy in Medieval Winchester*, Winchester Studies 7, 328–49 |
| Dobson, B., 1984 | 'Mendicant ideal and practice in late medieval York', in Addyman, P.V. and Black, V.E. (eds), *Archaeological Papers from York presented to M.W. Barley* (York), 109–22 | Goodall, I.H, 1990b | 'Locks and Keys', in Biddle, M., *Object and Economy in Medieval Winchester*, Winchester Studies 7, 1001–36 |
| | | Green, F., 1979 | 'Phosphate mineralisation of seeds from archaeological sites', *J. Archaeol. Sci.* 6, 279–84 |
| Doucet, P.V., 1953 | 'Le Studium Franciscain de Norwich en 1337 d'après le MS Chigi BV66 de la Bibliotheque Vaticane', *Archivum Franciscanum Historicum* 46, 85–98 | Green, N.A. and Batty Shaw, A., 1981 | 'Bladder stones in children. The Norwich School of Lithotomy', *European Urology* 7, 126–31 |

| | | | |
|---|---|---|---|
| Greene, J.P., 2001 | 'Strategies for future research and site investigation', in Keevill, G., Aston, M. and Hall, T., *Monastic Archaeology* (Oxford), 4–8 | | S., *Waterfront Excavation and Thetford Ware Production, Norwich*, E. Anglian Archaeol. 17, 74–91 |
| Gregory, A.K. and Metcalf, D.M., 1994 | 'The coins', in Ayers, B., *Excavations at Fishergate, Norwich 1985*, E. Anglian Archaeol. 68, 13–14 | Jones, A., 1983 | 'Fish remains', in Ayers, B. and Murphy, P., 'A waterfront excavation at Whitefriars Street Car Park, Norwich 1979', in Atkin, M., Ayers, B. and Jennings, S., *Waterfront Excavation and Thetford Ware Production, Norwich*, E. Anglian Archaeol. 17, 32–34 |
| Grigson, C., 1982 | 'Sex and age determination of some bones and teeth of domestic cattle: a review of the literature', in Wilson, B., Grigson, C. and Payne, S. (eds), *Ageing and Sexing Animal Bones from Archaeological Sites*, Brit. Archaeol. Rep. Brit. Ser. 37–54, 7–23 | Jones, A.K.G. and Scott, S.A., 1985 | 'The fish bones', in Atkin, M., 'Excavations on Alms Lane (Site 302N)', in Atkin, M., Carter, A. and Evans, D.H., *Excavations in Norwich 1971–1978 Part II*, E. Anglian Archaeol. 26, 144–260, 223–8 & microfiche MFT 26 |
| Gryspeerdt, M., 1981 | 'The pottery', in Williams, J.H., 'Excavations in Chalk Lane, Northampton', *Northamptonshire Archaeol.* 16, 87–135 | Keevill, G., 2001 | 'Past approaches to the archaeological study of monastic sites', in Keevill, G., Aston, M. and Hall, T., *Monastic Archaeology* (Oxford), 1–3 |
| Hadley, D.H., 2001 | *Death in Medieval England* (Stroud) | | |
| Hajnalová, E. (ed.), 1991 | 'Palaeoethnobotany and archaeology, Acta interdisciplinaria', *Archaeologica* 7 | Keller, C., 1995 | 'Pingsdorf-type ware: an introduction', *Medieval Ceramics* 19, 19–28 |
| Hale, R. and Rogers, M., 1991 | *The Greyfriars of Norwich* (Norwich) | Kennedy, M., 1954 | *The Sea Angler's Fishes* (London) |
| Harcourt, R.A., 1974 | 'The dog in prehistoric and early historic Britain', *J. Archaeol. Sci.* 1, 151–75 | Kilmurry, K., 1980 | *The Pottery Industry of Stamford, Lincs. c. AD 850–1250*, Brit Archaeol. Rep. Brit. Ser. 84 |
| Harman, M., 1985 | 'The human remains', in Lambrick, G., 'Further excavations at the second site of the Dominican Priory, Oxford', *Oxoniensia* 50, 188–90 | Kilmurry, K., 1984 | 'Stamford ware', in Rogerson, A. and Dallas, C., *Excavations in Thetford 1948–59 and 1973–80*, E. Anglian Archaeol. 22, 68–75, 124–5 |
| Hatting, T., 1975 | 'The influence of castration on sheep horns', in Clason, A.T. (ed.), *Archaeological Studies*, 345–51 (Amsterdam) | Kirkpatrick, J., 1845 | *History of the religious orders and communities and of the hospitals and castle of Norwich (c. 1725)* |
| Hayward, S., 2001 | *St Bartholomew's Church, Greens Norton, Northamptonshire*, Northamptonshire Archaeol. Rep. | Kruse, S.E., 1992 | 'Late Saxon balances and weights from England', *Medieval Archaeol.* 36, 67–95 |
| | | Lambrick, G., 1985 | 'Further excavations at the second site of the Dominican Priory', *Oxoniensia* 50 |
| Hinton, R.W.K., 1956 | *The Port Books of Boston 1601–1640*, Lincoln Rec. Soc. 50 | Lawson, A.J., 2000 | *Potterne 1982–5: Animal Husbandry in Later Prehistoric Wiltshire* (Salisbury) |
| Hodder, M.A., 1991 | 'Excavations at Sandwell Priory and Hall 1982–8', *Trans. S. Staffordshire Archaeol. Hist. Soc.* 31 | Lawson, G., 1995 | *Pig Metapodial Toggles and Buzz-Discs: traditional musical instruments*, Finds Research Group 700–1700, data sheet 18 |
| Hudson, W., 1892 | *Leet jurisdiction in the city of Norwich during the XIII and XIV centuries with a short notice of its later history and decline*, Selden Soc. 5 | Lawson, G. and Margeson, S., 1993 | 'Musical instruments', in Margeson, S, *Norwich Households: the medieval and post-medieval finds from Norwich Survey excavations 1971–78*, E. Anglian Archaeol. 58, 211–15 |
| Hudson, W., 1910 | 'The stone bridge by the horsefair in St Faith's Lane, Norwich; with some account of the ancient history and topography of the adjoining street', *Norfolk Archaeol.* 17, 117–42 | Leah, M., 1994 | *The Late Saxon and Medieval Pottery Industry of Grimston, Norfolk: Excavations 1962–92*, E. Anglian Archaeol. 64 |
| Hurst, J.G., 1959 | 'Middle Saxon pottery', in Dunning, G.C., Hurst, J.G., Myres, J.N.L. and Tischler, F., 'Anglo-Saxon Pottery: a symposium', *Medieval Archaeol.* 3, 1–78 | Litten, J., 1992 | *The English Way of Death: the common funeral since 1450* (London) |
| | | Locker, A., 1987 | 'The fish remains', in Ayers, B., *Excavations at St Martin-at-Palace Plain, Norwich 1981*, E. Anglian Archaeol. 37, 114–17 |
| Hutton, E., 1926 | *The Franciscans in England 1224–1538*, (London) | | |
| Jenkins, H.J.K., 1993 | 'Medieval barge traffic and the building of Peterborough Cathedral', *Northamptonshire Past and Present* 8, 255–61 | Locker, A., 1994 | 'Fish bones', in Ayers, B., *Excavations at Fishergate, Norwich 1985*, E. Anglian Archaeol. 68, 42–4 |
| Jennings, S., 1981 | *Eighteen Centuries of Pottery from Norwich*, E. Anglian Archaeol. 13 | Locker, A., 2001 | *The Role of Stored Fish in England AD 900–1750: the evidence from historical and archaeological data*, unpubl. Ph.D. thesis, University of Southampton |
| Jennings, S., 1982 | 'Pottery', in Atkin, M., '29–31 St Benedict's Street (Site 147N)', in Carter, A. (ed.), *Excavations in Norwich 1971–1978 Part I*, E. Anglian Archaeol. 15, 7–9 | | |
| | | Locock, M., 2000 | 'The analysis of historical bone assemblages: is big beautiful? and animal bones and the urban economy: 30 years of archaeozoology in Coventry', *Curr. Recent Res. Osteoarchaeol.* 2, 8–16 |
| Jennings, S., 1983 | 'The pottery', in Atkin, M., Ayers, B. and Jennings, S., 'Thetford-Type Ware Production in Norwich', in Atkin, M., Ayers, B. and Jennings, | | |

Luard, H.R., 1859 'Bart de Cotton, Monaci Norwicensis', *Historia Anglicana, Rolls Series*

MacGregor, A., 1982 *Anglo-Scandinavian finds from Lloyds Bank, Pavement and Other Sites*, Archaeol. York 17/3

MacGregor, A., 1985 *Bone, Antler, Ivory and Horn. The Technology of Skeletal Materials since the Roman Period* (London)

Margeson, S., 1985a 'The small finds', in Atkin, M., 'Excavations on Alms Lane (Site 302N)', in Atkin, M., Carter, A. and Evans, D.H., *Excavations in Norwich 1971–1978 Part II*, E. Anglian Archaeol. 26, 144–260, 201–13

Margeson, S., 1985b 'The small finds', in Evans, D.H. and Carter, A., 'Excavations on 31–51 Pottergate (Site 14 9N)', in Atkin, M., Carter, A. and Evans, D.H., *Excavations in Norwich 1971–1978 Part II*, E. Anglian Archaeol. 26, 52–66

Margeson, S., 1993 *Norwich Households: the medieval and post-medieval finds from Norwich Survey excavations 1971–78*, E. Anglian Archaeol. 58

Margeson, S. and Williams, V., 1985 'The artefacts', in Ayers, B., *Excavations within the North-East Bailey of Norwich Castle 1979*, E. Anglian Archaeol. 28, 27–48

Mayer, J.J. and Brisbin, I.L., 1988 'Sex identification of *Sus scrofa* based on canine morphology', *J. Mammalogy* 69 (2), 408–12

McCarthy, M.R. and Brooks, C.M., 1988 *Medieval Pottery in Britain AD 900–1600* (London)

Migne, J-P., 1849–55 *Patrologia Latina, series secunda*, vols 72–217 (Paris)

Moffett, L., 1991 'The archaeobotanical evidence for free-threshing tetraploid wheat in Britain', in Hajnalová, E. (ed.), Palaeoethnobotany and archaeology, Acta interdisciplinaria, *Archaeologica* 7, 233–43

MPRG, 1995 *Guide to the Classification of Ceramic forms*, Medieval Pottery Research Group: Ocasional Paper 1

Murphy, P., 1983 'Plant macrofossils', in Ayers, B. and Murphy, P., 'A Waterfront Excavation at Whitefriars Street Car Park, Norwich 1979', in Atkin, M., Ayers, B. and Jennings, S., *Waterfront Excavation and Thetford Ware Production, Norwich*, E. Anglian Archaeol. 17, 40–4

Murphy, P., 1985 'The plant remains', in Atkin, M., 'Excavations on Alms Lane (Site 302N)', in Atkin, M., Carter, A. and Evans, D.H., *Excavations in Norwich 1971–1978 Part II*, E. Anglian Archaeol. 26, 228–34

Murphy, P., 1991 *Calvert Street, Norwich, Norfolk (840N): plant remains from Late Saxon to Early Medieval deposits*, English Heritage AML Rep. 67/91

Murphy, P., 1994 'Plant macrofossils (excluding wood and mosses)', in Ayers, B., *Excavations at Fishergate, Norwich 1985*, E. Anglian Archaeol. 68, 54–58

Murphy, P. and Macphail, R., 1985 'Plant macrofossils', in Ayers, B., *Excavations within the North-East Bailey of Norwich Castle 1979*, E. Anglian Archaeol. 28, 60–2

Noddle, B., 1980 'The animal bones', in Wade-Martins, P., *Excavations at North Elmham Park 1967–72*, E. Anglian Archaeol. 9 (2), 375ff

North, J.J., 1991 *English Hammered Coinage* 1

O'Connor, T.P., 1982 *Animal Bones from Flaxengate, Lincoln c. 870–1500*, Archaeol. Lincoln 18/1

O'Connor, T.P., 1993 'Birds and the scavenger niche' *Archaeofauna* 2, 155–62

O'Connor, T.P., 1994 '8th–11th century economy and environment in York', in Rackham, J. (ed.), *Environment and Economy in Anglo-Saxon England*, Counc. Brit. Archaeol. Res. Rep. 89, 136–47

O'Connor, T.P., 2000a 'Human refuse as a major ecological factor in medieval urban vertebrate communities', in Bailey, G., Charles, R. and Winder, N. (eds), *Human Ecodynamics* (Oxford), 15–20

O'Connor, T.P., 2000b *The Archaeology of Animal Bones* (College Station, Texas)

Orton, C., 1998–9 'Minimum Standards in Statistics and Sampling', *Medieval Ceramics* vol 22–3, 135–8

Ottaway, P., 1992 *Anglo-Scandinavian Ironwork from Coppergate*, Archaeol. York 17/6

Page, W., 1906 *Victoria County History of the County of Norfolk*, 2

Payne, S., 1973 'Kill-off patterns in sheep and goats: the mandibles from Asvan Kale', *Anatolian Stud.* 23, 281–303

Pearce, J.E., Vince, A.G. and Jenner, M.A., 1985 *A Dated Type-Series of London Medieval Pottery Part 2: London-Type Ware*, London Middlesex Archaeol. Soc. Spec. Pap. 6

Perdikaris, S., 1996 'Scaly heads and tales: detecting commercialisation in early fisheries', *Archaeofauna* 5, 21–33

Prummel, W., 1978 'Animal bones from tannery pits of 's-Hertogenbosch, Berichten', *ROB* 20, 399–422

Rackham, J. (ed.), 1994 *Environment and Economy in Anglo-Saxon England*, Counc. Brit. Archaeol. Res. Rep. Brit. Ser. 89

Rahtz, P., 1978 'Grave orientation', *Archaeol. J.* 135, 1–14

Reichstein, H. and Pieper, H., 1986 *Untersuchungen an Skelettresten von Vögeln aus Haithabu (Ausgrabung 1966–1969)*, Berichte über die Ausgrabungen in Haithabu, Berichte 22, (Neumünster, Karl Wachholtz Verlag)

Roest, B., 2000 *A History of Franciscan Education c. 1210–1517* (Leiden and Boston)

Rogerson, A. and Dallas, C., 1984 *Excavations in Thetford 1948–59 and 1973–80*, E. Anglian Archaeol. 22

Rojo, A., 1986 'Live length and weight of cod (*Gadus morhua*) estimated from various skeletal elements', *N. American Archaeol.* 7 (4), 329–51

Saunders, A.D., 1980 'Lydford Castle, Devon', *Medieval Archaeol.* 24, 123–86

Scull, C., 1990 'Scales and weights in early Anglo-Saxon England', *Archaeol. J.* 147, 183–215

Serjeantson, D. and Waldron, T. (eds), 1989 *Diet and Crafts in Towns*, Brit. Archaeol. Rep. Brit. Ser. 199

Serjeantson, R.M., 1911 *The Northampton Friaries* (Northampton)

Shepherd Popescu, E., forthcoming *Excavations at Norwich Castle 1989–98*, E. Anglian Archaeol.

| | | | |
|---|---|---|---|
| Simmonds, N.W., 1976 | *Evolution of Crop Plants* (London) | Wade, K. and Brown, N., 2000 | 'Strategy', in Brown, N. and Glazebrook, J. (eds), *Research and Archaeology: a framework for the eastern counties, 2. research agenda and strategy*, E. Anglian Archaeol. Occ. Pap. 8 |
| Smith, J.C., 1895 | *Wills proved in the Prerogative Court of Canterbury, II: 1383–1558* | Wade-Martins, P., 1980 | *Excavations at North Elmham Park 1967–72*, E. Anglian Archaeol. 9 |
| Smith, R.N., 1969 | 'Fusion of ossification centres in the cat', *J. Small Animal Practice* 10, 523–30 | Wade-Martins, P., 1983 | *Two Post-Medieval Earthenware Pottery Groups from Fulmodestone*, E. Anglian Archaeol. 19 |
| Soden, I., 1995 | *Excavations at St Anne's Charterhouse, Coventry 1968–87*, Coventry Mus. Monogr. 4 | Waterman, D.M., 1959 | 'Late Saxon, Viking and early medieval finds from York', *Archaeologia* 97, 59–105 |
| Soden, I., 2000a | 'A story of urban regeneration: excavations in advance of development off St Peter's Walk, Northampton, 1994–7', *Northamptonshire Archaeol.* 28, 61–128 | Weatherley, E.H. (ed.), 1936 | *Speculum Sacerdotale*, EETS Original Ser. 200 |
| Soden, I., 2000b | *Excavations on St Faiths Lane, Norwich 1998: Assessment and updated project design*, Northamptonshire Archaeology Rep. | West, S.E., 1964 | 'Excavations at Cox Lane (1958) and at the Town Defences, Shire Hall Yard, Ipswich (1959)', *Proc. Suffolk Inst. Archaeol. Hist.* 29, 233–303 |
| Soden, I., 2005 | *Coventry: the hidden history* (Stroud) | Wheeler, A., 1977 | 'Fish bone', in Clarke, H. and Carter, A., *Excavations in King's Lynn 1963–1970*, Soc. Medieval Archaeol. Monogr. 7, 403–8 |
| Stace, C., 1991 | *New Flora of the British Isles* (Cambridge) | Wheeler, A., 1997 | *The Pocket Guide to Saltwater Fishes of Britain and Europe* (London) |
| Sternberg, M., 1992 | *Osteologie du Loup Dicentrarchus labrax (Linnaeus 1758)*, Fiches l'Osteologie Animale pour l'Archeologie Serie A: Poissons No 7, Centre de Recherches Archeologiques du CNRS | Wheeler, A. and Jones, A.K.G., 1976 | 'Fish remains' in Rogerson, A., *Excavations at Fuller's Hill, Great Yarmouth*, E. Anglian Archaeol. 2, 208–24 |
| Stilke, H., 1993 | 'Die fruhmittelalterliche Keramik von Oldorf, Gde. Wangerland, Ldkr. Friesland', *Nachrichten aus Niedersachsens Urgeschichte* 62, 135–68 | Williams, J.H., 1981 | 'Excavations in Chalk Lane, Northampton', *Northamptonshire Archaeol.* 16, 87–135 |
| Stirland, A. forthcoming | *Criminals and Paupers: the graveyard of St Margaret Fybriggate in combusto, Norwich*, E. Anglian Archaeol. | Williams, J.H., Shaw, M. and Denham, V., 1985 | *Middle Saxon Palaces at Northampton*, Northampton Dev. Corp. Archaeol. Monogr. 4 |
| Stroud, G. and Kemp, R.L., 1993 | *Cemeteries of the Church and Priory of St Andrew, Fishergate*, Archaeol. York 12/2 | Williams, V., 1987 | 'Bone, antler and ivory objects', in Ayers, B., *Excavations at St Martin-at-Palace Plain, Norwich 1981*, E. Anglian Archaeol. 37, 100–6 |
| Stuart-Macadam, P., 1986 | 'Health and disease in the monks of Stratford Langthorne Abbey', *Essex J.* 21, 67–71 | Wilson, C.A., 1976 | *Food and Drink in Britain from the Stone Age to Recent Times* (London) |
| Tannahill, R., 1973 | *Food in History* (New York) | Wilson, C.A., 1989 | 'Preserving food to preserve life: the response to glut and famine from early times to the end of the Middle Ages', in Wilson, C.A. (ed.), *Waste Not, Want Not: food preservation from early times to the present day* (Edinburgh), 5–31 |
| Tanner, N.P., 1984 | *The Church in Late Medieval Norwich 1370–1532* (Toronto) | | |
| Teichert, M., 1975 | *Osteometriche Untersuchungen zur Berechnung der Widderisthohe bei schafen.* Archaeological Studies 1975 | Wilson, D.G., 1975 | 'Plant foods and poisons from medieval Chester', *J. Chester Archaeol. Soc.* 58, 57–67 |
| Thorpe, B., 1848 | 'Florentii wigorniensis monachi chronicon ex Chronicii II. London', *English Hist. Soc.* 13(2) | Wilson, D.M. (ed.), 1976 | *The Archaeology of Anglo-Saxon England* (London) |
| Trotter, M. and Gleser, G.C., 1958 | 'A re-evaluation of estimation of stature based on measurements of stature taken during life and long bones after death', *American J. Physical Anthropology* 16, 79–123 | Wilson, D.M. and Hurst, J.G., 1965 | 'Medieval Britain in 1964', *Medieval Archaeol.* 9, 170–220 |
| Trow-Smith, R., 1957 | *A History of British Livestock Husbandry to 1700* (London) | Wilson, J., 1978 | 'Where to fish: Norfolk', *Marshall Cavendish Fisherman's Handbook* (London), 1406–13 |
| Ubelaker, D.H., 1979 | 'Skeletal evidence for kneeling in prehistoric Ecuador', *Amer. J. Physical Anthropology* 51, 679–85 | Woolgar, C. M., 2000 | '"Take this penance now, and afterwards the fare will improve": seafood and late medieval diet', in Starkey, D.J., Reid, C. and Ashcroft, N. (eds), *England's Sea Fisheries: the commercial sea fisheries of England and Wales since 1300* (London), 36–44 |
| van Neer, W. and Ervynck, A., 1996 | 'Food rules and status: patterns of fish consumption in a monastic community (Ename, Belgium)', *Archaeofauna* 5, 155–64 | | |
| von den Dreisch, A. and Boessneck, J., 1974 | 'Kritische Anmerkungen zue Widderisthöhenberechnung aus Langenmassen vor-und frühgeschichlicher Tierknochen', *Saugetierkundliche Mitteilungen* 22, 345–8 | Wright, S. M., 1992 | 'Millstones', in Rahtz, P. and Meeson, R., *An Anglo-Saxon Watermill at Tamworth: excavations in the Bolebridge Street area of Tamworth, Staffs in 1971 and 1978*, Counc. Brit. Archaeol. Res. Rep. Brit. Ser. 83, 72–3 |

# Index

Page numbers in *italics* denote illustrations. Streets and locations are in Norwich unless indicated otherwise.

Alms Lane 3
animal bone
  assemblage 41
  discussion
    craft/industrial activities 45
    diet 43–4
    environment 43
    fisheries 44–5
  preservation 41
  species description
    cattle 41
    dog/cat 42
    fish 42–3
    goat 42
    pig 42
    sheep 41–2
antler 34, 45; *see also* bone and antler working
architectural fragments 22
ash burials *20*, 22, 53, 54–5
axehead 34, 37, *39*, 40

balances 37–9, *39*, 40, 51
bell 36
Benedict XII 53
Bergen (Norway) 51
Bernard, St 52
bolt, sliding 35, 37, *38*, *39*
bone *see* animal bone; human bone
bone and antler working 34, 45, 51
Boniface VIII 54
bowl, stone 34, 37, *38*, *39*
Brackley, John, Friar 53, 54
brooches 35, 36, *38*, *39*
Brunham, William de, Prior 4
buckles 34, 35, *38*, *39*, 50
Building A 9, *9*, 13, 34, 52
Building B 9–10, *9*, 34, 52
*burh* 3
burial fees 4, 5, 53
burials
  character *17–20*, 20–2
  discussion 53–5, 57
  excavation evidence 13, 14–20, *14*, *21*
  excavation methodology 6
  orientation 55
  plan *16*
  *see also* human bone
Butler, L.A.S. 56–7
buzz bones 34, 36, 52

Calvert Street 49
Cambridge (Cambs), *studium* 53
Castle
  construction 4, 50
  pottery 31, 33
Cathedral 4, 50
Cathedral Priory 4, 53, 56
cellar 22
cemetery
  discussion 53–5, 56–7
  excavation evidence *10*, 13–22, *14*, *15–19*, *20*, *21*
  excavation methodology 6
  *see also* burials; human bone
charnel pit 20
churches *see* St John de Berstrete; St Margaret in combusto; St Vedast
Cleer, Thomas, map by 5
clench bolts 34, 37
coffin nails 20, 35, 37
coffins 20, 54
coins 36, 37
combs 34, 36, *38*, *39*

Conesford 3, 4, 5, 52
copper alloy working 34, 37, 51
Coslany 3
Coventry (W Mids), Greyfriars 55
craft *see* industrial activities
crop-processing 11, 48, 49
crucibles 27, 37, 51

Dallingflete 4, 44
dating evidence 22
diet 43–4, 48–9, 51
Dissolution 5, 22, 55–6
ditches *10*, 13, 20, 22; *see also* gullies
double graves 23

East Bergholt (Suffolk) 6
Edward the Elder 3
excavation
  background 1
  description
    Phase 1 (Late Saxon) 8–10, *8*, *9*, *11*
    Phase 2 (early medieval) *8*, 10–13, *10*, *11*, *12*
    Phase 3 (medieval cemetery) 13–22, *14*, *15–19*, *20*, *21*
    Phase 4 (post-medieval) 22
  discussion
    pre-Friary 50–2
    Friary 52–6
    site context and future research 56–7
  environmental evidence *see* animal bone; plant remains
  finds
    discussion 36–40, *38*, *39*
    summary 34–5
    *see also* human bone; pottery; slag
  location 1, *2*, *3*
  methodology 6
  research priorities 7
  *see also* dating evidence; historical background

Fastolf, Sir John 54
finger ring 34, 36, *38*, *39*
fish bone 42–3, 44–5, 51
Fishergate 26, 31, 49
fletching 45, 51
flints 34
Florence of Worcester 52
forge 9–10, 34
fowling 51
France, links with 50
friary
  discussion 52–7
  historical background 4–5
  *see also* cemetery
fuel 11, 48, 49

gardens 5, 22, 55, 56
geology and topography 1
grave markers 14, 55
Great Yarmouth (Norfolk) 44, 45
greenhouses 5
Gregory XI 54
Greyfriars Creek 4
Greyfriars Road, pottery 31
gullies 10–11, *10*; *see also* ditches

hammerscale 40
Haverel 53
Hely, Adam 53
Henry III 4
historical background 3–6
Hochstetter, Anthony, map by 5
hornworking 45, 51
horseshoe 34, 39
horseshoe nail 39
Hudson, W. 5
human bone

63

demography 23–4
discussion 24–5
overview 23
pathology 24

industrial activities, pre-Friary 51; *see also* bone and antler working; copper alloy working; fletching; hornworking; ironworking; leadworking; textile manufacture
industrial zones, medieval 3–4
ironworking 4, 8, 9–10, 34, 50, 51; *see also* slag

jetton 36, 37

key 35, 37, *38*, 39
King Street 31, 52
Kirkpatrick, J. 4, 5
knives 34, 35, 37, *38*, 39

lace chapes 35–6
lead fragments 34
leadworking 34
Little/Nether Conesford 4
locks 37, *38*, 39; *see also* bolt, sliding
Losinga, Herbert de, Bishop of Norwich 4
Luttrell Psalter 54

malting 48
Mann Egerton site 7, 50, 51, 52
*mos teutonicus* 54
mounts 36
Mousehold Heath 49

nails 34, 35, 37; *see also* coffin nails; horseshoe nail
Needham 3
needles 37, *39*, 40
Nicholas of Assisi 53
Norfolk, Duke of 5
Norfolk Archaeological Unit 1, 6
Norfolk Landscape Archaeology 6
Northamptonshire Archaeology 1, 6
Norwich School 1, 6

orchard 5
Oxford (Oxon), Greyfriars 24

Pardon Cloister 4, 5
Paston, Sir John I 53, 54
pathology *see under* human bone
pathways 11, 13, 22
pentice 20, 22
Pigaz, Ralph 53
pinbeater 34, 37, *39*, 40, 52
pins *see* shroud pins
pipe/flute, bone 36–7, *38*, 39, 52
pit cover 37
pits
    Phase 1 8, 9, 34, 37
    Phase 2 10, *10*, 11, *11*, *12*, 13, 34
    Phase 3 13–14, *15*, 20
    *see also* charnel pit; plant remains; sand quarries
plant remains
    compared 48–9
    discussion 47–8
    methodology 47
    results 46, 47
    samples 45–7
post-holes
    Phase 1 8, 9
    Phase 2 10, 11, 13
    Phase 3 14, 20
Pottergate 3–4
pottery
    assemblage 26
    chronology 32
    discussion 30–2
    fabrics
        Andenne/Huy-type wares 30
        Badorf-type ware *28*, 29–30
        Cambridge Sgraffito ware 29
        Developed Stamford ware *28*, *29*, 29

Early Medieval Sparse Shelly ware 27
Early/Middle Saxon hand-made wares 26, *28*
Flemish Grey wares 30
'Frisian' ware 30
German stonewares 30
Grimston ware 27–9, *28*, *29*
Ipswich ware 26
Local Medieval Unglazed ware 27, *29*
London-type ware 29
Low Countries earthenwares *28*, 30
Miscellaneous Early Medieval Sandy wares 27
Normandy Gritty wares *28*, 30
North French/Low Countries wares *28*, 30
Pingsdorf ware *28*, 30
Red earthenwares 30
Rhenish Grey wares *28*, 30
Rouen ware *28*, 30
St Neots ware 27, *28*
Scarborough ware 29
Stamford ware 27, *28*, *29*
Thetford-type ware 26–7, *28*, *29*
Tin-Glazed earthenware 30
    fragmentation analysis 33
    methodology 26
    occurrence 32–3
    trade 50–1
    vessel use 33
    *see also* crucibles
pottery production 3–4
precinct wall 6, 50, 55
    excavation evidence 13, *14*, 20, 22
Prince of Wales Road 5, 31
Purcell Miller Tritton and Partners 6

quadruple grave 23
querns 34, 37

Repps, Bartholomew de 53
Rose Lane 4–5, 31
Roseth, Roger 53

St Benedict's Street 31
St Faith's Lane
    background and origins 1, *3*, 4–6, 50, 56
    buildings fronting 8, 52
    pottery 31
St John de Berstrete church 24
St Margaret in combusto church 56
St Martin-at-Place Plain 31, 33
St Vedast church 4
sand quarries 10, 13–14, *15*, 55
scaffolding, evidence for 20
Seven Coal Row 4
Sevencote Rowe 4
shroud pins 20, 35, 36, 54
shrouds 20, 54
Skerning, Roger de, Bishop of Norwich 4
slag 40, 51
slots 8, 9, 11–13
Southampton (Hants), pottery 31, 32
spindle-whorls 34, 37, *39*, 40, 52
stake-holes 8, 9, 10
Standysshe, Dr James 55
staples 37
Statute of Alienation in Mortmain 5
Stratford Langthorne abbey (G London) 24
street layout 4, 50
*studium* 53, 54

terrace 13, 55
textile manufacture 34, 37, 52
Theophilus 51
Tombland 4, 52
topography *see* geology and topography
trackway 13–14, *14*, *15*, 50, 55
trade, evidence for 30–2, 34, 50–1
triple graves 20, 23
tuyere plates 40

Wallace King warehouse 1, 5–6

64

Wensum, River  4, 44, 49
Westwick  3
wheel ruts  13, *14*, *15*, 55
Whitefriars Street  31
wills  53–4
window glass  37

Wodeham, Adam  53
Wood, Lawrence  5
woodworking  34, 37
Wymbergh, Robert  5

Yare, River  44, 45

**East Anglian Archaeology**
is a serial publication sponsored by ALGAO EE and English Heritage. It is the main vehicle for publishing final reports on archaeological excavations and surveys in the region. For information about titles in the series, visit www.eaareports.org.uk. Reports can be obtained from:
Oxbow Books, 10 Hythe Bridge Street, Oxford OX1 2EW
or directly from the organisation publishing a particular volume.

*Reports available so far:*

|  |  |  |
|---|---|---|
| No.1, | 1975 | Suffolk: various papers |
| No.2, | 1976 | Norfolk: various papers |
| No.3, | 1977 | Suffolk: various papers |
| No.4, | 1976 | Norfolk: Late Saxon town of Thetford |
| No.5, | 1977 | Norfolk: various papers on Roman sites |
| No.6, | 1977 | Norfolk: Spong Hill Anglo-Saxon cemetery, Part I |
| No.7, | 1978 | Norfolk: Bergh Apton Anglo-Saxon cemetery |
| No.8, | 1978 | Norfolk: various papers |
| No.9, | 1980 | Norfolk: North Elmham Park |
| No.10, | 1980 | Norfolk: village sites in Launditch Hundred |
| No.11, | 1981 | Norfolk: Spong Hill, Part II: Catalogue of Cremations |
| No.12, | 1981 | The barrows of East Anglia |
| No.13, | 1981 | Norwich: Eighteen centuries of pottery from Norwich |
| No.14, | 1982 | Norfolk: various papers |
| No.15, | 1982 | Norwich: Excavations in Norwich 1971–1978; Part I |
| No.16, | 1982 | Norfolk: Beaker domestic sites in the Fen-edge and East Anglia |
| No.17, | 1983 | Norfolk: Waterfront excavations and Thetford-type Ware production, Norwich |
| No.18, | 1983 | Norfolk: The archaeology of Witton |
| No.19, | 1983 | Norfolk: Two post-medieval earthenware pottery groups from Fulmodeston |
| No.20, | 1983 | Norfolk: Burgh Castle: excavation by Charles Green, 1958–61 |
| No.21, | 1984 | Norfolk: Spong Hill, Part III: Catalogue of Inhumations |
| No.22, | 1984 | Norfolk: Excavations in Thetford, 1948–59 and 1973–80 |
| No.23, | 1985 | Norfolk: Excavations at Brancaster 1974 and 1977 |
| No.24, | 1985 | Suffolk: West Stow, the Anglo-Saxon village |
| No.25, | 1985 | Essex: Excavations by Mr H.P.Cooper on the Roman site at Hill Farm, Gestingthorpe, Essex |
| No.26, | 1985 | Norwich: Excavations in Norwich 1971–78; Part II |
| No.27, | 1985 | Cambridgeshire: The Fenland Project No.1: Archaeology and Environment in the Lower Welland Valley |
| No.28, | 1985 | Norfolk: Excavations within the north-east bailey of Norwich Castle, 1978 |
| No.29, | 1986 | Norfolk: Barrow excavations in Norfolk, 1950–82 |
| No.30, | 1986 | Norfolk: Excavations at Thornham, Warham, Wighton and Caistor St Edmund, Norfolk |
| No.31, | 1986 | Norfolk: Settlement, religion and industry on the Fen-edge; three Romano-British sites in Norfolk |
| No.32, | 1987 | Norfolk: Three Norman Churches in Norfolk |
| No.33, | 1987 | Essex: Excavation of a Cropmark Enclosure Complex at Woodham Walter, Essex, 1976 and An Assessment of Excavated Enclosures in Essex |
| No.34, | 1987 | Norfolk: Spong Hill, Part IV: Catalogue of Cremations |
| No.35, | 1987 | Cambridgeshire: The Fenland Project No.2: Fenland Landscapes and Settlement, Peterborough–March |
| No.36, | 1987 | Norfolk: The Anglo-Saxon Cemetery at Morningthorpe |
| No.37, | 1987 | Norfolk: Excavations at St Martin-at-Palace Plain, Norwich, 1981 |
| No.38, | 1987 | Suffolk: The Anglo-Saxon Cemetery at Westgarth Gardens, Bury St Edmunds |
| No.39, | 1988 | Norfolk: Spong Hill, Part VI: Occupation during the 7th–2nd millennia BC |
| No.40, | 1988 | Suffolk: Burgh: The Iron Age and Roman Enclosure |
| No.41, | 1988 | Essex: Excavations at Great Dunmow, Essex: a Romano-British small town in the Trinovantian Civitas |
| No.42, | 1988 | Essex: Archaeology and Environment in South Essex, Rescue Archaeology along the Gray's By-pass 1979–80 |
| No.43, | 1988 | Essex: Excavation at the North Ring, Mucking, Essex: A Late Bronze Age Enclosure |
| No.44, | 1988 | Norfolk: Six Deserted Villages in Norfolk |
| No.45, | 1988 | Norfolk: The Fenland Project No. 3: Marshland and the Nar Valley, Norfolk |
| No.46, | 1989 | Norfolk: The Deserted Medieval Village of Thuxton |
| No.47, | 1989 | Suffolk: West Stow: Early Anglo-Saxon Animal Husbandry |
| No.48, | 1989 | Suffolk: West Stow, Suffolk: The Prehistoric and Romano-British Occupations |
| No.49, | 1990 | Norfolk: The Evolution of Settlement in Three Parishes in South-East Norfolk |
| No.50, | 1993 | Proceedings of the Flatlands and Wetlands Conference |
| No.51, | 1991 | Norfolk: The Ruined and Disused Churches of Norfolk |
| No.52, | 1991 | Norfolk: The Fenland Project No. 4, The Wissey Embayment and Fen Causeway |
| No.53, | 1992 | Norfolk: Excavations in Thetford, 1980–82, Fison Way |
| No.54, | 1992 | Norfolk: The Iron Age Forts of Norfolk |
| No.55, | 1992 | Lincolnshire: The Fenland Project No.5: Lincolnshire Survey, The South-West Fens |
| No.56, | 1992 | Cambridgeshire: The Fenland Project No.6: The South-Western Cambridgeshire Fens |
| No.57, | 1993 | Norfolk and Lincolnshire: Excavations at Redgate Hill Hunstanton; and Tattershall Thorpe |
| No.58, | 1993 | Norwich: Households: The Medieval and Post-Medieval Finds from Norwich Survey Excavations 1971–1978 |
| No.59, | 1993 | Fenland: The South-West Fen Dyke Survey Project 1982–86 |
| No.60, | 1993 | Norfolk: Caister-on-Sea: Excavations by Charles Green, 1951–55 |
| No.61, | 1993 | Fenland: The Fenland Project No.7: Excavations in Peterborough and the Lower Welland Valley 1960–1969 |
| No.62, | 1993 | Norfolk: Excavations in Thetford by B.K. Davison, between 1964 and 1970 |
| No.63, | 1993 | Norfolk: Illington: A Study of a Breckland Parish and its Anglo-Saxon Cemetery |
| No.64, | 1994 | Norfolk: The Late Saxon and Medieval Pottery Industry of Grimston: Excavations 1962–92 |
| No.65, | 1993 | Suffolk: Settlements on Hill-tops: Seven Prehistoric Sites in Suffolk |
| No.66, | 1993 | Lincolnshire: The Fenland Project No.8: Lincolnshire Survey, the Northern Fen-Edge |
| No.67, | 1994 | Norfolk: Spong Hill, Part V: Catalogue of Cremations |
| No.68, | 1994 | Norfolk: Excavations at Fishergate, Norwich 1985 |
| No.69, | 1994 | Norfolk: Spong Hill, Part VIII: The Cremations |
| No.70, | 1994 | Fenland: The Fenland Project No.9: Flandrian Environmental Change in Fenland |
| No.71, | 1995 | Essex: The Archaeology of the Essex Coast Vol.I: The Hullbridge Survey Project |
| No.72, | 1995 | Norfolk: Excavations at Redcastle Furze, Thetford, 1988–9 |
| No.73, | 1995 | Norfolk: Spong Hill, Part VII: Iron Age, Roman and Early Saxon Settlement |
| No.74, | 1995 | Norfolk: A Late Neolithic, Saxon and Medieval Site at Middle Harling |
| No.75, | 1995 | Essex: North Shoebury: Settlement and Economy in South-east Essex 1500–AD1500 |
| No.76, | 1996 | Nene Valley: Orton Hall Farm: A Roman and Early Anglo-Saxon Farmstead |
| No.77, | 1996 | Norfolk: Barrow Excavations in Norfolk, 1984–88 |
| No.78, | 1996 | Norfolk:The Fenland Project No.11: The Wissey Embayment: Evidence for pre-Iron Age Occupation |
| No.79, | 1996 | Cambridgeshire: The Fenland Project No.10: Cambridgeshire Survey, the Isle of Ely and Wisbech |
| No.80, | 1997 | Norfolk: Barton Bendish and Caldecote: fieldwork in south-west Norfolk |
| No.81, | 1997 | Norfolk: Castle Rising Castle |
| No.82, | 1998 | Essex: Archaeology and the Landscape in the Lower Blackwater Valley |
| No.83, | 1998 | Essex: Excavations south of Chignall Roman Villa 1977–81 |
| No.84, | 1998 | Suffolk: A Corpus of Anglo-Saxon Material |
| No.85, | 1998 | Suffolk: Towards a Landscape History of Walsham le Willows |
| No.86, | 1998 | Essex: Excavations at the Orsett 'Cock' Enclosure |
| No.87, | 1999 | Norfolk: Excavations in Thetford, North of the River, 1989–90 |
| No.88, | 1999 | Essex: Excavations at Ivy Chimneys, Witham 1978–83 |
| No.89, | 1999 | Lincolnshire: Salterns: Excavations at Helpringham, Holbeach St Johns and Bicker Haven |
| No.90, | 1999 | Essex:The Archaeology of Ardleigh, Excavations 1955–80 |
| No.91, | 2000 | Norfolk: Excavations on the Norwich Southern Bypass, 1989–91 Part I Bixley, Caistor St Edmund, Trowse |
| No.92, | 2000 | Norfolk: Excavations on the Norwich Southern Bypass, 1989–91 Part II Harford Farm Anglo-Saxon Cemetery |
| No.93, | 2001 | Norfolk: Excavations on the Snettisham Bypass, 1989 |
| No.94, | 2001 | Lincolnshire: Excavations at Billingborough, 1975–8 |
| No.95, | 2001 | Suffolk: Snape Anglo-Saxon Cemetery: Excavations and Surveys |